Daytrips, Getaway Weekends, and Vacations in New England

"A dependable, well-arranged guide."
—*Sunday Cape Cod Times*

"An excellent guide to New England's many attractions and will save many an argument about which restaurant to try or what route to take."
—*New England Living* magazine

"The planned itineraries will save travelers arduous time spent poring over maps, gathering information and deciding on a route."
—*Cape Cod Times*

"This useful guidebook offers detailed itineraries through the New England states. One of the most helpful aspects of the book is the appendices—two directories—one of major campgrounds and the other of bed and breakfast establishments organized by location. That feature alone makes the book a worthwhile investment for the New England traveler. Whether you are going on a daytrip or two week vacation, this book is sure to come in handy on the road."
—*Hudson Valley* magazine

"If you are looking for the perfect getaway and a superb traveling companion, look no further than **Daytrips**. Extensive work and loving care make this a book worth owning."
—The *Rhode Island Herald*

"Here is an excellent resource to short and extended excursions for those with modest resources as well as those with unlimited funding. When travelling in New England take the book with you; if you are on business it will make your day more interesting; if for pleasure you will gain knowledge of exciting opportunities that you would otherwise simply pass by."
—The *Counselor*

"Its good representation of activities in this area gives one an idea of how well it handles other regions with which we are less familiar."
—The *Berkshire Courier*, Great Barrington, MA

"It does not just identify the touristed hot spots; it exposes the little-known, little-traveled cubbyholes of tradition and caches of avant-garde."
—The *Cambridge* (MA) *Express*

"Has a little something for everyone."
—*F.Y.I.*, Eastern Airlines Review

Daytrips, Getaway Weekends, and Vacations in New England

by

Patricia & Robert Foulke

A Voyager Book

THE GLOBE PEQUOT PRESS
CHESTER, CONNECTICUT

Cover photograph taken by Oliver Denison at Mystic Seaport® of Mystic, Connecticut.
Cover design by Barbara Marks.
Book design by Kathy Michalove.

Library of Congress Cataloging-in-Publication Data

Foulke, Patricia.
    Daytrips, getaway weekends, and vacations in New England
Patricia and Robert Foulke—2nd ed.
        p.   cm.—(A Voyager book)
    Rev. ed. of: Daytrips and budget vacations in New England. 1st ed.
c1983.
    Includes index.
    ISBN 0-87106-734-X
    1. New England—Description and travel—1981—Guide-books.
2. Family recreation—New England—Guide-books. 3. Automobiles—Road guides—New England. I. Foulke, Robert, 1930- .
II. Foulke, Patricia. Daytrips and budget vacations in New England.
III. Title. IV. Title: Daytrips, getaway weekends, and vacations in
New England. V. Series.
F2.3.F68 1988
917.4'0443—dc19   87-37947
                                                               CIP

Manufactured in the United States of America
Second Edition/First Printing

Contents

Photo Credits

ACKNOWLEDGMENTS

We wish to thank those who have contributed expertise, time, enthusiasm, and encouragement to enhance this book: Phyllis and Alexander Aldrich, Jo and Verner Alexanderson, Susan Allen, Ruth Alsin, Craig Altschul, Ted Austin, Peter Bachelder, Anne and William Barclay, Barbara and Carl Beehner, Vondee and David Beeman, Ann and Werner Berthoff, Pamela Black-Boer and Westin Boer, Ralph Bloom, Marilyn Bosare, Becky Bovelsky, Sally Bray, Constance Carlson, Grethe and Maria Certain, Judith Christenson, Betty and Woodbridge Constant, Dick Courcelle, Richard Cutts, Shirley Barrie and George Davidson, Beth DeLong, Shirley and Howard DeLong, Anne and Terence Diggory, Cynthia and David DuPre, Judith and Bruce Eissner, Peter Fallon, Alberta and Jack Feynman, Jack Fenners, Joan Fina, Patricia Fiorelli, Patricia and Thomas Fox, Grace Friary, Stuart Frank, Michael Frucci, Gay and Alvin Gamage, Sue and Robert Gorton, Anne Gwynn, Diane and William Hall, Jerry Hall, Thomas Holmes and Phyllis Roth, Tracy Hendrickson, Elizabeth Hibbard, Judy Hilliard, Judy Hudson, Bette Hunt, Jonathan Hyde, Dave Iavonne, Amy Jordan, Cherie Keemar, Conrad Kelfos, Nancy and John Kendall, Albert Klyberg, Katherine Kinderman, Lizabeth King, Madeline and Paul Kruzel, Linda and Benjamin Labaree, Barnet Laschever, Angela LeBlanc, David Lee, Carol Levesque, Ardyth Lewis, Thor Loberg, Polly and Chuck Longsworth, Mary Maynard, Janet and Curt Mayott, Sharon McCanna, Carol and Bud McKeon, Marjorie and Bard McNulty, Virginia and Stephen Minot, Charlotte Moore, Thomas Murphy, Elaine Murray, Tom Myers, Linda Naiss, Mab and Charles Owen, Anne and Joseph Palamountain, Bette Perreault, Barbara Pitnof, George Potter, Judith and James Potter, Elizabeth and David Ratcliff, Elaine Raymond, Celeste Reid, Jean and Donald Richards, Fred Roehrig, Polly Rollins, Kenneth Rothwell,

Mary Rulison, Rosemary Ryan, Jane and Karl Sabo, Judy Salsbury, Juliet Saunders, Ardene Scroggy, Janet Serra, Mary and Sanford Sistare, Jane Snaider, Vivian Stanley, Mark Stenning, Eileen and Elwood Stitzel, Mary Lou and Robert Strode, Jean and Leonard Tomat, Scott Van Pelt, Theresa Waite, Alex Warden, Phillip West, Alan Wheelock, Frank Whitman, Brad Williams, Helen and Gunther Winkler, Nancy Wurlitzer, and Frederick Zivic.

Introduction

When you feel the urge to travel, whether for a day or a month, you want to move about the world a bit and satisfy your curiosity about what is there. We hope that this book will arouse your historical imagination, inspire you to explore a variety of interesting places, and provide you with some details about what you might want to see and do. Some travelers want to hit only the highlights; others prefer poking around in places off the beaten track. In either case, once you are on your way, you will want to strike a nice balance between knowing what you are looking for and having the fun of discovering something unknown to most travelers. This book provides much of what you need to know, and the people you meet and circumstances of the day will often lead to the most surprising and memorable experiences.

Travelers are notorious for returning home with bags stuffed full of purchases. We would like to suggest a different kind of collecting—not of things but of the sights and sounds of places and the people who live in them. To make places come alive, one must be open to the sensations they offer and notice details that all of us pass by in the rush of ordinary living. We learned this lesson many years ago on a meandering walk through a rather undistinguished section of Hartford with Constantinos Doxiadis, a noted Greek city planner. He poked into alleys, inspected backyards, sniffed the smells coming through kitchen windows, retraced footsteps across lawns, looked at the furniture on front porches, and seemingly missed no clue to the way of life all these signs indicated. His acute powers of observation and openness to experience taught him more about the district in a few hours than we had learned in years.

Perhaps he taught us the difference between tourists and travelers. Tourists roar through "sights," ask no questions, buy souvenirs, meet schedules, and often complain about the food or accommodations. Travelers learn to be in touch with their own sensations, to follow their inclinations, to shape each day as they move through its experiences, to be alert for the unexpected beauty of a storm, the insight provided by a random conversation, or the new territory unfolded by a detour. Travelers make plans to avoid the frustrations of aimless wandering, but they are willing to alter them and flow with circumstances. They understand that the value of travel is the freedom to move about the world as they wish, exploring what is strange and new or looking again at the old and familiar with fresh eyes. They balance the impulse of Melville, who opens *Moby Dick* with a portrait of city dwellers restlessly seeking the shore and the unknowns beyond it, against that of Thoreau, who found enough to explore in the environs of Concord to last a lifetime.

A New England daytrip, weekend, or vacation offers remarkable variety to the imaginative traveler. Whether you live around the corner or across the country, something new awaits you on each trip. You may enjoy an Atlantic sunrise or a Green Mountain sunset, undisturbed saltwater marshes or busy village greens, fresh lobster in Maine or local cheese in Vermont. You can hike the Appalachian Trail, run white water on the Allagash, climb in the Presidential Range, and surf on Cape Cod beaches. Or you can explore whaling museums and reconstructed colonial villages, walk historic trails in old cities, trace local legends and the lore of shipwrecks, and collect valuable memories everywhere.

For almost forty years we have enjoyed these many pleasures of New England. During this time we have traveled with babies and toddlers, children and teenagers, and alone. We have discovered the pleasures of traveling light and the problems of carrying too much in a backpack or the trunk of a car. At times we have tried to do too much, planning our trips in great detail; at others we have simply taken off on an impromptu journey with vague destinations. But no matter how we have traveled, and no matter how often we have visited a place, we have never exhausted the possibilities of this region blessed by mountain, sea, city, and a rich cultural heritage. If this book helps you to enjoy New England as much as we have, we will be content.

TRIP PLANNING   This book suggests a variety of activities to suit travelers with different inclinations. For those with strong historical interests, we have interviewed people with great expertise on the staffs of the museums and old houses listed in each itinerary. Often these individuals have provided more information than we can use in a book of this size, but we have included enough of it to whet your appetite and give you some background for your visit to each site.

For those who want to build a trip around doing more than seeing, we have indicated special opportunities—climbing the ravines of Mount Washington or running wild white water on the West River in Jamaica, Vermont—and have made quite specific suggestions for using recreational areas. For example, we have included our own personal recommendations to downhill skiers who are visiting some of New England's largest ski areas for the first time. Usually the experts head off for trails marked with a black diamond, beginners start on slopes marked with green circles, and the intermediates are supposed to choose among the large number of trails marked with blue squares. Realistically, intermediates comprise a group with a wide span of skills, ranging from advanced beginner to near expert. They may head off on a blue trail only to find it is terrifying, especially on the first day. Therefore we have suggested a first run for any intermediate, followed by several more that we have skied and enjoyed.

Within a city or region, we have tried to cluster or group sites together so that you will know what is available nearby. We don't like to drive or walk back and forth randomly looking for something, and know you won't want to either. For your convenience, we have also suggested a place or two for lunch or dinner in many areas. The appendix also lists some interesting inns, bed-and-breakfast homes, and established campgrounds so that you can call ahead to make a reservation if you wish; large hotels or well-known motel chains are not included. These suggestions for meals and accommodations are **not** comprehensive for any area or evaluative, either by inclusion or omission. We are not involved in rating places to eat or stay, by price or by quality, but those listed do represent ones that we or our friends have enjoyed.

ITINERARIES

Styles of travel involve choices that ultimately reflect personality. We opt for a flexible mode of travel midway between the carefully integrated schedule of a business trip and the total freedom of impulsive wandering. Our planned itineraries will save you the time and trouble of gathering information and deciding on a route in a new region, but they need not confine you. You can choose to travel all or part of any trip or combine parts of several. The itineraries are grouped by states, and you can connect easily from one itinerary to another within or between states. Maps show the route from place to place so that you can visualize the possible connections and permutations that are most appealing to you.

Each itinerary contains sightseeing tips and a good bit of detail about places of special interest. The description is not meant to be comprehensive, but it represents a selection of the highlights of each site or place, as well as some little noticed details that may convey some sense of its ambience. At times our enthusiasm runs away with us and we write a great deal; in those cases we hope you will enjoy sharing our bent for personal discovery. We also hope that our tracks will lead to new ones of your own making. We never intended "doing" New England and tying it up in a neat package to be unwrapped by docile readers. We know that there is much that we have missed, whole areas unopened to our imaginations, and much that we can revisit with benefit. The value of travel lies in the process, not the product.

A: Western Circuit of Connecticut. Wind through the hills of western Connecticut where time seems to stand still as you walk along streets filled with historic clapboard homes, visit Indian exhibits, relax on quiet lakes, or swish down the Housatonic River in a canoe. This dormant region of New England is now being rediscovered by those who value the combination of great natural beauty with sophisticated culture.

B: Central Connecticut. From Hartford, with its Mark Twain house, insurance companies, and historic homes, side trips radiate like the spokes of a wheel. The offerings range from arts centers, horse shows, canoe routes, nature preserves, an herb farm, and major museums to Dinosaur State Park.

C: Connecticut's Shore. Outside New York City and across the border in Connecticut, colonial cities grew as shipbuilding and overseas trade first made them prosperous, to be followed by pioneering manufacturing industries and the establishment of colleges. Now linked to New York, Providence, and Boston by major transportation networks, the shore is becoming a year-round home for many who do not have to commute to cities every day. But this region contains far more than exurban sprawl for those who know where to look, particularly in university centers like New Haven and in river towns like Old Lyme, Essex, and East Haddam.

D: Rhode Island Shore and Providence. The shore has an unbroken ocean beach conjoined with one of the most beautiful and intricate bays in New England. At the mouth of the Narragansett Bay lies Newport, a yachting center that was the site of America's Cup matches for many years after its earlier glory as a summering place for high society, and at the head of the Bay, Providence still lives and works in the buildings of its "Mile of History."

E: Southern Massachusetts Shore, Cape Cod, and the Islands. From the whaling port of New Bedford through the coves and harbors of Buzzards Bay and out to the elbow and tip of the Cape, this is maritime territory par excellence. Cape Cod provides excellent beaches all around its hooked arm, and the offshore islands of Martha's Vineyard and Nantucket are rich in history and shipwreck lore.

F: Historic Boston and the Bay Colonies. This area, stretching from Plymouth to Newburyport, was the beachhead for many of the first settlements in our country. Here you can trace our early history: the relationship between Indians and Pilgrims, the problems of the early colonists, the development of education and culture, the battles between theocracy and democracy, the growth of early industries, the tensions leading to the Revolutionary War, and the beginnings of the Industrial Revolution in America.

G: The Berkshires of Massachusetts. The rolling hills and quiet valley towns of western Massachusetts are touched during the summer by marvelous music, theater, and art transplanted from the city. Historic towns represent different strains of nineteenth-century culture ranging from the elegance of Lenox and Stockbridge to the simplicity of Hancock Shaker Village.

H: The New Hampshire Shore. Settlers arrived, after months at sea, to find wild strawberries growing along the banks of the Piscataqua River. Historic homes in Portsmouth and surrounding towns reflect the evolution of seacoast life through four centuries.

I: The Lake District and Southern New Hampshire. Formed by glaciers, the lakes of central New Hampshire are dotted with islands and carved with coves that make them perfect for summer holidays. Midway through the southern tier of the state, the broad valley of the Merrimack gives way to the ridges and hills surrounding Mount Monadnock.

J: The White Mountains of New Hampshire. The highest mountains in New England provide a challenge for skiers and climbers, as well as an extensive network of huts and trails for hikers. Many of their wide vistas and unusual rock formations are also accessible by road, aerial tramway, and cog railway.

K: Down East Along the Coast of Maine. Sailors ran downwind in prevailing southwesterlies as they moved northeastward along this coast, thereby creating the otherwise incomprehensible phrase "Down East." This rugged coastline of fjords created by long peninsulas with secure harbors and saltwater farms has always been more accessible by sea than by land, and its interpenetration of land and sea continues to attract artists, sailors, and travelers.

L: The Lakes and Mountains of Maine. The justly famous shore is not all there is to Maine. Its vast interior filled with large lakes, mountain ranges, and river networks provides the most extensive wilderness area in New England, stretching from the Longfellow Mountains, Baxter State Park, and the Allagash Wilderness Waterway to the Canadian border.

M: The Green Mountains of Vermont and the Champlain Valley. Ethan Allen's beautiful ridge of mountains—the backbone of Vermont separating the rest of New England from the Champlain Valley—is prized today by skiers, hikers, and sightseers who want to admire contours of rounded beauty. To their west Lake Champlain provides a major waterlink between the St. Lawrence and the Hudson that played a large part in determining the outcome of the French and Indian War and the American Revolution.

N: Southern Vermont. In the southern tier of Vermont, mountains and valley towns merge into an extraordinary landscape that pleases the eye at every curve of the road. There is more fine skiing and hiking here, as well as lots to see—covered bridges, country stores, picturebook villages surrounding greens, churches with layered steeples, cheese factories, bowl mills, potteries, and maple sugar huts.

THE ARMCHAIR TRAVELER

As we traveled doing the research for this book we became increasingly excited by the rare opportunity we have—to learn more about the rich historical heritage of these states and then to have the fun of writing about it for others. As children we had a smattering of historical background about this part of the country from books, but we had no sense of the blending of past and present that we now feel as we walk the streets of most New England towns. Whether you will be taking a trip or traveling vicariously from your armchair, we hope to intrigue you with historical tales of real people who lived long ago.

It's impossible to think about New England without thinking about the history of the area— a history embellished with centuries-old folktales and legends. Throughout the book we've scattered sea chanteys, ghost stories, local tall tales, and anecdotes—all to whet your appetite for this marvelous region of our nation.

ACCOMMODATIONS

For the past thirty-four years we have traveled in many parts of the United States and have lived in Europe every seventh year while on sabbatical leave from teaching. In our younger years in Europe we camped most of the time or stayed in bed and breakfast establishments, enjoying occasional splurges such as a castle in France with our children one New Year's Eve. We were able to stretch our budget and build up memories at the same time. Now that B&Bs have become popular in the United States, inexpensive and pleasant accommodations can be combined with the pleasure of meeting people who live where you want to travel. B&B hosts are noted for offering specific local knowledge that you would never hear about in any other way. Inns, with their history, hospitality, and good food, offer another opportunity for discriminating travelers. Some travelers "collect" inns, spurred on by yet another one to investigate. Check our appendices for the inn and B&B list. We offer a selection of both along the itinerary routes for your convenience. This selection does not pretend to be a comprehensive list for each region, but includes some that we have enjoyed. We also list a number of large, established campgrounds that may provide good summer accommodations along the routes for those who are equipped to live outdoors.

We usually begin by attacking the travel section in our local library, with a sturdy canvas bag in hand to carry home our selections. Later we buy some of these books to take on the trip, along with other new books we've found in local bookstores. Then we may visit a travel agency for free brochures and information.

INFORMATION

State tourist offices offer maps, information about historic sites, and lists of campgrounds and other accommodations, restaurants, and sightseeing suggestions. It's a good idea to write before you go.

Connecticut: Connecticut Division of Tourist Information, 210 Washington Street, Hartford

06106. Phone: 203-566-3948; recording 800-243-1685 from Maine to Virginia, 800-842-7492 in Connecticut.

Maine: State Development Office, State House, Augusta 04333. Phone: 207-289-2423.

Massachusetts: Massachusetts Department of Commerce and Development, 100 Cambridge Street, Boston 02202. Phone: 617-727-3201 or 800-632-8038 in Massachusetts, or 800-343-9072 in the Northeast.

New Hampshire: New Hampshire Office of Vacation Travel, State House Annex, Box 856, Concord 03301. Phone: 603-271-2665; 800-258-3608 in New England and New York.

Rhode Island: Rhode Island Department of Economic Development, 7 Jackson Walkway, Providence 02903. Phone: 401-277-2601; 800-556-2484 from Maine to West Virginia.

Vermont: Vermont Travel Division, 61 Elm Street, Montpelier 05602. Phone: 802-828-3236.

You can also write to individual chambers of commerce in the towns you intend to visit. They too offer maps and information about historic houses in the area (days and times sites are open), restaurants, accommodations, and special activities.

A number of organizations publish information about wildlife sanctuaries, wilderness expeditions, hiking trails, and outdoor recreation.

The **Appalachian Mountain Club** (5 Joy Street, Boston, MA 02108; 617-523-0636) is the oldest conservation club in the United States. It publishes guidebooks on hiking trails and canoe routes, a monthly newsletter, and a semiannual journal. The **National Audubon Society** (950 Third Avenue, New York, NY 10022; 212-832-3200) maintains wildlife sanctuaries all over the country. Its programs include conservation education, research on current wildlife issues, and natural history films. The society also operates libraries and stores where you can buy nature-related gifts. The **Green Mountain Club** (Box 889, Montpelier, VT 05602; 802-223-3463) maintains and protects the Long Trail system and offers guidebooks and maps. **American Youth Hostels** (132 Spring Street, New York, NY 10012; 212-431-7100) offers hiking and bicycle tours and a network of low-cost hostels.

BEFORE YOU GO

When you have considered where you want to go, weather and road conditions, crowds in high season, ferry schedules (if applicable), and any other contingencies, you're ready to get organized. We find it useful to make a list of the areas we want to cover, the activities we would like to enjoy, and possible side trips. A destination for each night with estimated mileage and driving time is the next step. Addresses and phone numbers we'll need along the route are added to the list. Then we put lists, brochures, travel articles, books, and other information we've collected into a large envelope for easy reference along the way.

MONEY

Plan to carry enough money in traveler's checks, credit cards, and cash to complete your trip. Bring your twenty-four-hour bank card, if you have one. Remember weekends and holidays if you need access to a bank to replenish your supply, unless you have access to automatic teller machines. We estimate expenses such as gas, tolls, ferry fares, entrance fees, meals, gifts, accommodations, and add a slush fund for miscellaneous expenses *plus* a reserve for emergencies. Of course, it's easy to spend a little more, but we find that preplanning saves us the annoyance of a frantic search for money once we're on our way.

FOOD   You will want to try the local cuisine as you travel. Be alert to special foods that are featured locally. Is there a special restaurant you've heard wonderful things about? It doesn't hurt to write or phone ahead for a reservation. We have listed phone numbers for our suggestions. Or, once you get into town, ask a native for a good place to eat. If you want to try regional foods and sample some terrific home cooking, look in the local papers or on bulletin boards around town for notices of church, grange, or special-event suppers. Craft fairs and bazaars often sell homemade baked goods as well.

ACTIVITIES   Enjoy! Let the ages and interests of your family set the focus of your trip. But leave some time free for relaxation (defined as time to do nothing) and flexibility (the freedom to change your mind according to weather and mood).

When our children were little, we chose activities to appeal to their interests and levels of understanding. We visited zoos, country fairs, beaches, whaling museums, aquariums, restored villages, dinosaur traces, amusement parks, and planetariums; we took train rides and steamboat trips; we saw theater and puppet shows, baseball games and historical reenactments; and we canoed and sailed and swam and rowed. Whenever we could we prepared them for an activity—showing them pictures and talking about the historic sites we intended to visit. They especially loved hearing stories about the children who once lived in these old houses.

We let them guide us through museums, picking out displays that intrigued them rather than stopping them (shifting from one foot to the other) in front of every exhibit. Then we would head for the museum shop and select postcards for our collections.

Children love nature trails with buttons to push and signs to read. They also love hikes, especially when they're well supplied with goodies for energy. Ours carried hard candies, raisins, fruit, gorp, and a jacket in a child-sized rucksack. And as we'd go along, we'd decorate the rucksack with souvenir patches from places we visited.

Whether you're traveling alone or with family, try something new on each trip. For starters, think about lake canoeing, white-water canoeing and kayaking, saltwater fishing, gliding, distance swimming, snorkeling, cross-country skiing, or something else that appeals to you.

Most of us have a strong impulse to return with some booty from our adventures. You may want to collect postcards, decals, demitasse spoons, T-shirts, local books, cookbooks, state emblems, shells, rocks, or things as various as forest leaves or colonial foodstuffs for a special hobby.

We wish to thank those who have contributed expertise, time, enthusiasm, and encouragement to enhance this book: Phyllis and Alexander Aldrich, Jo and Verner Alexanderson, Susan Allen, Ruth Alsin, Craig Altschul, Ted Austin, Peter Bachelder, Anne and William Barclay, Barbara and Carl Beehner, Vondee and David Beeman, Ann and Werner Berthoff, Pamela Black-Boer and Westin Boer, Ralph Bloom, Marilyn Bosare, Becky Bovelsky, Sally Bray, Constance Carlson, Grethe and Maria Certain, Judith Christenson, Betty and Woodbridge Constant, Dick Courcelle, Richard Cutts, Shirley, Barrie and George Davidson, Beth DeLong, Shirley and Howard DeLong, Anne and Terence Diggory, Cynthia and David DuPre, Judith and Bruce Eissner, Peter Fallon, Alberta and Jack Feynman, Jack Fenners, Joan Fina, Patricia Fiorelli, Patricia and Thomas Fox, Grace Friary, Stuart Frank, Michael Frucci, Gay and Alvin Gamage, Sue and Robert Gorton, Anne Gwynn,

Diane and William Hall, Jerry Hall, Thomas
Holmes and Phyllis Roth, Tracy Hendrickson,
Elizabeth Hibbard, Judy Hilliard, Judy Hudson,
Bette Hunt, Jonathan Hyde, Dave Iavonne,
Amy Jordan, Cherie Keemar, Conrad Kelfos,
Nancy and John Kendall, Albert Klyberg,
Katherine Kinderman, Lizabeth King, Madeline
and Paul Kruzel, Linda and Benjamin Labaree,
Barnet Laschever, Angela LeBlanc, David Lee,
Carol Levesque, Ardyth Lewis, Thor Loberg,
Polly and Chuck Longsworth, Mary Maynard,
Janet and Curt Mayott, Sharon McCanna, Carol
and Bud McKeon, Marjorie and Bard McNulty,
Virginia and Stephen Minot, Charlotte Moore,
Thomas Murphy, Elaine Murray, Tom Myers,
Linda Naiss, Mab and Charles Owen, Anne and
Joseph Palamountain, Bette Perreault, Barbara
Pitnof, George Potter, Judith and James Potter,
Elizabeth and David Ratcliff, Elaine Raymond,
Celeste Reid, Jean and Donald Richards, Fred
Roehrig, Polly Rollins, Kenneth Rothwell, Mary
Rulison, Rosemary Ryan, Jane and Karl Sabo,
Judy Salsbury, Juliet Saunders, Ardene Scroggy,
Janet Serra, Mary and Sanford Sistare, Jane
Snaider, Vivian Stanley, Mark Stenning, Eileen
and Elwood Stitzel, Mary Lou and Robert
Strode, Jean and Leonard Tomat, Scott Van Pelt,
Theresa Waite, Alex Warden, Phillip West, Alan
Wheelock, Frank Whitman, Brad Williams, Helen and Gunther Winkler, Nancy Wurlitzer, and
Frederick Zivic.

ITINERARY A: WESTERN CIRCUIT OF CONNECTICUT

FIRST CONGREGATIONAL CHURCH

ITINERARY A

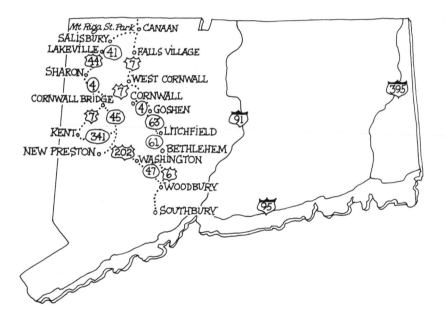

Western Circuit of Connecticut

Connecticut's topography divides the state into three areas: the western highland, with its small mountains and hills; the central lowland, a long wide valley centered on the Connecticut River; and the eastern highland, along waves of gently rolling wooded hills running north and south.

The formation began in Precambrian times, about 620 million years ago, with a major shifting of the earth's crust. Two more shifts, during the Paleozoic era, 230 to 500 million years ago, created a fault along the eastern side of the lowland that produced mountains. These mountains and those in the western part of the state developed a basalt crust (you can still see a basalt ridge at Talcott Mountain, west of Hartford).

A later shift of the earth's crust tilted the land, sloping it from northwest to southeast, producing cliffs on one side and a gradual slope on the other. Streams and rivers, their velocity increased by the tilt, began to erode the plain of the central lowland. Glaciers carried soil from northern New England, depositing it in Connecticut's valleys; boulders, too, scraped along, scouring rocks and leaving scratches you can still see today. Centuries later the smaller rocks were used to build the stone walls that line the roads and farms of the area; the larger ones stand where they've stood for hundreds and thousands of years, mute remnants of a bygone age.

This itinerary through western Connecticut begins in the lovely town of Litchfield, a living museum of eighteenth-century life. Our route heads south through Bethlehem and Woodbury (with perhaps a side trip to Southbury), continues northwest through Washington to New Milford and New Preston, and then swings west to Kent. The Appalachian Trail and the Housatonic River parallel part of the trip north from Kent to Cornwall Bridge, then we head west to Sharon and north through Lakeville and Salisbury into Mount Riga State Park for a climb and a picnic. We retrace our steps south again to Salisbury, then northeast to Canaan, turning back south through Falls Village, the Cornwells, and Goshen, to complete the circuit back to Litchfield.

LITCHFIELD The Pootatuck Indians gave title of land in the western hills of Connecticut to the residents of Hartford and Windsor, who named it Litchfield. The early settlers, led by John Marsh and John Buell in 1719, built churches, gristmills, a school, and houses on the rolling hills. Litchfield's location along natural routes from

New York, Albany, Hartford, and Boston later made the town a busy center of commerce.

During the American Revolution the town played a major role as a communication and supply link. Litchfield residents, including Oliver Wolcott, Ethan Allen, Seth Warner, Ephraim Kirby, Bezaleel Beebe, and Benjamin Tallmadge, played active parts in the American cause during that time. According to local legend, a lead statue of King George II was seized from its spot on Bowling Green in New York, brought to the woodshed behind Oliver Wolcott's house, melted down by the women and girls in town, and made into bullets. George Washington had breakfast with Oliver Wolcott during one of his trips to Litchfield.

The village today is a living museum that has been maintained by its residents through the generations. You can see this care in the facades of elegant white clapboard homes that line North and South streets; most of these homes are still privately owned. A walk or drive on North Street passes the 1760 home of **Benjamin Tallmadge**, an aide to George Washington; **Sheldon's Tavern**, where George Washington (who else?) slept when he came to town; the 1775 birthplace of **Harriet Beecher Stowe**; and the first academy for girls, **Pierce Academy**, founded in 1792.

South Street takes you by the **Tapping Reeve House and Law School**. In the house you'll find hand-stenciled walls in the front hall, a lovely paneled dining room, and fine period furnishings, many of which belong to the Reeve family. The school, one hundred feet from the house, is a one-room building where legal education in this country began in 1784. Among its graduates were Aaron Burr, John C. Calhoun, Horace Mann, and many members of Congress. Also on South Street is the 1799 home of Oliver Wolcott, Jr.

The **Congregational Church**, facing the

**Tapping Reeve
House and Law
School
South Street
Litchfield
203-567-5862**

north end of the green, is a majestic structure. It was built in 1829 by the First Ecclesiastical Society of Litchfield. The architecture has been changed several times, and the church was once moved several hundred feet. The weathervane is the original one; and one of the pew doors, found in the basement, is also original.

Litchfield Historical Society
East and South Streets
Litchfield
203-567-5862

The **Litchfield Historical Society**, at one corner of the green, houses a fine collection of early American paintings, furniture, decorative arts, galleries of special exhibits, and a research library.

When you're ready for lunch head east on Route 202, to **Toll Gate Hill Inn** (203-482-6116), which was once a way station between Litchfield and Hartford in the late eighteenth and early nineteenth centuries. Dating from 1745, the building is also called the "Captain William Bull Tavern."

White Memorial Conservation Center
Route 202
Litchfield
203-567-0857

Two miles west of town on Route 202 is the **White Memorial Conservation Center**, the largest nature center in the state. On its 4,000 acres visitors will find trails for hiking, horseback riding, cross-country skiing, and snowshoeing, and a special trail for the handicapped marked in braille. The former residence of the White family, "Whitehall" is a combined nature center and museum, containing a natural history library, classrooms for educational programs, giftshop, and bookstore.

Haight Vineyards and Winery
Chestnut Hill Road
Litchfield
203-567-4045

The **Haight Vineyards and Winery** is one mile east of town off Route 118. The first Rieslings and Chardonnays were produced here in 1979 from fifteen acres of grapes. The winery offers vineyard walks, winery tours, and wine tasting.

Lourdes in Litchfield Shrine
Route 118
Litchfield
203-567-8434

The **Lourdes in Litchfield Shrine** is also located on Route 118. The Montfort Missionaries created there a thirty-five-acre shrine that includes a replica of the Grotto of Our Lady of

Lourdes in France and a trail leading past stations of the cross to a crucifixion scene.

White Flower Farm (203-507-0801) is located on Route 63, three miles south of town. Avid gardeners make pilgrimages there every year to select plants from exotic gardens and greenhouses.

BETHLEHEM

Drive south from Litchfield on Routes 63 and 61 to Bethlehem. The town is famous for its special "Bethlehem" Christmas postmark and for the Christmas Festival. For a very unusual and moving experience continue south on Route 61 to **Regina Laudis Abbey**, on Flanders Road. An eighteenth-century Neopolitan nativity scene is on display there. It's the sort of exhibit you can look at for a long time without assimilating every figure into your mind. The Benedictine nuns offer handmade goods in their gift shop.

WOODBURY

Flanders Nature Center
Flanders and Church Hill Roads
Woodbury
203-263-3711

Not far away is the **Flanders Nature Center,** which was founded in 1963 on the Van Vleck estate. This 200-acre farm estate features a sheep farm, trails, aboretum, a forest sanctuary, gift shop, maple syrup house, and a full schedule of special events. Parts of the estate are located in several sections of Woodbury.

Continue south on Route 6 into the center of Woodbury, one of the oldest of the western towns in Connecticut. It was purchased from Chief Pomperaug of the Pootatuck Indians, who lies buried in the center of town.

Today Woodbury is known for having more antique shops per square mile than any other spot in the state. **Woodbury Pewterers** (203-263-2668) offers discounts of twenty to fifty percent on factory seconds. Come for pewter bowls, candlesticks, coffeepots, mugs, tankards, and teapots.

Glebe House was built as a minister's farm

**Glebe House
Hollow Road
Woodbury
203-263-2855**

in 1771. During a secret meeting at the house in 1783, Samuel Seabury was proposed for consecration as bishop in the Episcopal church. After a year of his time and a trip to Scotland, he was finally consecrated by the Scottish church, in Aberdeen, Scotland, in 1784, beginning the Episcopal church in the New World. When you visit the house, ask about the secret tunnel once used as an escape route into the hills.

**Hurd House
Hollow Road
Woodbury**

Hurd House dates from 1680 and is one of the oldest houses in town. Once two houses, the southern half was moved from its foundation on the river in 1798. It is owned by the **Old Woodbury Historical Society** and contains period furniture donated to the society.

If you're ready for lunch head for the **Curtis House** (203-263-2101) on Route 6, which is Main Street in Woodbury. First opened as Orenaug Inn in 1754, it was later called Kelly's Tavern.

SOUTHBURY

For a side trip to Southbury continue south on Route 6. Southbury was part of the Woodbury land purchase of 1673 from the Pootatuck Indians. Deacon Minor, one of the first to explore Southbury, camped on an Indian trail under a large white oak tree during his visit. The current White Oak district is now an historic area.

**Bullet Hill School
Route 6
Southbury
203-264-2993**

Bullet Hill School, built in 1787 of bricks made from local clay on Bullet Hill, is one of the oldest schools in Connecticut. It is listed in the National Register of Historic Places.

**Old Town Hall
Route 172
South Britain
203-264-2993**

The **Old Town Hall** is now used as a museum. Manuscripts, books, and local artifacts are displayed there.

WASHINGTON

From Woodbury take Route 47 to Hotchkissville, continue to Route 199, and look for signs leading to the **American Indian Archaeological Institute.** Exhibits include a 12,000-year-old mastodon skeleton, 10,000-year-old Indian artifacts including a "clovis type" spear point, a simulated archaeological site, and a reconstructed Algonquian village. A longhouse is furnished with sapling-supported bunks covered with skins and contains birchbark carriers, pottery, tools, games, and clothing. The Quinnetukut habitat trail meanders through the woods.

The institute also conducts archaeological digs in prehistoric campsites near Brookfield, Washington, and East Canaan. You can sign up as a participant and learn about mapping, collecting, screening, and recording information. Educational programs are held around the year for children and adults. Ever wanted to learn flintknapping or finger weaving? Here is the place, along with workshops on pottery, leather, quillwork, and basketry.

American Indian Archaeological Institute
Curtis Road
Washington
203-868-0518

The **Gunn Historical Museum** is located in a 1781 house. The collection includes dolls, dollhouses, period furnishings, needlework, and spinning wheels.

Gunn Historical Museum
Wykeham Road on Route 47
Washington
203-868-7756

Route 47 north and Route 202 west will bring you to New Preston and the Lake Waramaug area. **Lake Waramaug State Park** is located on Route 478 on the northwest shore. The Indian name, Waramaug, means "good fishing."

NEW PRESTON

North of the lake, **Hopkins Vineyard** grows French-American hybrid wine grapes. As a visitor you can tour and taste in a nineteenth-century restored barn, or bring a picnic and purchase wine for lunch.

Hopkins Vineyard
Hopkins Road
Warren
203-868-7954

Route 45 north and Route 341 west will lead you to Kent. Just north of Kent, the **Sloane-Stanley Museum** is located in a rustic barn. There is a replica of Eric Sloane's studio, exhibits of his work, and an extensive collection of wooden tools, some dating back to the seventeenth century. The ruins of a Kent iron blast furnace on

KENT
Sloane-Stanley Museum
Route 7
Kent
203-927-3849 or
203-566-3005

the grounds help to complete the picture of work in early Kent.

The **Fife and Drum** (Main Street, 203-927-3509) is a handy place for lunch after touring the Sloane-Stanley Museum. Eric Sloane prints hang on the walls of the Tap Room.

Kent Falls State Park, with its 200-foot cascade, is located on Route 7 in North Kent. Visitors can walk along a winding path up to the head of the falls.

SHARON

Northeast Audubon Center
Route 4
Sharon
203-364-0520

Continue on Route 7 to Cornwall Bridge, then take Route 4 northwest to Sharon. The **Northeast Audubon Center** is a 684-acre sanctuary on the grounds of the former home of Mrs. Clement R. Ford. There are eleven miles of self-guided trails, an herb garden, and a museum shop. Come in late July for the **Sharon Audubon Festival.**

Sharon was settled in 1739 on the plateau east of the Taconic Mountains. Along Main Street and Route 41 you will pass elegant estates and mansions, some from Revolutionary War days. The **Clock Tower** and **Congregational Church** face the green, the site of the **Clothesline Art Show** in August. The green is busy all summer and fall with flea markets and antiques fairs. The **Gay-Hoyt House** nearby is made of brick; its fireplaces angled into the end walls are characteristic of the regional architecture.

Gay-Hoyt House
Main Street
Sharon
203-364-5688

LIME ROCK

Lime Rock Park
Route 112
Lakeville
203-435-2571

Sports car enthusiasts may want to continue north from Sharon on Route 41, then detour on Route 112 to **Lime Rock Park.** Even if you are not a racing aficionado, you may still want to make the trip. This is one of Paul Newman's favorite tracks!

SALISBURY

Retrace your way back to Route 41 and head north for Salisbury. This resort town in the hills was settled by the Dutch from New York state.

WOODBURY

Black-faced sheep are some of the many domestic animals at the Van Vleck Farm Sanctuary in Woodbury.

LAKEVILLE

Heart-stopping stock car racing is just one of the numerous events happening at Lime Rock Park, summer and fall.

NEW PRESTON

Wine-tasting at the Hopkins Vineyard can be doubly enjoyable, as the vineyard overlooks tranquil Lake Waramaug.

Later, during the Revolutionary War, the town's furnaces produced cannon, cannonballs, muskets, swords, sabers, shot, and grenades. In front of the site of the old and beautiful Town Hall, which burned in 1987, is a triphammer that once pounded hot iron as a part of Salisbury's industrial past.

North of town, off Route 41, in **Mount Riga State Park**, you can also see the **Mount Riga Furnace**. This furnace was abandoned when a breakdown in the bellows cooled material in the furnace into one solid mass, called a "salamander." A salamander wasn't uncommon in blast furnace operations and could sometimes be removed by firing into the furnace with a small cannon, but the Mount Riga Furnace did not have enough money to start up again.

Most mountain towns have their legends about local recluses or isolated communities tucked into "coves," and Salisbury is no different. Near Mount Riga live the "Raggies," descendants of the furnace workmen, who keep apart from modern society. In stark contrast to this remnant of the past, contemporary Salisbury has become a very exclusive area that includes many celebrities as part-time residents of the community.

CANAAN

Housatonic Railroad
Routes 7 and 44
Canaan
203-824-0339

FALLS VILLAGE

Route 44 will take you northeast from Salisbury to Canaan for a pleasant ride along the Housatonic River by train. The **Housatonic Railroad** offers trips departing from the oldest train station still in use in the United States.

Alternatively, turn south from Route 44 onto Route 126 to Falls Village for a canoe trip on the Housatonic River with **Riverrunning Expeditions** (Main Street, 203-824-5579). The trip begins in Falls Village and ends at either West Cornwall or Cornwall Bridge, with some mild whitewater along the way and a short, more challenging patch at the bridge. You can choose to paddle the upper Housatonic for flat water or more downstream to Kent for more extensive whitewater.

Whether by land or river, continue south to West Cornwall where, at the junction of Route 7 and 128, you can see and photograph the one-lane covered bridge that won a national award for restoration in 1973. Originally designed by Ithiel Town in 1827, it is the longest of the four covered bridges over the Housatonic.

Routes 128 and 125 lead southeast to Cornwall. **Cathedral Pines**, a forest of 200-year-old pines, is a couple of miles from town. Head west on Route 4, and about a half mile beyond the junction of Route 125 turn left on Bolton Hill Road, then right on Jewell Street. At the next fork turn left and watch for the white blazes that mark the Appalachian Trail. The trees here in Cathedral Pines reach as high as 150 feet, some with diameters of over three feet. Look for the many woodpeckers who find more than enough insects to lure them to this lush forest.

In the Cornwalls you will undoubtedly hear about the controversy over **Dudleytown**. As one of the few ghost towns left in Connecticut, its legends linger on. The town, built on a plateau above the Housatonic River on the Appalachian Trail near Cornwall Bridge, was founded in 1747 and was populated until 1900. Today only parts of collapsed stone walls, foundations, and wells remain. Who knows if it is haunted? Life in Dudleytown was not easy. The mountains surrounding the village kept the sunlight out, so the land couldn't be farmed. Instead villagers depended on charcoal for their livelihood. And there is the legend of the Dudleytown Curse, with odd happenings and bizarre deaths as proof. The story of the curse seems to start with the Dudley brothers, early residents of the town,

THE CORNWALLS

who were descended from Edward and John Dudley, the dukes of Northumberland who plotted against the English monarchy during the fifteenth and sixteenth centuries.

Just before the turn of the nineteenth century, Gershom Holister was killed when he fell from the roof of a barn during a barnraising. A string of other deaths claimed residents over the years. During the remainder of the century, when charcoal was the town's main industry, the residents may well have been affected by heavy concentrations of carbon monoxide in the air that could have caused brain damage. One story tells about a man who caught mussels in Spectacle Pond, let them sit until they were rancid, then made them into a stew. He gave the stew to a family he was feuding with, and when they died he hanged himself. Although the town languished and then disappeared in the twentieth century, its reputation lives on.

GOSHEN

From Cornwall continue southeast on Route 4 into Goshen, a farming village where the first commercial hard cheese in America was made. Several miles outside of town you will find the entrance to **Mohawk State Forest.** You can drive in 2¹/₂ miles to a wooden observation tower for a panoramic view around the compass. Park your car and walk to the tower; then follow the blue-blazed **Mattatuck Trail** to the ruins of a great stone tower. You can climb to the top of the trail—1,683 feet, straight up—for views of the Riga Plateau (Mounts Everett, Race, and Bear), the Catskills, Canaan Mountain, and Mount Tom. Then you can follow the trail for 3¹/₄ miles back to your car.

Route 63 leads you south back to Litchfield. Or, if you would like to continue into Itinerary B, take Route 8 south, I-84 west to Danbury, and

Route 7 south to Norwalk. Alternatively, you can meander through the country on a series of pleasant local roads to the shore. If you plan to head east to central Connecticut, Routes 202 and 4 will take you into Hartford. Another alternative is to link up with Itinerary G into the Berkshires of Massachusetts.

ITINERARY B: CENTRAL CONNECTICUT

MARK TWAIN HOUSE

ITINERARY B

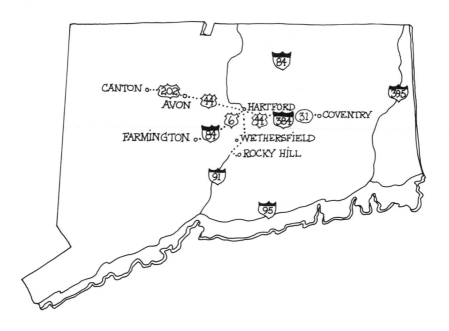

Central Connecticut

Connecticut, originally named Quinnetukut from an Indian word meaning "beside the long tidal river," is called the Constitution State because it was the first colony to have a written constitution. More informally it's also called the Nutmeg State, for the peddlers who once traveled door to door selling spices. (Now and again customers would find little carved wooden pellets instead of the spices they had paid for.)

It is in Hartford, the state capital, where we begin this itinerary through central Connecticut. The itinerary is patterned in the shape of a wheel. Hartford lies at the center, and each spoke leads to destinations— Farmington to the southwest, Avon and Canton to the west, Coventry to the east, and Wethersfield and Rocky Hill to the south. Visit a house that is "part medieval fortress, part Mississippi riverboat, part cuckoo clock," hike up to the Heublein Tower for a view all the way to Long Island on a clear day, have lunch at an herb farm, or catch up on dinosaur lore.

HARTFORD

Fort Good Hope was founded by Dutch fur traders from Nieuw Amsterdam in 1623. In 1635 settlers from Cambridge, Massachusetts, arrived with John Steel as their leader. They changed the Indian name for the area—Suckiag—to Newtowne. (It was named Hartford two years later in honor of Reverend Samuel Stone, who hailed from Hertford, England.) A year later Thomas Hooker led more settlers here from Cambridge, on a two-week journey. He bought the land from Sequassen, sachem of the Suckiaug Indians. This was the second time the land was bought: In 1633 the Pequot Indians had sold it for "one piece of duffell [a heavy woolen fabric] 27 ells long [an ell is an old Dutch unit of measurement], six axes, six kettles, eighteen knives, one sword blade, one pair of shears, some toys and a musket."

Settlers from Windsor, Wethersfield, and Hartford drew up a constitution in 1639. The eleven articles in the Fundamental Orders of Connecticut later served as a model for the Constitution of the United States.

Early settlers made good use of the Connecticut River, their outlet to the sea. Their source of trade: furs, timber, fish, game, and tobacco. This busy trade created a new industry. The people who financed the ships, worried about possible wrecks, storms, and fire damage, began to set aside a portion of their profits to insure against possible losses. When shipping ended during the War of 1812, the insurance companies shifted their focus from marine insurance to fire insurance for homes and buildings. A disastrous fire in New York City in 1835 was a bonanza for the Hartford Fire Insurance Company. Claims in excess of $17 million forced its New York competitors into bankruptcy; the Hartford firm paid every one of its claims. Suddenly new clients wanted policies, and the boom was on. And it's still on. Hartford even today is dominated by insurance and banking companies that retain their reputation for reliability and profitability.

As you enter Hartford from West Hartford, your first stop, and our favorite place in the city, is the **Mark Twain House**. The house—"part medieval fortress, part Mississippi riverboat, part cuckoo clock"—was described by Twain this way:

**Mark Twain House
351 Farmington
 Avenue
Hartford
203-525-9317**

> This is the house that Mark built,
>   These are the bricks of various hue,
> And shape and position, straight and askew,
>   With the nooks and angles and gables too,
> Which make up the house presented to view,
>   The curious house that Mark built.
>
> This is the sunny and snug retreat,
>   At once both city and country seat,
> Where he grinds out many a comical grist,
>   The author, architect, humorist,
> The auctioneer and dramatist,
>   Who lives in the house that Mark built . . .
>
> Samuel L. Clemens his maiden name;
>   As a humorist not unknown to fame,
> As author or architect all the same,

At auction or drama always game,
An extravagant wag whom none can tame:
He lives in the house that Mark built.

Here is the Innocent Abroad,
The patron too of the lightning rod;
And here disports the Jumping Frog,
Roughing it on his native log;
Tom Sawyer, with his graceless tricks,
Amuses the horse-car lunatics;
And here is the grim historic sage,
Who hurled in the facts of the Gilded Age,
In this curious house that Mark built.

And below is the alias autograph
Over which he has given you many a laugh,
This author, architect, humorist,
This auctioneer and dramatist,
Who still keeps grinding his comical grist
In his cozy, sunny and snug retreat,
At once both city and country seat,
Made up of bricks of various hue,
And shape and position, straight and askew,
With its nooks and angles and gables too,
The curious house that Mark built.

The Victorian-Gothic house is definitely unusual. It sits on a knoll above Farmington Avenue, a large red and black brick structure with gables, porches, and chimneys. Samuel Langhorne Clemens built the house in 1874. Nostalgia for his days on the Mississippi riverboats later prompted him to add a section in the rear shaped like a wheelhouse, complete with nautical doors and an intercom. The servants' quarters were built on the front of the house, so that they could keep track of anyone passing by without running through the house—a plan Twain claimed saved wear on his rugs. The author's study, which was also known as the billiard room, was on the top floor of the house. He worked here all day at his desk, which faced the wall, not the street, using a pigeonhole system for storage—a system so confusing he actually lost the manuscript for *Huckleberry Finn.* There's a large billiard table in the middle of the room, and stenciled billiard balls, cues, and pipes on the ceiling. In the library there's a 12-foot carved mantelpiece that Twain bought in Scotland. It's decorated with carved flowers, fruits, baronial arms, and a bronze plate inscribed "The ornament of a house is the friends who frequent it." The house was decorated by Louis Tiffany and Company, and is filled with Oriental, Turkish, Indian, and American objects. Every one of the twenty rooms has something unusual or interesting about it. And the guides add flavor to your visit with their repertoire of stories about Twain.

The **Harriet Beecher Stowe House**, nearby, is decorated with her paintings and some original furnishings and is filled with the kinds of plants the author loved.

Harriet Beecher Stowe House Forest Street Hartford 203-525-9317

Both Twain and Stowe houses are part of **Nook Farm**, a nineteenth-century writers' colony. Also here: the **Nook Farm Research Library** (twelve thousand volumes, including valuable manuscripts) and the **Nook Farm Museum Shop** (books and gifts).

Nook Farm 77 Forest Street Hartford 203-525-9317

Before you go to Hartford, write the Greater Hartford Convention and Tourist Bureau (One Civic Plaza, Hartford) for **The Walk**—a pamphlet that describes a walking tour of the city. Banners on lampposts mark tour highlights in the downtown area.

Greater Hartford Convention and Tourist Bureau One Civic Center Plaza Hartford 06103 203-728-6789

Follow Farmington Avenue into downtown Hartford, where you'll find parking, shopping, and restaurants at the **Hartford Civic Center**. This is the downtown sports center—the home of the **Aetna World Cup** tennis tournament and the **Hartford Whalers**.

Hartford Civic Center One Civic Center Plaza Hartford 203-727-8080

Leave your car and walk down Asylum Street to the **Old State House**, on Main Street.

**Old State House
800 Main Street
Hartford
203-522-6766**

Charles Bulfinch designed the building. There's an information center on the first floor; legislative chambers, with original furnishings, on the second.

Around the corner, down State Street, you'll see **Constitution Plaza**, one of the first urban-renewal projects in New England, on your left; the **Phoenix Life Insurance Building**, the green curved-glass "hyperbloid" that's stirred up quite a controversy, on your right.

Turn down Prospect Street, and head for the **Travelers' Tower** and a bird's-eye view of the city. The green light atop the 527-foot tower, the tallest in New England until Boston's Prudential Tower was completed in 1965, is a landmark for visitors and townspeople.

**Travelers' Tower
One Tower Square
Hartford
203-277-2431**

The tower sits on the site of the old Zachary Sanford Tavern. On October 31, 1687, Sir Edmund Andros, the Crown-appointed governor, came to a meeting here and demanded the return of a liberal charter that had been granted the Hartford Colony in 1662 by King Charles II. Before Andros had the charter in his hands, all of the candles "miraculously" blew out, and the charter was gone! One of the colonists, Joseph Wadsworth, took it and hid it in the trunk of an old tree. That tree was called the Charter Oak Tree until it blew down in 1856. Mark Twain once listed some of the objects that were said to have been made from its wood: "A walking stick, dog collar, needle case, three-legged stool, bootjack, dinner table, tenpin alley, toothpick, and enough Charter Oak to build a plank road from Hartford to Salt Lake City."

The arts are alive and well in Hartford. The Connecticut Opera Association, the Hartford Symphony, and the Hartford Ballet all perform at the **Horace Bushnell Memorial Auditorium** on Capitol Avenue. Also here: films, lectures, Broadway shows, and a rotating art exhibit in the Promenade Gallery.

**Bushnell Memorial
Hall
166 Capitol Avenue
Hartford
203-246-6807**

And there's neighborhood theater and music in town too. Our favorite: the **Hartford Stage Company** on Church Street.

At the **Wadsworth Atheneum**, right next to the tower, you'll find the Nutting collection of early American furniture, the J. P. Morgan collection of antique bronzes, European porcelains and paintings, ship models, a library of art reference books, a museum shop, and a restaurant. Come for a lecture, a tour, or a special program.

Farther down Main Street is one of the few surviving eighteenth-century houses in Hartford. The **Butler-McCook Homestead**, built in 1782, houses paintings, silver, dolls, toys, and a collection of Japanese armor. Part of the house was once a blacksmith's shop; that room later became Dr. Daniel Butler's kitchen.

The **Noah Webster House**, in West Hartford is now a national historic landmark. When it was built in 1676, the farmhouse had just two rooms; a later addition turned the house into a saltbox. In the museum wing you can buy pewter and apothecary jars at the museum shop.

Don't miss the **Science Museum of Connecticut**, where kids enjoy the hands-on aquarium, the life-size model of a 60-foot sperm whale, and the **Gengras Planetarium**.

There are many places of interest surrounding Hartford. Route 4 or 84 will lead you southwest to Farmington, the scene in mid-May of the annual **Children's Services, Horse Show and Country Fair.**

The **Farmington Museum** is in the **Stanley-Whitman House**, which was built in 1660. The Elizabethan and Jacobean architecture of the original house has been fully restored, and the building is filled with seventeenth-century furnishings. Also here: displays of old manuscripts, glass, china, silver, and pewter.

Hartford Stage Company
50 Church Street
Hartford
203-527-5151

Wadsworth Atheneum
600 Main Street
Hartford
203-278-2670

Butler-McCook Homestead
394 Main Street
Hartford
203-522-1806

WEST HARTFORD

Noah Webster House
227 South Main Street
West Hartford
203-521-5362

Science Museum
960 Trout Brook Drive
West Hartford
203-236-2961

FARMINGTON

Farmington Museum
37 High Street
Farmington
203-677-9222

Hill-Stead Museum
35 Mountain Road
Farmington
203-677-4787

The **Hill-Stead Museum** is in the elegant mansion designed by Stanford White for millionaire Alfred Pope. You'll see paintings by Manet, Monet, Degas, Cassatt, and Whistler, among others, and a collection of Ming dynasty porcelains.

Enjoy canoeing? Then you'll love the 9½-mile trip from Farmington to Weatogue on the lower Farmington River. This stretch is smooth, and there are no portages. Spot one car in Weatogue, at the end of the bridge along Route 185. (There's a large lot at the east end of the bridge a few yards down Nod Road.) Then head back to Route 4 in Farmington to start off. The trip takes you past tall maples, sycamores, and oaks, a couple of golf courses; then more woods. Look for kingfishers, sandpipers, orioles, woodchucks, and muskrats; you might even spot a deer, fox, or raccoon. On your right you'll see Talcott Mountain, Heublein Tower marking its summit. At the bend in the river toward the right, just as you come abreast of the tower, look for the cave at the northern end of the ridge. Legend has it that King Philip directed the burning of Simsbury from this spot in 1676.

Farther west, the upper Farmington River between Riverton and New Hartford is also popular (sometimes too popular—it gets crowded on nice days). You can take a 4½-mile trip, with some small rapids, from the Riverton picnic area west of the Route 20 bridge (across the highway from the Hitchcock Chair Factory), to the bridge on Route 318. Or go on another 5 miles, to the take-out above the Route 44 bridge.

Along the way: some rapids interspersed with flat stretches, islands, woods, and fast water, and several picnic areas and a campground. The general rule seems to be stick to the right side, which is clearer; on the left you'll find rocks. A stand of tall pines on the left bank signals one set of rapids; then, just after the river curves to the left, you'll see a stretch of boulders. The first bridge you come to is Route 318, the site for the first take-out. The second bridge is Route 219; where you'll have to dodge some rocks.

Don't go beyond the bridge at Route 44 unless you're a white-water expert; the heavy rapids in the gorge at Satan's Kingdom demand a rubber raft or inner tube. River Run apartments, on the right, signal the take-out. Once you've landed, walk along the shore below the bridge to see what you've missed—the river cascading into the gorge between cliffs on both sides.

AVON

From Hartford you can head west on Route 44 into Avon. Hikers will enjoy a day along the **Metacomet Trail**. From Routes 44 and 10, follow Route 44 a little bit over 2 miles to the sign for Reservoir 6. Park in the lot, and walk to the far end, bearing left on the dirt road, where you'll see blue-blazed signs marking the trail. The path leads to **Heublein Tower**, an ornate observation tower built in 1914. The view from the top on a clear day reaches as far as Mount Monadnock to the north, Long Island Sound to the south. Follow the trail along the other side of the reservoir on your way back.

Hungry? Stop for a meal at the **Avon Old Farms Inn** (203-677-2818) at the intersection of Routes 44 and 10. The Sunday brunch here is delicious. Then visit the **Farmington Valley Arts Center** in an historic stone building, once an explosives plant. Here you'll find artists' studios, a gallery, and a bookstore—and wonderful exhibitions and programs.

Farmington Valley Arts Center
Avon Park North
Avon
203-678-1867

Routes 44 and 202 lead to Canton, to visit the **Roaring Brook Nature Center**. You'll find interpretive displays with year-round nature exhibits, a store, a resource room, and 115 acres of woodland trails.

CANTON
Roaring Brook Nature Center
Gracey Road
Canton
203-693-0263

One of the trails—the **Tunxis Trail**—winds for almost 8 miles through Satan's Kingdom, a very steep gorge. It begins 2½ miles west of the junction of Routes 202 and 179. From the parking lot follow the blue-blazed signs along Pine Hill Road and Tipping Rock Ledge (where a glacial rock did in fact tip over) to Queen Mary Ledge and Rome Spare Outlook. Look for the sign that reads "Charcoal Kiln." It marks the spot where wood was cut, piled into a circle, covered with earth, and burned (with very little air)—all to produce charcoal. When you come to the end of the trail at Rome Spare Outlook, retrace your steps to Tipping Rock Ledge; then continue down to Satan's Kingdom Road, which leads back to Pine Hill.

COVENTRY

Heading east, follow Route 84 and 384 to Route 44, to Route 31 into Coventry, about 26 miles east of Hartford. This seventeenth-century town is much like its counterpart in England, with woods, hills, lakes, and ponds.

**Nathan Hale Homestead
South Street
Coventry
203-742-6917 or
247-8996**

Come mid-May to mid-October, when you can visit the **Nathan Hale Homestead**. Deacon Richard Hale, the patriot's father, built the home in 1776; and the family lived here until 1832. The ten rooms are furnished with family heirlooms and other antiques. The long table in the dining room was originally in a local tavern. It's said that when George Washington came through town, he had breakfast at this table.

During the Revolutionary War, Nathan Hale joined Knowlton's Rangers. When Washington needed information behind the British lines, Hale volunteered. He was caught and executed. His last words on the scaffold: "I regret that I have but one life to lose for my country."

Stop for lunch and more at **Capriland's Herb Farm** (203-742-7244) on Silver Street, off Route 44A. Your visit (reservations are a must) begins at 12:30 with a lecture and a tour of the

CANTON

Curious kids play with a turtle at the Roaring Brook Nature Center in Canton.

HARTFORD

The Wadsworth Atheneum, founded in 1842 by Daniel Wadsworth, is the oldest civic art museum in the country with a collection of nearly 40,000 objects.

COVENTRY

The Nathan Hale Homestead (c. 1776).

twenty-eight herb gardens; the delicious lunch is served at 1:30. During the meal, the owner, Adelma Simmons, appears in a cape and decorated skullcap to talk about each course. After lunch, head for the gift shop for kitchen wreaths, cornhusk scarecrows, sandalwood powder, handmade soaps, and pomanders.

WETHERSFIELD
Webb-Deane-Stevens
  Museum
211 Main Street
Wethersfield
203-529-0612

From Hartford head south on I-91 to Wethersfield. Here you'll find the **Webb-Deane-Stevens Museum**, actually three houses. The **Webb House** was once called Hospitality Hall, because officers of the Continental Army were entertained here during the Revolution. This national historic landmark, built in 1752 by Joseph Webb, was where George Washington and Count de Rochambeau met to plan the Yorktown campaign. It contains period furnishings, silver, and porcelain. Mrs. Webb redecorated in a flurry with a French red-flocked wallpaper just before Washington arrived; you can still see the paper on the walls of the room where he slept. The **Silas Dean House** was built in 1766 by a commissioner to France who was also a member of the First Continental Congress. It's furnished with elegant period pieces. The **Isaac Stevens House**, built in 1788, features toys, ladies' bonnets, handwrought fixtures, and an herb garden.

Buttolph-Williams
  House
Broad and Marsh
  Streets
Wethersfield
203-529-0460

The **Buttolph-Williams House**, built in 1692, is the oldest restored house in Wethersfield. It was considered a mansion in its day. Look for Pilgrim Century chairs and tables, pewter and Delft, a curved settee, and authentic implements in Ye Greate Kitchin.

ROCKY HILL
Dinosaur State
  Park
West Street
Rocky Hill
203-529-8423

From Wethersfield continue south on I-91 to exit 23 in Rocky Hill. At **Dinosaur State Park** you'll see hundreds of tracks from the Triassic period, 200 million years ago. These tracks, left in the soft mud of shallow ponds, later hardened into rock. They were uncovered in 1966, and now are protected by a geodesic dome.

More dinosaur lore? Drive up to Granby, Massachusetts, where you'll find **Granby Dinosaur Museum**. (Take I-91 north to Route 202 east.) There are fine collections nearby at **Amherst College** and **Mount Holyoke**. Or head south to New Haven, where a gigantic dinosaur skeleton can be found at the **Peabody Museum**.

From Rocky Hill, return to Hartford to complete the circle. Or, if you haven't visited the Connecticut shore yet, head south on I-91 to New Haven and join Itinerary C in progress, or you can continue west on I-95 to Norwalk, the beginning of the itinerary.

ITINERARY C: CONNECTICUT'S SHORE

MYSTIC SEAPORT MUSEUM

ITINERARY C

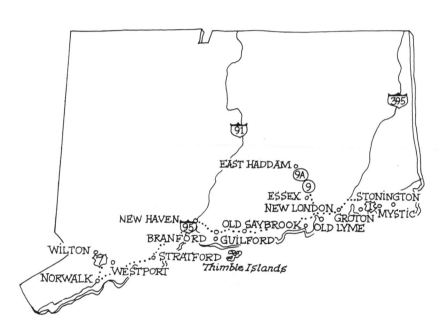

Connecticut's Shore

This itinerary begins in southern Connecticut, where features of the coast—a semiprotected sound, good harbors, and the mouth of a great river—made exploration and settlement inevitable. In 1614 Adriaen Block, a Dutch explorer and navigator, sailed through Long Island Sound, up into the lower reaches of the Connecticut River. Farther upstream the river separates the Berkshires from central Massachusetts, and Vermont from New Hampshire, linking north and south. Settlers used the river to reach Windsor, Hartford, and Wethersfield from their homes in Massachusetts as early as 1633.

Blow, Ye Winds

'Tis advertised in Boston, New York, and Buffalo
Five hundred brave Americans a-whaling for to go.

> Blow, ye winds, in the morning,
> And blow, ye winds, high-O!
> Clear away your running gear,
> And blow, ye winds, high-O!

They send you to New Bedford, that famous whaling port,
And give you to some land-sharks for to board and fit you out.

They send you to a boarding house, there for a time to
    dwell,
The thieves they there are thicker than the other side
    of hell!

They tell you of the clipper ships a-going in and out,
And say you'll take five hundred sperm, before you're
    six months out.
Now we have got him turned up, we tow him alongside;
We over with our blubber-hooks and rob him of his hide.

Now the boat-steerer overside the tackle overhauls,
The Skipper's in the main-chains, so loudly he does
    bawl!

Next comes the stowing down, my boys; 'twill take
    both night and day,
And you'll all have fifty cents apiece on the hundred
    and ninetieth lay.

Now we are bound into Tonbas, that blasted whaling
port,
And if you run away, my boys, you surely will get
caught.

Now we are bound into Tuckoons, full more in their
power,
Where the skippers can buy the Consul up for half a
barrel of flour!

But now that our old ship is full and we don't give
a damn,
We'll bend on all our stuns'ls and sail for Yankee
land.

When we get home, our ship made fast, and we get
through our sail,
A winding glass around we'll pass and damn this
blubber whaling!

And the winds can still whip up a storm along the Connecticut shore of Long Island Sound. The growth of manufacturing cities along parts of this shore in the nineteenth century, and the growth of exurban residential and commercial development in the twentieth, hide an economic past dependent upon good ports. You won't glimpse a clipper ship booming down the Sound in a northeaster, but you can visit three maritime museums to see a variety of vessels from this coast's extensive seafaring heritage. Excursion boats will take you out to see islands once favored by Captain Kidd—who knows where he buried treasure? Visit the secluded courtyards and superb museums of a famous university town or a medieval-style castle high on a hill.

We suggest you start your exploration of the coast at Norwalk, in the outer layer of New York suburbs that fill the southwestern corner of the state, and move east along the water, with one excursion up the lower reaches of the Connecticut River. (For suggestions about places to visit in western and central Connecticut, see Itineraries A and B.)

NORWALK

Up until the American Revolution, Norwalk was an agrarian and industrial center. During the Revolution, until 1779, Norwalk had not had any major raids by the British, although apprehension was felt all along the coast. In June of that year, forty-one British boats assembled in Long Island Sound, preparing to attack one of the towns on the Connecticut shore. Because winds kept the fleet from sailing east, a revision of plans named Norwalk as the target for attack. Major General Tryon gathered his forces just outside the Norwalk Islands and then landed at Calf Pasture after sunset on July 12. Joined by other regiments, they marched into Norwalk and set fire to much of the town.

When you visit Norwalk, you will hear a lot about the Lockwood family. The first was Ephraim Lockwood, who settled there in 1664. His great-grandson, Eliphalet Lockwood, who was born in 1741, was the first of the family to collect family treasures. In 1779 Eliphalet and Susanna St. John Lockwood escaped from the British raid of July 12 with their silver and their Bible. A single line sums up the disaster: "The Town Burnt by ye Enemy July 12, 1779." Instead of rebuilding their home on North Avenue, the Lockwoods spent money rebuilding their family business near the east end of the bridge in town. As merchant-bankers they were involved in the West Indies trade with their ships *Eagle* and *Esther*, sailing out with lumber and returning with rum and sugar. Their sons, Buckingham and William, carried on the family business until 1842.

Lockwood House
141 East Avenue
Norwalk
203-866-0202

Lockwood House is also the Museum of the City of Norwalk. It was built in 1971 to house collections. Look for the mantels that were taken from Colonel Buckingham Lockwood's house, built in 1785. The building houses English and American furniture and silver of the eighteenth and nineteenth centuries as well as Oriental and French antiquities. The Norwalk Historical Reference Library has a collection of maps, charts, prints, photographs, manuscripts, diaries, and ledgers for research use.

The **Lockwood-Mathews Mansion Museum** was built by LeGrand Lockwood from 1864 to 1868. This four-story mansion has an octagonal rotunda with a parquetry floor and a grand staircase leading up to the top. Ceilings, windows, walls, and doors were constructed using gilt, marble, inlaid and carved wood, and etched glass. Architects and designers were brought from Europe to design this blend of a French château and a Scottish manor house. After Mr. Lockwood died in 1871 the Charles Mathews family lived in the house for three generations. Restoration has been in progress since the 1960s. When we visited there was an unusually rich collection of music boxes on the second floor under the auspices of the Musical Box Society International.

Lockwood–Mathews Mansion Museum
295 West Avenue
Norwalk
203-838-1434

SoNo is an historic district that is seeing renewed life with restaurants, shops, and art galleries. The steamboat and the railroad were originally responsible for growth in the area; from Stroffolino Bridge you can see the dock area and also a railroad bridge. Steamboats once landed at Quintard's Wharf on Marshall Street and at Steam Boat Landing, south of the bridge. In the nineteenth century many shippers sailed in and out of Norwalk. In 1853 there was a disaster involving both steamboats and the railroad. The Boston Express raced through South Norwalk at 20 MPH and straight off into the air; the drawbridge was up at the time because a steamboat had passed through minutes earlier.

SoNo
Washington and
  South Main
  Streets
Norwalk
203-866-1102

For those who love maritime museums, one more is being developed on the waterfront and will be ready in 1988. The Maritime Center at Norwalk will be "part history exhibit, part aquarium, part IMAX theater, and part recreated working waterfront." Visitors will be encouraged to see, hear, touch, and taste objects and concepts from the sea and understand the development and change in regional maritime activity. The aquarium will include a tidal pool, examples of marine life from the salt marsh to the ocean, and a seascape tank to exhibit how the Gulf Stream winds through the Atlantic. Displays about nineteenth-century coastal communities will provide a setting for visitors to understand what life was like in those days.

Still a seafaring community, Norwalk offers an oyster festival on the weekend after Labor Day every year. This event includes seafood cooked on an open fire, arts and crafts exhibits, entertainment, fireworks, and tours on vessels such as *The Lady Joan* (203-838-9003), a replica of a stern paddlewheeler. Information on the festival is available from the **Norwalk Seaport Association, Inc.**

Norwalk Seaport Association, Inc. 81 Washington Street South Norwalk 06854 203-838-9444

Sixteen islands are scattered around the Connecticut shore of Long Island Sound off Norwalk harbor, with a lighthouse at each end of the group. Adriaen Block, the Dutch explorer, discovered them in 1614, entering in his log "off the port bow appeared some islands with trees." Later, families lived on the islands raising cattle; they included one sheepherder living on Sheffield Island who decided to separate his rams from his ewes by placing the rams on so-named Ram Island. Nathan Hale spent some of his last days hiding in the islands—soon after he left he was caught by the British and hanged. Rumrunners, smugglers, and pirates have also used the Norwalk Islands for refuge.

Tavern Island was once the home of Billy Rose, who imported five statues of Grecian maidens; built a saltwater tidal pool as a home for peacocks, African crown cranes, and other rare birds; and raised a herd of European fallow deer. Garsham Smith, who lived on Sheffield Island, often had to row around from island to island to milk cows that had wandered across at low tide. Chimon Island is known for its heron rookery. Legend says that Captain Kidd buried treasure there.

Although many new restaurants are appearing in the area, local inhabitants recommend these: **Meson Galicia** (250 Westport Avenue Country Mall, 203-846-0223) for Northern Spanish cuisine; **Maria's Trattoria** (172 Main Street, 203-847-5166) for homemade pasta; **Jasper's Oyster Bar** (2–3 South Main Street, 203-852-1716); and **SoNo Seaport Seafood** (100 Water Street, 203-854-9483), which is next door to a fish market so you know your dinner is fresh. A short drive out of town will bring you to **Silvermine Tavern** (Silvermine Avenue, 203-847-4558) for lunch, dinner, or wonderful Sunday brunch. Not far from Silvermine Tavern, you will find **Silvermine Guild Arts Center**. The Guild houses a school of art, several galleries, and a shop. You can take classes there, hear lectures, or attend an evening of chamber music.

Silvermine Guild Arts Center
1037 Silvermine Road
Norwalk
203-966-5617

From Silvermine Guild you can take a side trip north on Route 106 to **June Havoc's Cannon Crossing**, where you will find a small village including a railroad station and a schoolhouse filled with shops. Miss Havoc has preserved a village atmosphere in this rural setting as a monument to early American settlers.

WILTON
June Havoc's Cannon Crossing
Cannondale
Wilton
203-762-7257

From Norwalk take either Route 1 or I-95 to Westport. The **Nature Center for Environmental Activities** is located on sixty-one acres of woods, fields, and streams interlaced with trails: Swamp Loop, which is popular for wildflowers; High Woods, including a "managed burn area"; Wadsworth Trail, which features ferns and wildflowers; Butterfly Trail, where butterflies are prolific; and a Sensitivity Trail, for the visually handicapped. Inside the center, local birds, animals, and flowers are placed in natural settings

WESTPORT
Nature Center for Environmental Activities
Woodside Lane
Westport
203-227-7253

for the visitor to inspect at close range. In fact, you can touch some of them!

Westport Country Playhouse (25 Powers Court, 203-226-0153) offers Broadway and pre-Broadway shows. For music—jazz, rock, or classical—try **Levitt Pavilion** (Saugatuck River of Jesup Road, 203-226-7600.

From Westport take I-95 to Stratford. The **American Shakespeare Theatre** has been in operation since 1955. Shakespearean plays are presented all summer with symphonies, ballet, opera, and Broadway shows replacing them during the fall and spring seasons.

I-95 will lead you east into New Haven.

NEW HAVEN

New Haven
 Convention and
 Visitors Bureau
155 Church Street
New Haven 06510
203-787-8367

In 1638, Reverend John Davenport and Theophilus Eaton came from England to New Haven after a brief stay in what they felt was a too liberal Boston. The two established harsh laws to govern the settlement through the church. They interpreted the Bible strictly and enforced its edicts rigidly.

Yale, founded in 1701 in Old Saybrook as the Collegiate School, moved to New Haven in 1716. Two years later the school was renamed for Elihu Yale, in appreciation for a £562 gift he made to the college. Tours of the university are available from Phelps Gateway off College Street, at the green. The **Yale Information Office** there provides maps and schedules.

Yale Information
 Office
341 College Street
New Haven
203-432-2302

The campus, with its separate enclosed colleges, is very much like Oxford University. A carillon in Gothic-style **Harkness Tower** fills the air with melody throughout the day. Inside, in the Memorial Room, you can follow the history of the college through a series of woodcarvings. From here, you can work your way through the many fine collections in the **Yale University Art Gallery**, the **Yale Center for British Art**, the Sterling Memorial Library, the **Beinecke Rare Book**

Yale University Art
 Gallery
1111 Chapel Street
New Haven
203-432-0600

and Manuscript Library, the Yale Collection of Musical Instruments, and the Peabody Museum (look for the dinosaur skeleton).

Bulldogs are everywhere in New Haven—on business signs, on clothing, even on gargoyled university buildings. It all began in 1892, when a bulldog named Handsome Dan was found in a local blacksmith's shop and was made the Yale mascot. The original Dan has been stuffed and is on display in a closely guarded glass box in the Payne Whitney Gymnasium. But his name lives on in each new bulldog, the living mascot.

The college green is like a European square, filled with people relaxing and talking with friends. It's also the site of two local celebrations. In late April or early May there's an historical reenactment of Powder House Day, the day Captain Benedict Arnold asked for the keys to the Powder House before he took his troops off to Boston to join the rebellion. The ceremony is complete with the Governor's Footguard in Revolutionary War uniforms. At the end of June, the Mayor's Festival, an ethnic fair, is celebrated here with crafts, dancing, food, and fireworks.

From the green, head west out Whalley Avenue to West Rock Park. West Rock is part of a basalt ridge that rises from New Haven and continues north 20 miles to Southington. Geologists believe it was formed 200 million years ago as lava was forced up through a crack in the red sandstone crust. This left a "dike" several hundred feet thick (most are only a few feet wide). The trail along the ridge offers views of cliffs and harbors, tracks of prehistoric animals, and marks of glacial movement in the sedimentary rocks.

One stop along the trail is Judges' Cave— home for three months to two British regicides. In 1661 Edward Whalley and William Goffe, who had signed a warrant for the arrest and execution of King Charles I fourteen years earlier,

Yale Center for British Art
1080 Chapel Street
New Haven
203-432-2800

Sterling Memorial Library
120 High Street
New Haven
203-436-1773

Beinecke Rare Book and Manuscript Library
Wall and High Streets
New Haven
203-436-8438

Yale Collection of Musical Instruments
15 Hillhouse Avenue
New Haven
203-432-0822

Peabody Museum
170 Whitney Avenue
New Haven
203-436-0850

fled for their lives when Charles II, the son of the beheaded king, offered a £100 reward for their capture. A plaque bolted to a nearby boulder tells the story:

> Here, May 15th 1661, and for some weeks thereafter, Edward Whalley and his son-in-law William Goffe, Members of Parliament, General Officers in the Army of the Commonwealth and signers of the death warrant of King Charles I, found shelter and concealment from the officers of the Crown after the Restoration. Opposition to tyrants is Obedience to God!

Regicides Trail, the path to Judges' Cave and out along West Rock, begins at the **West Rock Nature Recreation Center**. Just follow the blue markers along the trail for about three-quarters of a mile. The center itself has two museum buildings, pens filled with small native animals (bobcats, raccoons, red foxes, deer, and turkeys), and a picnic area.

West Rock Nature
  Recreation Center
Wintergreen
  Avenue
New Haven
203-787-8016

When you leave the park, take Route 10 toward the city, and follow it to Long Wharf Drive. The **Long Wharf Theater** offers excellent theater—repertory and Broadway tryouts—in a converted warehouse building. Nearby, the *Liberty Belle*, a 250-passenger ship, makes short trips around the harbor.

Long Wharf
  Theater
Sargent Dr.
New Haven
203-787-4282

Liberty Belle
Long Wharf
New Haven
203-562-4163

When you're ready for a meal try **Fitzwilly's** (338 Elm Street, 203-624-9438) in a renovated firehouse. Yale students like the informality there. Also **Gentree, Ltd.** (194 York Street, 203-562-3800), which specializes in prime rib. **Delmonaco's** (232 Wooster Street, 203-865-1109) offers Italian cuisine and is popular with locals who know where the best cooking can be found.

EAST HAVEN

From New Haven take Route 1 to East Haven. **Lighthouse Park Community Beach** is located right off Route 142. It's a wonderful beach for children: The surf is gentle and the drop-off is gradual. The sand is rocky with shells.

In town the **Shoreline Trolley Museum** contains ninety trolleys dating from 1878 to 1940. There are exhibits and guided tours, and you can ride back and forth to Short Beach at the end of the line, as often as you like.

Shoreline Trolley Museum
17 River Street
East Haven
203-467-6927

Continue on Route 1 to Branford, once a busy shipping center in its own right, now an industrial satellite and residential suburb of New Haven. The New Haven Colony purchased Totoket, as it was then called, from the Indians in 1638. It was later named Branford after Brentford, a town in England.

BRANFORD

Bittersweet Farm (203-488-4689), on Route 1 between exits 56 and 57 off I-95, is a group of arts and crafts shops in redesigned poultry farm buildings. Here you'll find a seemingly unlimited array of wood carvings, jewelry, books, handwoven goods, stained glass, pottery, paintings, metal sculpture, ship models, leather, silk-screened products, and miniature furniture. And there's a cafe on the grounds. The **Bittersweet Farm Arts and Crafts Festival** is held over the Fourth of July.

May through mid-October, you can take a cruise on the *Volsunga III*, from Branford to the Thimble Islands. There are 365 islands, 32 of them populated, in the group named by Stony Creek Indians for the thimbleberry (similar to the gooseberry). Indians used the islands' pink glacial deposit for arrowheads; later it was quarried to make foundations for the Statue of Liberty and the Brooklyn Bridge.

THIMBLE ISLANDS

Volsunga III
Stony Creek Public Dock
Branford
203-481-3345,
203-488-9978

Captain Kidd used one of the islands, **High Island,** to hide from the colonists. Legend says he left gold in an underwater cave, perhaps on **Money Island**; treasure hunters are still searching for it.

The populated islands are all privately owned. But you might see the Jolly Roger flying and catch black motifs on homes, boats, and docks.

GUILFORD

From Branford wind along Route 146 for about 8 miles, to Guilford. The town, named for lovely Guilford in Surrey, England, has a green surrounded by carefully preserved buildings dating from the early eighteenth to the late nineteenth century. Reverend Henry Whitfield, vicar of Ockley Parish, Saint Margaret's Church, in Surrey, led twenty-five young families from their homes in one of the most beautiful regions of England, and settled them here in 1639. He built his home of stone—in late medieval English style—the oldest stone house in New England. It has been restored and is open today as the **Henry Whitfield Museum**.

Henry Whitfield Museum
Old Whitfield Street
Guilford
203-453-2457

Two other early homes open for visits are **Hyland House**, a seventeenth-century home, restored and furnished; and the **Thomas Griswold House Museum**, with its costumes of the 1800s, historical exhibits, and period gardens.

Hyland House
84 Boston Street
Guilford
203-453-9477

The **Guilford Handcraft Center**, on Route 77 just north of exit 58 off I-95, displays the products of two hundred artists and craftsmen. During the third week in July you can see craftsmen at work at the **Guilford Handcraft Exposition and Sale** on the green.

Thomas Griswold House Museum
171 Boston Street
Guilford
203-453-3176

The **Trails of the Guilford Westwoods** lead hikers through terrain that ranges from low and marshy to high and spectacular. Pick up a map from the **Guilford Recreation Department**. The park, with six hiking trails and a bridle path, is right off Boston Post Road (Route 1).

Guilford Handcraft Center
411 Church Street
Guilford
203-453-5947

Friends recommend **Chello Oyster House** (203-453-2670) on Route 1. Here you can buy a clam chowder base that, when mixed with water or milk, is absolutely delicious—"almost as good as my mother's was!" Or try **Dock House**, Lower Whitfield Street (203-453-6884).

Hammonasset Beach State Park (exit 62 off I-95; 203-245-2785) is the largest shoreline park in Connecticut. There are two miles of beach, with campgrounds and picnic areas.

MADISON

Route 1 will lead you east to Clinton, a popular place in mid-August during the Bluefish Festival. Clinton was the home of the first rector of Yale University, Abraham Pierson, who held classes in his home.

CLINTON

The Stanton House dates from 1790. The Marquis de Lafayette stayed there in 1824, and the bed he slept in is still there to prove it! The house is furnished with eighteenth- and early nineteenth-century pieces, including Staffordshire dinnerware.

Stanton House
63 East Main Street
Clinton
203-669-2793

From Clinton take Route 1 east to Old Saybrook, originally called "Pashbeshauke," which means "the place at the river's mouth." Settled first by Dutch traders in the early seventeenth century, the town was finally named Saybrook after Viscount Saye & Sele and Lord Brooke, who controlled the Saybrook Company in town.

OLD SAYBROOK

In addition to shipbuilding, the town carried on a lively fishing trade.

The **General William Hart House** was built in 1767. Count them—there are eight corner fireplaces in the house. One is especially interesting with Sadler & Green transfer-print tiles that depict Aesop's Fables. Colonial gardens and an award-winning herb garden are on the grounds.

General William
Hart House
350 Main Street
Old Saybrook
203-388-2622

From Old Saybrook, follow Route 154 northwest to Essex.

The area along the Connecticut River is a yachtsman's paradise, with beautiful harbors in

ESSEX

Old Saybrook, Old Lyme, and Hamburg Cove.

Essex, on the west shore, has preserved the romance of its maritime and architectural past. The town became a shipbuilding center in the 1720s. The *Oliver Cromwell*, a twenty-four-gun vessel, was given to the patriots by the town during the Revolutionary War. In 1814 men from the British naval squadron blockading Long Island Sound arrived to destroy the shipping industry here. They burned twenty-two ships. Today the waterfront is bustling with sloops, ketches, schooners, and yawls.

Although shipping was the backbone of Essex's commercial growth, another industry was rooted here as well. At one time Essex was famous for its piano keys. In fact, Ivoryton, as it came to be called, was known to piano manufacturers around the world. Of course, there came a time when plastic keys replaced ivory ones, and yet another oldtime industry ended. Today the town thrives through its real estate, yachting facilities, and tourist attractions.

Walk along Main Street, past lovely colonials and Federal homes built during the early years of the nineteenth century. The **William Pratt House**, nearby, is even older. The original building, which dates from 1725, was one room. Later it was enlarged to four rooms with a gambrel roof. The house is filled with early American furnishings.

The **Griswold Inn** (767-0091), built in 1776, has a collection of Currier and Ives prints, marine oils, and firearms in the Gun Room, a nostalgic setting for lunch or dinner. The Tap Room, once a one-room schoolhouse, is now decorated by a potbellied stove, steamship prints on the walls, and captain's chairs for seating at round tables. And guess where the lumber for the covered bridge room came from.

The **Connecticut River Foundation** has displays of shipbuilding, steamboats, relics from

William Pratt House
20 West Avenue
Essex
203-767-8987

Connecticut River Foundation
Main Street
Essex
203-767-8269

sunken vessels, marine paintings, and other memorabilia. One of the most interesting exhibits includes a replica and diagrams of David Bushnell's one-man submarine, the *Turtle*, which looks like the shells of two turtles fastened together. Although some people were skeptical, he had the encouragement and approval of both George Washington and Benjamin Franklin to build it in 1776. The *Turtle* tried to destroy the much larger HMS *Eagle*, with its powerful sixty-four guns, without success. A model of the *Oliver Cromwell*, built in Essex in 1776, is also on display. She captured nine British ships before she was finally captured by the British and recommissioned as the *Restoration* in the Royal Navy. Don't miss the *City of Hartford*, a Connecticut River steamboat with an elegant interior; as you look at the model you'll see the little figures waving from the deck. This Victorian ship met disaster when it struck the Middletown railroad bridge and sank.

Essex sits near the base of the Connecticut Valley, the beautiful countryside bordering the Connecticut River. To see the area, take the **Valley Railroad** steam train from Essex Depot to Chester. There you can connect with a riverboat for a one- or two-hour cruise on the river.

Valley Railroad
Railroad Avenue
Essex
203-767-0103

From Essex follow Route 154 through Chester to Tylerville, to Route 82 into East Haddam. In town, the **Goodspeed Opera House**, which was built in the days of river steamboats, has been beautifully restored and now presents musical shows each season. *Annie* and *Man of La Mancha* originated here.

EAST HADDAM

Goodspeed Opera House
The Plaza
East Haddam
203-873-8668

Follow Route 82 to Mount Parnassus Road (Route 434) to get to **Devil's Hopyard State Park**. In the spectacular 860-acre park you'll find the turbulent **Eight Mile River**, the **Devil's Oven** (a small cave), groves of huge hemlocks, and **Chapman Falls** (a 60-foot waterfall). Legend says the

Devil's Hopyard State Park
Route 434
East Haddam
203-873-8566

devil sat high above the falls playing his violin while he directed the witches mixing hops into magic potions in the potholes below. Also here: 15 miles of hiking trails, and facilities for picnicking, fishing, and camping.

Retrace your steps to Route 82 and go east to Route 148 and Hadlyme, where you'll see signs to **Gillette Castle State Park**. William Gillette, an actor, built his medieval castle on a hilltop overlooking the river. It took five years to build. Its granite walls are 4 to 5 feet thick, and each of its twenty-four rooms is unique. Gillette designed, not only the structure, but also the heavy oak furniture. One piece, the dining room table, runs on a track. Also here: an art gallery and a collection of theater memorabilia (playbills, scrapbooks, magazine articles, even a stage set for a Sherlock Holmes play in which Gillette starred).

Gillette Castle State Park
River Road
East Haddam
203-526-2336

At one time there was a train that ran around the property to amuse the actor's guests. You can take a 2-mile hike beginning at "Grand Central Station," once the main terminal for Gillette's Seventh Sister Shortline. Follow the flagstone ramp to the sign reading "Loop Trail to River Vista, 0.5 mile." Turn left and walk through the woods. The trail follows the old railroad bed—sometimes crossing it, sometimes running parallel to it.

When you've finished exploring the park, you can follow Route 148 to the Connecticut River, where you can take the ferry to Chester from April through October. Then pick up Route 154 south to Essex and Route 9 south to I-95 where you head east over the bridge to Old Lyme. Or, take Route 82 to Route 156, which will lead you into Old Lyme.

OLD LYME

Old Lyme, originally named for a similar seaside community in England, Lyme Regis, once had a sea captain and his family living in every house in town. The lovely old houses re-

The Goodspeed Opera House, built in 1876 and restored in 1963, offers performances of American musicals, a number of which go on to Broadway.

EAST HADDAM

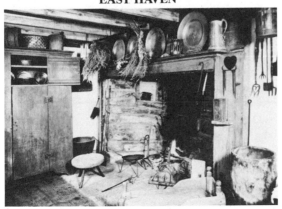

Branford's #629N restored and operating at the Branford Trolley Museum.

EAST HAVEN

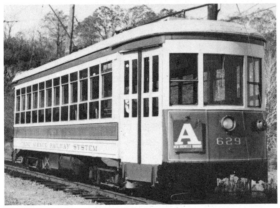

The Hempstead House, built in 1678, is listed on the National Register of Historic Places. Joshua Hempstead's "kitchen" contains many rarities.

NEW LONDON

**Florence Griswold
Museum
96 Lyme Street
Old Lyme
203-434-5232**

**Lyme Art
Association
70 Lyme Street
Old Lyme
203-434-7802**

**Lyme Academy of
Fine Arts
84 Lyme Street
Old Lyme
203-434-5232**

NEW LONDON

main, and the town is a fine example of early America.

The **Florence Griswold Museum** is located in a stately Georgian mansion. Florence Griswold inherited the house from her father, Robert Griswold, who was a sea captain. In 1899, she started to take artists as summer boarders; some of them presented her with their work on fireplace mantelpieces, dining room panels, and doors. When Woodrow Wilson was president of Princeton University, he used to escape to Old Lyme as a guest in the Griswold home. Other guests recalled his skill as a storyteller. Exhibits in the museum include American Impressionism, decorative arts, and paintings of the Old Lyme art colony and local history.

The **Lyme Art Association** is adjacent to the Griswold House. Five major shows are held each summer. The **Lyme Academy of Fine Arts** has changing exhibits of sculpture, and contemporary and traditional paintings. Year-round programs are offered to both professional artists and students.

After your excursion in the lower reaches of the Connecticut River, take I-95 or Route 156 from Old Lyme to New London. The Thames River (*thaymes*, not *tems*) gives New London one of the best deep-water ports in New England. The harbor is large, fairly well protected, and busy with traffic from all kinds of vessels—navy and coast guard ships, submarines, fishing trawlers, ferries, and yachts.

In the seventeenth century, farmers used the river to ship their produce; a hundred years later, whalers began bringing home their fortunes along it. During the Revolutionary War a number of New London vessels, privateers, raided British merchant ships. The devastating attack on the town in 1781 was retribution: Thirty-two British ships with seventeen hundred men, led by turncoat Benedict Arnold, destroyed the city.

In the 1860s almost eighty whaling ships called New London home; by 1900 the fleet was gone. Several New London whalers were in a group caught near Alaska by a Confederate warship during the Civil War; the rest of the fleet was gradually sold off or abandoned after the development of oil fields in Pennsylvania made whale oil less valuable. You can still see the hull of a schooner and the remains of other ships in the marine graveyard near the shipyard.

Today New London is still a marine center, home to the **U.S. Coast Guard Academy**. On the academy's grounds are a visitors' center and a museum. You can also tour the *Eagle*, a three-masted training bark, whenever it's in port (usually fall through spring). The *Eagle*, once a German sail-training ship, was confiscated as a war prize, restored, and then given its present name.

U.S. Coast Guard Academy
Mohegan Avenue
New London
203-444-8270

If you enjoyed the Coast Guard Academy, try a visit to the **USS *Nautilus* Memorial** (off Route 12). The USS *Nautilus*, the first nuclear-powered ship in the world, was finished in Groton. Mamie Eisenhower swung the bottle of champagne over her bow in 1954. The ship is now resting in her permanent berth after retiring from active service. Visitors are welcome to explore her torpedo room, dining area, operations deck, and crew quarters. The **Submarine Force Library and Museum** is located at the north end of Building 83 adjacent to Gilmore Hall. Visitors will see the development of the submarine from a one-man wooden hand-powered vessel during the Revolution to modern nuclear-powered ships. Exhibits include a model wall, original battle flags, pennants, paintings, drawings, simulators, diaries, and letters.

USS *Nautilus* Memorial
Naval Submarine Base
Groton
203-449-3174 or
203-449-3290

Red and white signs point the way to historical New London tourist attractions. The **Deshon-Allyn House**, built in 1829 by a whaling captain, contains an impressive collection of original Federal furnishings. Right down the street, the **Lyman Allyn Museum** displays a charming collection of dolls, dollhouses, doll furniture, and toys. **Hempstead House**, built in 1678, is one of the few intact seventeenth-century houses still standing in Connecticut. On its grounds is the **Nathaniel Hempstead House**, built in 1759, one of two houses of mid-eighteenth-century cut-stone architecture in the state. The **Shaw Mansion**, a restored 1756 building, was used as Connecticut's naval office during the Revolutionary War. The **Nathan Hale Schoolhouse** is where Hale taught before he enlisted in the army.

Contact the office of the Southeastern Connecticut Tourism District for more information and maps, and for current schedules for ferry service to Fishers Island, Block Island, and Orient Point on Long Island.

A few miles south of the city, off Route 213, is **Ocean Beach Park**. The beach here is sandy and clean, and there's gentle surf, no undertow, and a gradual drop-off. Ocean Beach Park also has an olympic-size outdoor pool, rides, an arcade, and miniature golf.

Harkness Memorial State Park was originally the summer home of the Edward S. Harkness family. The forty-two-room mansion was elegantly furnished with pieces chosen while the family was abroad. Rex Brasher's watercolor paintings of birds are displayed in the house. A summer music program is offered at Harkness. (Call 203-422-9199 or 203-566-2304.) The gardens were designed to provide a succession of color and range from Oriental to Southern Mediterranean in style. About half of the estate was

Deshon-Allyn House
613 Williams Street
New London
203-443-2545

Lyman Allyn Museum
625 Williams Street
New London
203-443-2545

Hempstead House
11 Hempstead Street
New London
203-443-7949
247-8996

Shaw Mansion
11 Blinman Street
New London
203-443-1209

Nathan Hale Schoolhouse
Captain's Walk
New London
203-269-5752

Southeastern Connecticut Tourism District
Ye Olde Towne Mill
8 Mill St.
New London, CT 06320
203-444-2206

Harkness Memorial State Park
Goshen Point
Waterford
203-443-5725

willed for use by handicapped persons who live in twenty-three cottages.

If you're ready for whale watching or fishing try **Captain John's Sport Fishing Center** (15 First Street, Waterford; 203-443-7259). You might be lucky enough to see a humpback, finback, or minke whale, and you're sure to see dolphins riding in the bow waves of the boat.

The **Eugene O'Neill Memorial Theater Center** houses the National Playwriter's Conference, the National Critics Institute, the Barn Theater, Amphitheater and Instant Theater, the National Theater Institute, and O'Neill Media. Original plays are produced here during the summer season.

Eugene O'Neill Memorial Theater Center 305 Great Neck Road Waterford 203-443-1238

O'Neill's boyhood home, **Monte Cristo Cottage**, is now open regularly. The house was the setting for *Ah, Wilderness* and *Long Day's Journey into Night*, and some of the rooms were reconstructed as sets for the plays. You can feel the sadness of O'Neill's childhood and the unhappiness of his mother, Ella, a withdrawn woman who secluded herself when O'Neill and his brother needed her. The boys went to boarding school but spent summers here with their actor father, James.

Monte Cristo Cottage 325 Pequot Avenue Waterford 203-443-0051

From New London take Route 1, or I-95 and then Route 27, to Mystic, one of the oldest shipbuilding and whaling ports in New England. Mystic was settled in 1654, its name derived from the Pequot Indian's Mistuket. Downtown Mystic is divided by the Mystic River: The Art Museum and many fine old homes lie on its west bank; Mystic Seaport, Mystic Marinelife Aquarium, and Olde Mistick Village, on the east bank.

MYSTIC

Olde Mistick Village is an interesting shopping center on Route 27, at I-95, which houses sixty shops in a recreated old New England village, nicely landscaped with a pond, a waterwheel, and ducks to feed. During June you can enjoy the craft exhibits here at the **Olde Mistick Village Art and Handcrafts Show** (203-536-4941).

Mystic Marinelife Aquarium
Mystic
203-536-3323

Follow signs from the shopping area to **Mystic Marinelife Aquarium**. Here you can watch demonstrations with whales, dolphins, and sea lions; visit the touch-and-feel exhibit, where children can handle live specimens and the 8-foot-long water table; and look through microscopes. The aquarium runs a summer program for children, among its other educational programs.

Mystic Seaport
Route 27
Mystic
203-572-0711

Mystic Seaport is a place we love to explore, and we go back year after year. This 17-acre village imparts the living history of land and sea. You can smell the fish and the pine tar used on sailing ships; you can hear the gulls squawking and crying, a foghorn in the distance, someone singing sea chanteys.

Mystic Seaport sponsors many activities: movies, lectures, demonstrations, sailing courses for children, and educational programs for all ages. It also offers accredited month-long or semester programs for college students. Students in the Williams Mystic program take courses in American maritime history, maritime literature, oceanography, marine ecology, and marine policy. They live in houses on the grounds but spend several weeks on board the schooner *Westward*, a research vessel, gaining practical experience in living and working at sea.

The Seaport offers individual and family memberships at reasonable rates, and it's money well spent. Members receive free admission, mooring facilities at the Seaport, and a magazine filled with interesting maritime articles and schedules of special membership activities and weekends.

You'll want to spend a full day at the Seaport. Most visitors start with a tour of the ships. The *Charles W. Morgan*, a nineteenth-century wooden whaler, is usually moored at Chubb's

Wharf. You can climb all over her, learn how whales were caught, and feel what it must have been like to live on board—the captain sleeping in a gimballed bed, the crew in the cramped, uncomfortable forecastle. The ship was built in 1841 in New Bedford, by Jethro and Zachariah Hillman. Over the next eighty years she completed thirty-seven whaling voyages. In 1941 she was towed to the Seaport for restoration. In recent years she's been refloated and extensively rebuilt at the shipyard on the grounds.

The *Joseph Conrad*, built in Copenhagen as a Danish sail-training ship in 1882, sailed under three flags before coming to Mystic in 1947. In 1905 she was rammed by a British freighter and sunk with the loss of twenty-two cadets. From 1934 to 1936 Alan Villiers and a group of students took the raised ship around the world on a 58,000-mile cruise. She is now permanently moored, a floating dormitory for visiting students. Look for demonstrations of sail setting and handling, and chantey singing, on board both the *Morgan* and the *Conrad*.

The third ship not to miss is the *L. A. Dunton*. She is the last Gloucester fisherman built primarily as a sailing vessel.

More than fifty other fishing vessels and yachts of specific historic types fill the Seaport's waterfront and boat sheds—it's a paradise for wooden boat aficionados. And, there are the shipyard and boat shop, too, where older methods of working in wood are still practiced. You'll leave with the scent of salt water, tar, and hemp, and perhaps a faint touch of the whale oil that permeated the being of whaling men.

The rest of the Seaport is a reconstructed village, with chapel, tavern, bank, general store, apothecary, and doctor's office to wander through. In the museum, along with several other magnificent exhibits, are "New England and the Sea," and the *Packard* exhibit, a reassembled salon and cabin section of a fine nine-teenth-century sailing ship. And there are several buildings housing collections of ship figure-heads, models, wheels, whaleboats, scrimshaw, paintings, even the toys of children who lived at sea.

There are also excellent rotating exhibits in the new art gallery and a scholar's collection of books and materials in the library. The planetarium offers programs on navigation, meteorology, and astronomy throughout the year. The boat shop offers classes in the disappearing art of wooden boat building, and there are sailing programs for both children and adults.

Every day the shops along Seaport Street have staff members practicing and happy to talk about the crafts that were a necessary part of colonial life: weaving, printing, marine iron-work, barrel making, sail making, rope making, and open-hearth cooking. And there are special programs throughout the year. Our favorites: the **Christmas Lantern Light Tours** in December and the **Chantey Festival** in mid-June, which draws singers from all over the world.

Sea chanteys are part of the rich heritage of seafaring. Although they tell a musical story, they were not sung for pleasure. A chanteyman was hired to lead the ship's crew as they worked.

Chanteys are not all alike. There are four types, each varying in beat and tempo, that correspond with the work done on board sailing ships. The *capstan* (windlass) *chantey* was used to weigh anchor or to unload cargo. A story unfolded as the chanteyman sat on the capstan head and the sailors pushed on the capstan bars to the continuous rhythm of the song. The *halyard* (long-haul) *chantey* did not have a steady marching beat; instead it used two accented beats to time the pull of the men on the line, allowing them to rest in between pulls. The halyard chantey was used for heavy work (hoisting sails and

yards). The *short-haul chantey* had a single accented beat for one pull, and was used for haul-
ing sheets or furling sails. The *walkaway*
(hand-over-hand) *chantey* was used for hoisting
smaller sails or for scraping barnacles from the
bottom of the ship.

From the Seaport dock you can board the
Sabino, a 1908 coal-fired steamboat, for a cruise
along the Mystic River. There are thirty-minute
cruises during the day; a ninety-minute cruise,
past Noank and Mason's Island toward Fishers
Island, at six; and Dixieland jazz cruises every
other Saturday during the summer. Several other
charter vessels operate from Old Steamboat
Wharf, and **Windjammer Cruises**, which runs
week-long cruises, has a wharf just north of the
drawbridge.

Williams Beach, which is privately owned, is
located off Route 1. The water is clean, with
gentle surf and no undertow; there is a steep
drop-off, but the area is roped.

On the north side of the Seaport, stop for
lunch or dinner at the **Seamen's Inne** (536-9649),
with its three dining rooms and oyster bar. The
seafood is great, and the Sunday brunch is famous. On our last trip, we discovered the **Landing** (203-572-0549), on Old Steamboat Wharf.
New owners have redecorated with nautical flair,
and the schooners berthed not 6 feet from your
chair offer a pleasant view. **Flood Tide, The Inn
at Mystic** (Route 1 and Route 27, 203-536-9604)
offers a never-ending Sunday brunch as well as
marvelous seafood for lunch or dinner.

Windjammer
Cruises
Whaler's Wharf
Mystic
203-536-4218

STONINGTON

From Mystic take Route 1 east to
Stonington, one of the most impressive old
towns on the New England coast. As its name
suggests, the land around Stonington was rocky,
and settlers had a difficult time producing food.
They also found it hard to keep wolves from nec-
essarily shallow graves. Eventually they began to

top each grave with a heavy stone slab. These **wolf stones** can still be seen in the cemetery near Wequetequock off Greenhaven Road, south of Route 1.

The compact town is laid out on a narrow peninsula, its fine captains' homes, many of them still in use, jammed together. This made Stonington particularly vulnerable during the War of 1812, when the British fleet shelled the town. (You can still see cannonballs in the beams of some of the old homes.)

For special seafood, try the **Harbor View Restaurant** (203-535-2720) on Water Street. Through the ornate wooden doors you step into a Victorian setting: dark paneled walls lined with antique plates, tiled fireplaces, and brass sconces. The cuisine is French and delicious, and served with a fine view of Stonington Harbor.

You've now completed your trip along most of the Connecticut shore. From Stonington, you're just a few miles from the Rhode Island border and the beginning of Itinerary D.

ITINERARY D: RHODE ISLAND SHORE AND PROVIDENCE

STATE HOUSE

ITINERARY D

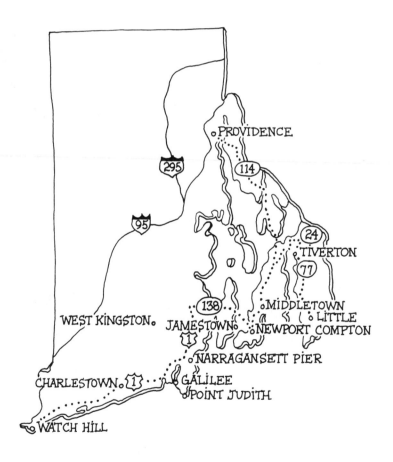

PROVIDENCE

295

114

95

24

TIVERTON

77

138

MIDDLETOWN

WEST KINGSTON.

JAMESTOWN

LITTLE

NEWPORT COMPTON

1

NARRAGANSETT PIER

CHARLESTOWN. 1

GALILEE

POINT JUDITH

WATCH HILL

Block Island

Rhode Island Shore and Providence

Although the state of Rhode Island stretches only 37 miles between the borders of Connecticut and Massachusetts, it has 400 miles of shoreline. Wind and waves modulate the quiet coves, beaches, rugged cliffs, and ponds—a mecca for sailors and fishermen.

During the Ice Age a glacier ground southward until it came to a stop just beyond the coast, along a line running through Nantucket, Martha's Vineyard, Block Island, and Long Island. Accumulations of rock and gravel kept piling up in a ridge (called a *terminal moraine*) along the northern coast of Cape Cod (the Sandwich Moraine), along the west coast of Buzzards Bay (the Buzzards Bay Moraine), and through western Rhode Island (the Watch Hill Moraine). Several lakes scattered around Rhode Island are remnants of this glacier.

Rhode Island was discovered in 1524 by Giovanni da Verrazano, an Italian explorer, and was settled a century later by a bull-riding clergyman named Roger Williams. Williams had been banished by the Puritan leaders of the Massachusetts Bay Colony in 1635 for religious nonconformity; a year later he arrived by canoe with several followers in what is now Providence. In 1663 the Colony of Rhode Island and Providence Plantation was chartered by Charles II. The name came from the Greek island Rhodes; it's also called Aquidneck Island.

Williams was adept at keeping peace with the Narragansett Indians, as well as at acquiring land from them. Unfortunately the peace ended after the Wampanoag chief, Massasoit, died in 1674. Massasoit's son Metacomet, or King Philip as the white men called him, knew the Indians were not being treated fairly. He convinced other chiefs to join him, and in 1675 went to war. During King Philip's War Indian warriors attacked towns in Connecticut, Massachusetts, and Rhode Island. Finally, in December, the colonists struck back at the Narragansett winter camp in a swamp near South Kingston, Rhode Island. They burned six hundred wigwams, killed a thousand Indians, and took hundreds of prisoners. Although Indians continued to ravage the countryside, this battle was the turning point in the war. In August 1676 King Philip's wife and son were captured and taken to Bermuda as slaves; Metacomet was killed in a swamp on Mount Hope Neck, and his head was placed on a stockade paling in Plymouth, where it stayed for twenty years.

Rhode Island, although pint-sized, packs a lot within its borders. You can swim and sun at one beach after another, take a trip out to Block Island, actually see the wind as the fog blows in over Beaver Tail Lighthouse, visit the mansions from the Golden Age, and walk along a "Mile of History." This itinerary begins inside the west border of the state, at Watch Hill, continues along the coast with a possible side trip to Block Island, then rolls into Newport. The historical city of Providence has undergone a renaissance and should not be missed.

WATCH HILL

Take Route 1 or I-95 into Rhode Island to Westerly, and follow the signs to Watch Hill. One of the coast's oldest resorts, Watch Hill sits on a narrow peninsula between the Atlantic and the Pawcatuck River. The town is filled with lovely old colonial homes, and newer summer colonies spread out along the shore to the east. There are yachts in the harbor, a Coast Guard station, and a lighthouse.

For swimming, there are saltwater ponds and the ocean. **Misquamicut State Beach** is open to everyone. The surf is gentle (an occasional undertow); the drop-off, gradual.

Misquamicut State Beach
Atlantic Avenue
Watch Hill
401-596-9097

Don't miss one of the oldest merry-go-rounds in the country, the **Flying Horse Carousel,** on Beach Street. When it was built, two white horses provided the power; they're gone, but the original red and black wooden horses are still there.

CHARLESTOWN

From Watch Hill take Route 1A to Route 1. A few miles west of Charlestown you'll find the Audubon Society's **Kimball Wildlife Refuge.** It's located on the southern side of **Burlingame State Park,** a great spot for camping.

Kimball Wildlife Refuge
Route 1
Charlestown

In town stop for information and a map at the booth on Route 1. Then walk through the **Royal Indian Burial Ground** for the sachems (great men) and their families of the Narragansett tribe.

Burlingame State Park
Cookestown Road
Charlestown
401-322-7337

The beaches here are beautiful. Take Charlestown Beach Road off Route 1 for the **Charlestown Community Beach. East Beach** is across the Charlestown Breachway in the Ninigret conservation area. There are several beaches,

Royal Indian Burial Ground
Narrow Lane
Charlestown

**East Matunuck
State Beach
Succotash Road
East Matunuck
401-789-8585**

too, along the sound from Charlestown to Matunuck, among them **East Matunuck State Beach,** with its 8- to 10-foot waves. (Sorry. Surfing isn't allowed.)

WEST KINGSTON

**Greater
Westerly-Pawcatuck-
Charlestown
Chamber of
Commerce
159 Main Street
401-596-7761**

From Charlestown take Route 2 north to West Kingston. Here you'll find **Indian Cedar Swamp,** now a 2,600-acre wildlife refuge, the scene of the Great Swamp Fight in December 1675. Every September there's an Indian pilgrimage to the granite shaft that marks the site of Indian fortifications during that decisive battle. For information about the refuge and the pilgrimage, contact the chamber of commerce.

GALILEE

From Route 1 take the exit for Galilee and Point Judith. Galilee is known for the annual **Rhode Island Tuna Tournament,** held for three days in late August. Anyone with a boat can enter for a small fee. The boats set out at dawn and come back between four and five each afternoon to crowds waving tuna flags and loudspeakers blaring out the latest results. In 1961 a 758³/₄-pound tuna broke the standing record.

A large fleet of charter and party fishing boats operates from Galilee, and the ferry for Block Island leaves from a pier in town.

Try **Georges** (401-783-2306) on Sand Hill Cove for great crabcakes to take out, and full lunches and dinners. Then head for **Roger Wheeler Memorial Beach** nearby. The sandy strip is protected from the surf by a jetty.

BLOCK ISLAND

Block Island, the "Bermuda of the North," was discovered in 1524 by Giovanni da Verrazano, but was named for Adriaen Block, the Dutch explorer who arrived in 1614. Actually the island has had a series of names: The Indians called it Manisses, Verrazano called it Claudia, and Dutch maps labeled it Adriaen's Eyland.

When Verrazano discovered the island, it was covered with trees; now it is almost barren. The **Mohegan Bluffs**, like the white cliffs of Dover, rise abruptly 200 feet above sea level. The cliffs spread along the southern coast for 5 miles, looking in spots like the profiles of Indians. They have long been a landfall for sailors.

The island has also been a mariner's nightmare, with at least two hundred wrecks remaining around it. The **Palatine Graves**, on the southwestern side, are relics of one of the most appalling. Whittier's poem tells the story of the ship that sailed from Rotterdam in 1732.

Although there are several versions of the story, some historians believe that polluted drinking water killed three hundred during the voyage; barely a hundred survived the crossing. Then, off Block Island, the ship foundered and caught fire. One woman stayed on board with her valuables, and legend says you can hear her screaming whenever the Palatine Lights appear, right before a storm.

Mooncussers may have played a part in the legendary wreck of the *Palatine*. These smugglers, pirates, and thieves would use lights to lure boats onto the rocks, and then would make off with their cargo. How did they come to be called mooncussers? That's easy. On moonlit nights— when ships couldn't be led onto the rocks—the thieves would cuss the moon.

Sailors now enjoy **New Harbor**, the well-protected, large harbor in Great Salt Pond. Originally there was a piece of land separating the pond from the ocean, but this has been cut through by a channel 100 feet wide and 12 feet deep (at mean low water). With such excellent shelter, Block Island is a favorite haunt of yachtsmen and the scene of a fabulous collection of ocean-racing yachts every other June, during **Block Island Week**.

The Palatine
John Greenleaf Whittier

Old wives spinning their webs of tow,
Or rocking weirdly to and fro
In and out of the peat's full glow,

And old men mending their nets of twine,
Talk together of dream and sign,
Talk of the lost ship Palatine,—

The ship that, a hundred years before,
Freighted deep with its goodly store,
In the gales of the equinox went ashore.

The eager islanders one by one
Counted the shots of her signal gun,
And heard the crash when she drove right on!

Into the teeth of death she sped:
(May God forgive the hands that fed
The false lights over the rocky Head!)

O men and brothers! what sights were there!
White upturned faces, hands stretched in prayer!
Where waves had pity, could ye not spare?

Down swooped the wreckers, like birds of prey
Tearing the heart of the ship away,
And the dead had never a word to say.

And then, with ghastly shimmer and shine,
Over the rocks and the seething brine,
They burned the wreck of the Palatine.

In their cruel hearts, as they homeward sped,
"The sea and the rocks are dumb," they said:
"There'll be no reckoning with the dead."

But the year went round, and when once more
Along their foam-white curves of shore
They heard the line-storm rave and roar,

Behold! again, with shimmer and shine,
Over the rocks and the seething brine,
The flaming wreck of the Palatine!

The island has something for everyone. For fishermen there are giant bluefin tuna, school tuna, swordfish, marlin, striped bass, and flounder in the waters off the island. For cyclists there are uncluttered roads with gradual inclines and beautiful views. And for swimmers there are superb beaches everywhere. The ones on the east side are better for swimming when the afternoon southwesterly is blowing hard. Try **Block Island State Beach**, which is within walking distance of the ferry. The surf is gentle, and the drop-off is gradual.

Block Island is 12 miles off the mainland, a short ferry ride from Galilee. (Ferries also make the longer runs from New London and Providence.) For a schedule contact **Interstate Navigation**. If you want to take your car, you must make a reservation and send a deposit.

Block Island State Beach
Water Street
Block Island
401-466-2611

Interstate Navigation
Galilee State Pier
Point Judith
401-789-3502 or
401-783-4613

Follow the road from Galilee to Point Judith. During the Revolution a Coast Guard station and tower beacon were located here, but the original wooden lighthouse was destroyed in the hurricane of September 1815. In its place the town built an octagonal brick lighthouse that's still standing. (That storm of 1815 devastated Providence, where large vessels, torn from their moorings, crashed into the bridge, rammed through buildings, and blocked streets. In Narragansett Bay the tide rose 11 feet 9 inches above mean high water.)

POINT JUDITH

Narragansett Pier, a few miles north of Point Judith, was once the site of Stanford White's Narragansett Casino. Only the Gothic twin towers remain; a storm in 1886 destroyed the rest of the pavilion.

Today beautiful homes and clubs line the shore, and there's a lovely sand beach in the center of town. **Scarborough State Beach** is just south of the town.

NARRAGANSETT PIER

Scarborough State Beach
Ocean Road
Narragansett Pier
401-783-1010

JAMESTOWN

From Narragansett Pier take Route 1A to Route 138, to Jamestown, or Conanicut Island, in Narragansett Bay. The island is connected to the mainland on the west by a free bridge; to Newport on the east by a high toll bridge with spectacular views.

Originally named for King James I, the island is rich in Revolutionary War history. In 1775 the British burned most of the town, but a few old houses are still standing. Captain John Eldred, who died in 1784, would harass the Redcoats from a spot on the eastern side of the island—his one gun sounding like a whole company. Much later, after the Civil War, during the "cottage" period, fashionable people from Philadelphia, New York, Washington, and Saint Louis would spend their summers here.

Old Friends Burial Ground
Eldred Avenue
Jamestown

Jamestown Museum
Narragansett Avenue
Jamestown
401-423-0784

In the **Old Friends Burial Ground**, on Route 138, half a mile west of North Main Road, are the graves of early settlers and Revolutionary War soldiers. In the **Jamestown Museum** the historical society has created several interesting exhibits about old Jamestown and a display on a succession of island ferries. The society has also put an old windmill in working order on North Road, off Route 138.

When you've finished walking around the town, drive out Fort Getty Road past Mackeral Cove and an interesting old farm complex with weathered cedar-shake buildings. At the end of Fort Getty Road, at the southernmost tip of the island, you come to one of the treasures of this part of the world—the **Beaver Tail Lighthouse** area. Terraced rock faces shot through with quartz receive the brunt of ocean waves as they crash over and over, sweeping and swirling down and back to sea. You can actually see the wind as the fog blows in.

Beaver Tail Lighthouse
Beaver Tail Road
Jamestown

The first lighthouse here was built in 1749; its foundation was uncovered by the hurricane of

1938. The present lighthouse was built next to the original in 1856.

As you head back to town along Beaver Tail Road, look on the right at the lovely weathered shingle homes facing Newport—our next stop.

Newport has enjoyed two major periods of prominence: as a center for world trade during colonial times, and as a fashionable resort during the Golden Age of the late nineteenth century. Over the last several decades the city has come alive again as the premier yachting center in New England—the site of the **America's Cup** races, the starting point for the **Bermuda Race** and many other class championships, and home of the **Newport Sailboat Show**, the largest in-water show in the country. And the city is also a center for various music festivals, starting with the **Newport Jazz Festival** over the Fourth of July.

From Jamestown cross the high bridge into Newport, and take Farewell Street to the center of town. Your first stop should be the **Tourism & Convention Authority at Gateway Center,** where you can get maps for self-guided tours and arrange bus tours and boat trips. Or stop at the chamber of commerce. Downtown highlights: **Hunter House** and its exhibits of original Goddard and Townsend furniture, silver, and portraits; **Old Colony House,** the colonial capital as well as a barracks, hospital, and jail; the **Wanton-Lyman-Hazard House,** a 1675 Jacobean house, the oldest in Newport; the **Touro Synagogue,** built in 1759, the first synagogue in the country; and **Trinity Church,** with its unusual wineglass pulpit set on three levels. George Washington's pew is marked.

Around the corner from Trinity Church is the mysterious **Old Stone Mill,** its origins clouded in legend. Some say both the tower and

NEWPORT

Newport Chamber
of Commerce
10 America's Cup
Avenue
Newport
401-847-1600

Old Colony House
Washington Square
Newport
401-846-2980

Wanton-Lyman-
Hazard House
17 Broadway
Newport
401-846-0813

Trinity Church
Queen Anne
Square
Newport
401-846-0660

Hunter House
54 Washington
Street
Newport
401-847-1000

Touro Synagogue
84 Touro Street
Newport
401-847-4794

Old Stone Mill
Mill Street
Newport

a skeleton discovered in New Bedford in 1831 were the remains of Viking explorations here between the tenth and twelfth centuries. And Longfellow agreed. In his poem "The Skeleton in Armor," the Viking tells of building "the lofty tower, which, to this very hour, stands looking seaward."

In the reconstructed wharf area of the old town are dozens of spots that invite leisurely strolling and shopping, including **Bowen's Wharf, Bannister's Wharf, Christie's Landing,** and the **Brick Market**. The **Armchair Sailor Bookstore** (401-847-4252), on Bannister's Wharf, has a fine collection of Newport books as well as new and used marine books, and a catalog of available marine works.

The Redwood Library and Athenaeum Bellevue Avenue Newport 401-847-0292

Across the street and to the left a bit from the Old Stone Mill stands **The Redwood Library and Athenaeum,** which can be identified by the fern-leaved beech tree spreading over the front lawn and a bronze statue of George Washington watching passersby. Built from 1748 to 1750, the library houses much of the original collection that cost Abraham Redwood 500 sterling. During the American Revolution, when the British occupied the library, the furniture was used for firewood and all of the books disappeared. A bookbinder in Bristol has been carefully restoring volumes as they find their way back.

If you think your modern watch has a lot of features, take a look at the 1723 Claggett grandfather clock that tells you a variety of details about each point in time. Eighteenth-century portraits line the high walls of each room, including some of Gilbert Stuart. Earlier users of the library include William and Henry James, Edith Wharton, and Ezra Stiles. Look up to see a 1663 painted flag that came from England with the original charter and was found hidden under the floorboards in a local attic.

Directly across from the Old Stone Mill you

will see the Griswold House, housing the **Newport Art Museum and Art Association**. Built in the "stick style" reminiscent of medieval half-timbered houses in Europe, the house was designed by Richard Morris Hunt and completed in 1864. Inside the library is elegant with walnut paneling, a Gothic blue ceiling studded with stars, and a delicate frieze over the mantel. The octagonal dining room contains two portraits of dogs and a parquet floor. The museum displays changing exhibitions as well as a permanent collection. Across the lawn you will come to the Cushing Memorial building, which houses special exhibits. We were especially entranced by the sculpture of a little girl, Mary Louisa Cushing.

Newport Art Museum and Art Association 76 Bellevue Avenue Newport 401-847-0179

Continue along Bellevue Avenue just past Memorial Boulevard to **The International Tennis Hall of Fame**. You can't miss the long shingled building with dark green trim, decorated with lattices and gingerbread. Inside, the floors are covered with bright grass-green carpeting, leading visitors on to the competition grass courts where you can watch or play yourself. The Heffernan Court, with the Clock Tower on one end, is used for croquet meets as well as tennis. The Horseshoe Piazza, on the other end, is the site for social gatherings. Professional tennis tournaments are played on the center court, with the grandstand above it. The museum contains beautiful polished silver trophies and racquets held by famous hands including the one Chris Evert used to win the 1982 U.S. Open. Exhibits give the visitor a picture of each of the 146 members of the Tennis Hall of Fame. Also on the grounds is the Casino Theater, designed by Stanford White, which is used for a variety of performing arts.

International Tennis Hall of Fame 194 Bellevue Avenue Newport 401-849-3990

In a bustling town like this one there are many places to dine, some on the water. **Le Bistro Newport** (Bowen's Wharf, 401-849-7778) offers fine French cuisine along with a view of

Newport Harbor. Diners can feast on French seasonal specialties as well as American dishes. The bar on the third floor serves a less expensive menu. **The Ark** (348 Thames Street, 401-849-3808) has a formal dining room on the second floor serving elegant fare and an English pub on the first floor which expands onto the terrace in the warm months. For real atmosphere and superb seafood try the **SS Newport**, a restored ship converted into a restaurant, with live entertainment in the bar and less formal dining below (Waite's Wharf, 401-846-1200). The same owners have recently opened a casual family-style, inexpensive restaurant next door—**Shore Dinner Hall** (401-848-5058). There you'll find blue-and-white-checked cloths on picnic tables in a warehouse open to a wide view along the harbor front. Lobsters, clams, mussels, and other shore treats are cooked to order. Walk up the ramp to see huge lobster tanks continuously flushed with sea water. Locals pour into **Yesterday's** (28 Washington Square, 401-847-0125) for lunch. You can choose from salads, sandwiches, quiche, ratatouille, omelettes, and Mexican specialties. For fine dining, friends also recommend **The Black Pearl** (Bowen's Wharf, 401-846-5264), **The Southern Cross** (348 Thames Street, 401-849-3808), and **White Horse Tavern** (Farewell at Marlborough Street, 401-849-3600).

There are few visitors to Newport who aren't fascinated by the fabled mansions of Bellevue Avenue, those elegant monuments to high society in one of America's most ebullient moments. The mansions that are open to the public are maintained by the **Preservation Society of Newport County,** where you can buy tickets for one or all, either by bus tour or on your own. Be prepared for long lines if you go during high season or on holiday weekends.

**Preservation
Society of
Newport County
118 Mill Street
Newport
401-847-1000**

The **Breakers**, built by Cornelius Vanderbilt in 1895, is one of the most magnificent of the homes. Look for the stained-glass ceiling in the Great Hall. **The Elms**, built by E. J. Berwind, a Philadelphia coal magnate, is modeled after an eighteenth-century château in France. On the grounds are marble tea houses, fountains, and a sunken garden. **Château-sur-Mer**, an elegant Victorian mansion, was owned by William S. Wetmore, who made a fortune in trade with China. **Rosecliff**, designed by Stanford White and built in 1902 for Herman Oelrichs, has the largest ballroom in Newport. The party in *The Great Gatsby* was filmed here. **Marble House** is a French palace built for William K. Vanderbilt in 1892. **Belcourt Castle**, designed in the style of Louis XIII for Oliver Belmont, contains fine collections of armor and stained-glass antiques, and a gold coronation coach. **Hammersmith Farm**, built by John W. Auchincloss in 1887, and once the home of Jacqueline Bouvier Kennedy Onassis, now is open to the public. Frederick Law Olmsted designed the lovely gardens.

If you'd like a taste of the "gilded age" with real live actors playing characters in a mansion, head for **The Astors' Beechwood**. Guests are met at the door, swept into the hall and back into the society of the 1890s. As you tour the mansion you will find yourself drawn into the life of the Astors and their guests.

For a view of both the mansions and the breakers below, follow **Cliff Walk** along the shore. The 3-mile path begins just west of Newport Beach, at Memorial Boulevard, and ends on a side street off Bellevue Avenue. This elegant walk was designated a national recreation trail in 1975.

There are a number of cemeteries in Newport, some with fine collections of eighteenth-century stonecutting. The **Common Burying**

The Breakers
Ochre Point
Newport

The Elms
Bellevue Avenue
Newport

Château-sur-Mer
Bellevue Avenue
Newport

Rosecliff
Bellevue Avenue
Newport

Marble House
Bellevue Avenue
Newport

Belcourt Castle
Bellevue Avenue
Newport

**Hammersmith
 Farm**
Ocean Drive
Newport
**401-846-7346 or
 401-846-0420**

**The Astors'
 Beechwood**
**580 Bellevue
 Avenue**
Newport
401-846-3772

**Common Burying
 Ground**
Farewell Street
Newport

Ground is one of the most interesting, and the churchyard at **Trinity Church** has a collection of carved stones laid flat on the ground.

The **America's Cup races** are one remnant of Newport's grand era. They were revived thirteen years after World War II ended, in 1958. Since then the challenge races have been held every three years in Rhode Island Sound off Newport, until the cup was won by Australia in 1983.

For a closer look at the connections between mansions and the history of yachting, head for **The Museum of Yachting**. Millionaires in the 1880s built two hundred "cottages" as well as large steam yachts and racing sloops and schooners. Having opened in 1985 in the nineteenth-century Fort Adams, the museum has a gallery with a variety of boats on display. A photo exhibit features the mansions and the family yachts. A number of yachts have been given to the museum, including *Cotton Blossom*, owned by Dr. and Mrs. Bruce Eissner of Marblehead, Massachusetts. The Museum now owns *Shamrock V*, built for Sir Thomas Lipton in 1930 and one of the few J-class yachts left in the world. At 119 feet in length, with a 162-foot mast, she is magnificent indeed, nearly twice the size of the Twelve Metres now used for America's Cup matches.

Have you heard about the Lime Rock lighthousekeeper's daughter who rescued a number of people during the 1860s? Idawalley Zorada Lewis became adept at rowing as she took her brothers and sisters from Lime Rock across the water to Newport where they went to school. Because her father, Hosea, had become incapacitated from a stroke, Ida and her mother had the responsibility of not only managing to keep the light operating, but also ferrying the children to town and bringing back equipment, food, and other supplies. Ida saved people from drowning in the sea, including four men who had

Museum of Yachting
Fort Adams
Newport
401-847-1018

WATCH HILL

The Coast Guard Light Station is located on a point on the north side of the east entrance to Fishers Island Sound.

NEWPORT

The dining room at The Elms. Built in 1901 for Philadelphia coal baron, Edward J. Berwind, this French style chateau is the best furnished of the society houses.

NEWPORT

The Marble House cost, including furnishings, a total of $11 million when it was built in 1892.

rocked a sailboat until it capsized—an inebriated sailor from Fort Adams and three Irish employees from August Belmont's estate who were chasing a valuable sheep who had plummeted off the pier in Newport. After saving the men she went back and rescued the floundering sheep. In 1879 she received the highest honor of all. She was named keeper of the Lime Rock Light. Although the Lime Rock Light is no longer shining for mariners, it lives on as the Ida Lewis Yacht Club.

MIDDLETOWN

Norman Bird Sanctuary
Third Beach Road
Middletown
401-846-2577

From Newport follow Memorial Boulevard into Middletown. The **Norman Bird Sanctuary** is one of the best birding areas in New England. (Over 250 species are recorded.) A nineteenth-century farm belonging to the Norman family, this 450-acre refuge has over 10 miles of trails. There's a wonderful view of Second Beach and the sea from 50-foot-high **Hanging Rock**. Stop at the museum for a guide to the ecology trail and for the *Norman Bird Flyer*, a magazine filled with interesting articles about wildlife and schedules of events.

Second Beach
Sachuest Point Road
Middletown

Third Beach
Sachuest Point Road
Middletown

After your hike, head for a swim at **Second Beach**, which has rolling surf and a gentle drop-off. The water at **Third Beach** (it's also called Navy Beach or Peabody's) is clean, but there's a steep drop-off in some areas.

Now you have a choice of city or country. You can choose to explore the capital city of Providence or drive the back roads through the lovely farm country and quiet beach settlements of eastern Rhode Island. If country is your choice, take Route 138 to Tiverton.

TIVERTON

We've tried a number of routes through this peaceful countryside, amused by the lack of either numbers or road names, and have created our own rule of thumb for coping with junctions: When in doubt, follow the yellow-lined road that seems to bend in the right general direction.

From Tiverton follow Route 77 south through Tiverton Four Corners. Watch for the road on the left to **Little Compton**. There are fine stones from early colonial days in the graveyard on the commons.

More meandering? Head back to Route 77 and go south to Sakonnet on the point. Or take the back roads up to Adamsville to visit **Stonebridge Dishes** (401-635-4441), a shop that carries imports at discount prices, and a 225-year-old gristmill that's still grinding corn for johnnycake meal.

You're in a backwater of modern civilization just a dozen miles south of the major highway that connects New Bedford and the Cape with Providence and New York. Yet, in Sakonnet, you're off the track in a rural world not unlike the English countryside. Enjoy!

From here, you can follow the signs to Westport Point and the start of the next itinerary, or go to Providence.

If you chose to go to Providence from the Newport area, there are several routes to take. You can take either Route 114 or Route 138 north, or cross on the bridge to Jamestown, continue on Route 138 west, and go north on Route 1. There is an interstate (I-95 and I-195) on each side of Narragansett Bay, but it may not be worth the effort to get to either highway for such a short drive.

We, like others, used to zip past Providence on the big highways. We were annoyed with construction and sometimes got lost late at night trying to follow labyrinthine detours. Now we have done an about-face after exploring the renaissance of Providence. During the 1920s, as

LITTLE COMPTON

PROVIDENCE

the textile industry moved to the southern part of the U.S., Providence went into a decline. By the 1950s neighborhoods were mostly slums. The amazing good luck is that the historic buildings in the city stood neglected for years, waiting to be given a fresh coat of paint and brought back to life. In 1956 the **Providence Preservation Society** was formed to combat federal urban renewal programs, which operated by means of the wrecker's ball. Hundreds of structures were saved, and today the lovely lines of Federal, Greek Revival, and Victorian buildings have reappeared.

**Providence
Preservation
Society
24 Meeting Place
Providence
401-831-7440**

Benefit Street, also called Providence's "Mile of History," is a place where people live and work in historic buildings. The street originally was planned in the 1760s to reduce overcrowding on Main Street; it was designed "for the common benefit of all." Today you can stroll past at least 200 buildings, admiring period lights, wrought-iron railings, gables, mansard roofs, cobblestone alleys, brick sidewalks, and gardens. Pick up a guide to Benefit Street at the Preservation Society, which is housed in a 1769 brick schoolhouse.

**John Brown House
52 Power Street
Providence
401-331-8575**

The **John Brown House** was called "the most magnificent and elegant mansion that I have ever seen on this continent" by John Quincy Adams. John Brown, a staunch supporter of the American patriots, led the attack in 1772 on the British revenue ship *Gaspee*, which had run aground in Narragansett Bay. Captain Lindsey of the *Hannah*, one of many vessels harassed by the British ship for months, purposely led the *Gaspee* into shallow water off Namquit Point (later called Gaspee Point) until she ran aground. Captain Lindsey then went into Providence to see John Brown, who gathered a group of men to surprise and capture the captain and crew of the tilting *Gaspee*. Not surprisingly, the wrecked vessel was set on fire and burned to the waterline.

John Brown had left the family business in 1771 to begin his own commercial enterprises in shipping. The house, built in 1786, was the first of the large three-story mansions to be built on the hill; the Browns had a clear view of their ships in the harbor below. It was eventually sold to others in 1851 and again in 1901 and was then bought back into the family in 1935 by John Nicholas Brown. He donated it in 1941 to the Rhode Island Historical Society. The house is filled with period furniture, reproductions of the original wallpapers, silver, paintings, porcelain, glassware, and pewter.

At the junction of Hopkins and Benefit streets is the **Governor Stephen Hopkins House**, which was first built in 1707. The house, moved from the foot of the hill on South Main Street, also has a colonial garden. George Washington slept in this house not once but twice!

Governor Stephen Hopkins House 15 Hopkins Street Providence

Continuing north on Benefit Street, you will come to the **Providence Athenaeum**. Founded in 1753 as the Providence Library Company, before the days of tax-supported free libraries, it merged with the Providence Athenaeum in 1836. A wing was added in 1979 to expand library services. The library includes special collections of rare books, prints, paintings, over 155,000 volumes, and other research materials. Its full roster of programs includes films, readings, festivals, and trips abroad. One program that tickled our fancy was the "Poe Bizarre," heralded by the raven, "Nevermore . . ." It is said that Edgar Allan Poe courted Sarah Helen Whitman in the library.

Providence Athenaeum 251 Benefit Street Providence 401-421-6970

A side trip up College Street will lead you to **Brown University**, founded in 1764. **University Hall** sits at the top of College Street at Prospect Street. Built in 1771, this four-story brick, hip-roofed building was copied from Nassau Hall at Princeton University. It was used as a barracks

Brown University College Street Providence 401-863-1000

and hospital during the American Revolution. Check for campus tours at Nicolson House, at 71 George Street.

A few blocks farther east, on Benevolent Street, is the **Museum of Rhode Island History at Aldrich House**. This museum opened in 1979 and is operated by the Rhode Island Historical Society. Originally the home of Nelson Aldrich, this 1822 Federal mansion overlooks landscaped gardens. Inside, there are changing exhibits of Rhode Island history.

Museum of Rhode Island History at Aldrich House
110 Benevolent Street
Providence
401-421-6567

Back on Benefit Street you will come to the **Museum of Art, Rhode Island School of Design,** which houses the major art museum in Rhode Island. Founded in 1877, the Rhode Island School of Design was begun with $1675 left over from the Rhode Island exhibition of the Philadelphia Exposition in 1876. It has since achieved renown as a school for architecture, design, and visual art.

Museum of Art, Rhode Island School of Design
224 Benefit Street
Providence
401-331-3511

Acquisitions to the museum date from one of the first, Asher B. Durand's *Chocorua Peak*. Winslow Homer exhibited his work in the museum in 1898 and in 1900 wrote, "I have a *very excellent* painting *On a Lee Shore*, 39 × 39 . . . I will send it to you if you desire to see it. *Good* things are scarce. Frame not ordered yet, but I can send it by the time McKinley is selected." Collections include Greek, Roman, Medieval, Oriental, and Renaissance sculpture, European decorative arts, nineteenth-century French painting, nineteenth- and twentieth-century American painting, contemporary art, and American Indian artifacts.

First Baptist Meeting House
75 North Main Street
Providence
401-751-2266

The **First Baptist Meeting House** was built in 1775, although the congregation was founded in 1638 by Roger Williams and other settlers. This was the first Baptist church in America. Its Waterford crystal chandelier dates from 1792.

Prospect Terrace
Congdon at Cushing Street
Providence

Prospect Terrace is the place to come for a picnic lunch. The view of the city and surrounding countryside is worth the trip. Roger Williams' grave and statue are in this park. Not far away is the **Roger Williams National Memorial** on the site of the first settlement in 1636. The Roger Williams Spring is now a well.

The **Old State House** has seen a whirl of social life beginning with George Washington and Lafayette. It was here, two months before the Declaration of Independence was signed, that Rhode Island ended its ties with King George III of England. The current **State House** was built of white Georgia marble. It has the second largest unsupported marble dome anywhere; the first is St. Peter's Basilica in Rome. A bronze statue of **Independent Man** perches on top of the dome.

The oldest enclosed shopping mall in the country was built in Providence in 1828—**The Arcade**. Located between Westminster and Weybosset streets at Peck Street, this Greek Revival building is unusual in having facades of different styles. Apparently two architects couldn't agree and so each designed his own. The building was originally called "Butler's Folly" or a "foolhardy dream." While you're involved in shopping you might like to also try **Davol Square Marketplace** between Point and Eddy streets. The building originally manufactured surgical supplies for the Davol Rubber Company. Besides shops and restaurants Davol offers fashion shows and various musical performances.

Stop in **Player's Corner Pub** (194 Washington Street, 401-621-8738) for dinner before attending the theater. It specializes in veal and also offers a full range of entrees. **Trinity Repertory Company** (201 Washington Street, Providence 02903; 401-351-4242) has been in business for almost twenty-five years. In 1968 it was the first American company invited to perform at the Edinburgh festival, held in Scotland every summer.

Roger Williams
National
Memorial
North Main and
Smith Streets
Providence
401-528-5385

Old State House
150 Benefit Street
Providence

State House
Smith, Gaspee, and
Francis Streets
Providence

When you're ready to continue into Massachusetts, either take I-95 toward New Bedford and Cape Cod (Itinerary E), or Plymouth and the South Shore of Boston (Itinerary F). If you want to head toward the heart of Boston, take I-95 north from Providence or Route 24 north from Fall River.

ITINERARY E: SOUTHERN MASSCHUSETTS SHORE

CAPE COD NATIONAL SEASHORE

ITINERARY E

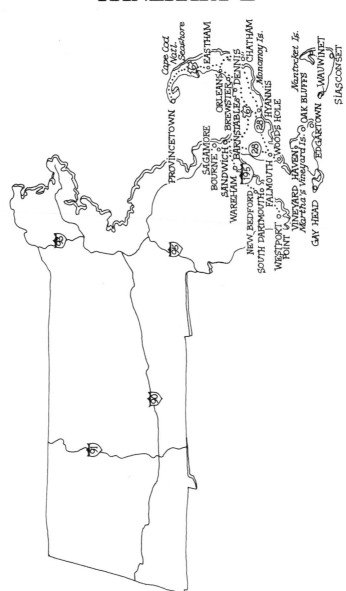

Southern Massachusetts Shore, Cape Cod, and the Islands

Cape Cod Chantey

Oh, Cape Cod girls they have no combs,
Heave away, heave away!
They comb their hair with codfish bones,
Heave away, heave away!

Heave away, you bully, bully boys!
Heave away, heave away!
Heave away, and don't you make a noise,
For we're bound for Australia!

Oh, Cape Cod boys they have no sleds,
They slide down hill on codfish heads.

Oh, Cape cod cats they have no tails,
They blew away in heavy gales.

From the end of the Revolution to the turn of the century Massachusetts developed both its shipping and whaling industries. Ports along the coast were booming with activity, creating individual fortunes and general prosperity. Although the War of 1812 disrupted that prosperity, for a time, shipbuilding, coastwise and long-distance trade, and whaling continued to generate wealth in ports like New Bedford and Salem throughout the first half of the century. But land-based industry—in the textile and manufacturing mills of Fall River and Lowell—was beginning to create an alternative base for the state's financial development. The Civil War and the hordes of immigrant workers who arrived after it, hurried the transition from sea to land. And by the end of the nineteenth century, Massachusetts dominated New England's industrial community.

The terrain in Massachusetts tilts from west to east, with high land from the Berkshire Mountains to the Connecticut River, and a gradual slope toward the shoals and rich fishing banks of the continental shelf in the eastern two-thirds of the state. Along that slope are forests, glacial lakes and ponds, the curiously shaped tail of Cape Cod, and such outposts as Nantucket, Martha's Vineyard, and the Elizabeth Islands.

Itinerary E will take you along the southern shore of Massachusetts past dune-lined beaches and into a former whaling town where you can follow the Moby Dick Trail and climb aboard a half-model of a whaling ship, or even take a cruise to spot real whales. Many people tend to head right from New York City or Connecticut to the Cape, bypassing this lovely section of Massachusetts. While you may not be coming from Rhode Island to begin this itinerary, you can connect to it from other points south and east on I-95 and I-195, or from the north and west via I-95 or Route 24 to I-195. A glance at the map will show you that the region is very compact; it does not matter much whether you begin exploring it in Fall River, where a bounty of factory outlet stores and a tour of the World War II battleship USS *Massachusetts* await, or in the historic district of New Bedford.

We have chosen, however, another starting point in the midst of a beautiful, relatively unknown part of the region that tourists who stick to the main roads will never see—the town of Westport Point. If you have been following the Rhode Island itinerary, take the road from Adamsville to Westport Point; coming from the north, reach Westport Point on either Route 81 from Fall River, via Adamsville, or more directly on Route 88 heading south from I-195.

WESTPORT POINT

Westport Point sits across the Westport River from Acoaxet. This area used to be called the Devil's Pocketbook because "the illusion of an unbroken coastline from the open sea made this harbor a haven for early smugglers and Revolutionists." It seems rum-running was a popular sport here at different times in history!

Friends recommend a small homey restaurant called **Ellie's Place** (617-636-5590), on the Main Road, about 3 miles north of the bridge. There are daily specials (corned beef and cabbage on Thursdays) and delicious home-baked desserts.

From Westport Point follow the signs to **Horseneck State Beach**. The dune-lined beach is 2 miles long. The water is clean and warm (about 70 degrees in summer), but the surf can be strong.

Horseneck State Beach
Route 88
Westport
617-636-8816

From the beach follow the coast road to East Beach Road for about a mile. Turn north on Old Horseneck Road, where you'll find the **Bayside Restaurant** (617-636-5882). Stop for quiche, homemade carrot cake, Indian pudding, and huge seafood platters.

**SOUTH
DARTMOUTH**

Continue jogging through the countryside, past rock walls and farms, on Old Horseneck Road, Russell's Road, Mills Road, and Gulf Road, to South Dartmouth. There are several interesting shops on Elm Street. We keep our family supplied with nylon duffle bags and sail-cloth ends from **Manchester Sail Makers** (617-992-6322). The **Packet** (617-944-0759) caters to yachtsmen, stocking everything from charts to sports clothes.

The **Sail Loft** (617-994-4542) has seafood meals and a great Sunday brunch. It's here we learned the story of Padanarum, the town's local name. It seems in the early eighteenth century Laban Thatcher, a well-to-do settler, saw similarities between his own life and fortunes and those of the Biblical Laban who lived in Paddan-Aram. So he named the area Padanarum. Unhappily, that later Laban "threw his weight around too much and the council of ministers, not to be discomfited by any mere mundane pressure, decided Laban had had it and brought against him 'eleven serious and grievous charges.' . . . Laban Thatcher was summarily excommunicated and, together with a few of his sympathizers, was packed off to Little Compton, Rhode Island."

NEW BEDFORD

From Padanarum, drive a few miles north on Dartmouth Street to New Bedford, one of the most interesting cities in New England because its history reflects the major stages of economic development and decline in the region.

Bartholomew Gosnold, a British explorer, sailed the *Concord* in 1602 to Cape Cod and Cuttyhunk Island, and finally landed near the mouth of the Acushnet River. In 1652 settlers bought the land from the Wampanoag Indians that included the area from Westport to New Bedford. That purchase didn't mean peace,

though: Over a number of years the Wampanoags continued to murder settlers and devastate
their lands.

Joseph Russell III founded Bedford Village
(new New Bedford to the west and Fairhaven to
the east of the Acushnet River) in the 1740s, and,
more significantly, started up the whaling industry here. In 1778 the British destroyed the village,
leaving the whaling industry at a standstill for a
number of years. Finally, in 1787, the rebuilt
town to the west of the river became New Bedford.

The town prospered and, by the middle of
the nineteenth century, was one of the most successful and powerful whaling ports in the world.
But that prosperity waned as whales grew scarce
and whaling voyages grew longer, and as the lure
of easy fortunes led many sailors to strike out for
California. During one disastrous cruise in 1871,
thirty-three New Bedford ships were locked in
Arctic ice. Their twelve hundred sailors survived,
but the financial loss to shareholders was irrepa-
rable.

With the decline of whaling and the increase
of industrial development, New Bedford turned
to textile mills, which created a booming econ-
omy from the 1880s through the late 1920s. But
with the depression, industrial development
turned elsewhere.

Today New Bedford is rehabilitating its
downtown section. The area is lit with gas lamps,
and the roads have been repaved with cobblestones (Wear comfortable shoes!). To begin your
self-guided walking tour of the **Waterfront Historic District**—an area filled with marine shops
and restored nineteenth-century architecture—
visit the chamber of commerce. Here you'll find
information about the **Moby Dick Trail** and
other attractions in the area.

New Bedford and whaling are irrevocably

New Bedford
Chamber of
Commerce
227 Union Street
New Bedford
617-999-5231

**New Bedford
  Whaling Museum
Johnny Cake Hill
New Bedford
617-997-0046**

associated with Herman Melville's *Moby Dick*. The story is told in the **New Bedford Whaling Museum**. Among the exhibits are an 8½-foot-high panorama of a worldwide whaling voyage that stretches around the room (it was painted in 1848); an authentic replica of a square-rigged whaler, an 89-foot-long half-model that you can climb aboard and explore; whaling relics and scrimshaw; and replicas of a rigging loft, sail loft, and cooperage shop. The museum also schedules whale-watching trips.

Did you know that there are two kinds of whales, toothed and toothless? Baleen whales are toothless; they use comblike fringed ridges of baleen to scoop plankton into their mouths. The blue whale and the right whale are both baleen whales. The right whale got its name because it floated after being killed, therefore it was the "right" one to catch. The sperm whale belongs to the toothed kind and lives by eating fish. Its sperm oil, the best kind for lamps, as well as for spermaceti, which is used to make candles, made this species particularly valuable to whalers.

"Thar she blows!" If you've wished you could have been born in the last century so you could have signed on a whaling ship, think again. Life on board a sailing ship sounds romantic, but it was often uncomfortable, dangerous, and even fatal. Living conditions were crowded, diet was unbalanced, boredom caused some to get into trouble, weather or reefs could destroy a ship, and the danger from hunting whales in small boats was unavoidable. Furthermore, men on a whaling cruise could be out for three years without setting their feet on home turf.

**Seamen's Bethel
15 Johnny Cake
  Hill
New Bedford
617-992-3295**

Across the street from the museum you'll find the **Seamen's Bethel**, filled with nautical memorabilia. Here is a photograph of Melville and the story of his voyages to the South Seas, where he "discerned the primordial beauty and terror of this world and the danger-ridden labors of whaling" that he later put into "the immortal saga of *Moby Dick*." The chapel, with boat-shaped pulpit, was built for sailors in need of a place for worship and rest; and Melville used it in *Moby Dick*, as the site of Father Mapple's sermon. Legend says that Enoch Mudge, a preacher in the 1840s, once took the bethel's organ, perched in a wheelbarrow, down to the docks to perform a last-minute service for departing seamen.

Next door is the **Mariner's Home**, bearing a characteristic plaque: "Latitude 41°-35°, Longitude 70°-55°." At night red and green port-and-starboard lanterns light up on either side of the door.

Mariner's Home
Johnny Cake Hill
New Bedford

At the foot of Union Street, at **State Pier**, sits the lightship *New Bedford*. The 133-foot ship, painted bright red, once marked a welcome landfall for ships returning from all over the world. During the summer you can go aboard and explore the vessel, imagining what life must have been like for the men who lived on her through the gales of winter. State Pier is also home to the **Blessing of the Fleet**, a ceremony held every August. A "dressed" fishing fleet passes in review, and prizes are awarded for the best decorations. New Bedford is now the fifth largest fishing port on the East Coast. You can watch the scallop auction at seven every weekday morning (the fish auction is at eight) at the Wharfinger Building on the waterfront.

New Bedford
State Pier
New Bedford

If you enjoy seeing ships, in nearby Fall River you can visit **Battleship Cove** (off I-95), to see four ships that are open for inspection: the battleship USS *Massachusetts*; World War II submarine USS *Lionfish*; destroyer USS *Joseph P. Kennedy, Jr.*; and *PT Boat 796*.

The New Bedford-Fall River area is a shopper's paradise. There are many factory outlets here, all listed in a booklet that's available at tourist offices and some stores.

From this area, follow signs to Cape Cod, to the Bourne Bridge or the Sagamore Bridge.

Cape Cod

During the Ice Age, as the sun melted the glacier advancing from the north, the power of the moving ice dissipated south of mainland New England. Rock continued to pile up with glacial momentum from the north, leaving a ridge (a terminal moraine) along Cape Cod, the Elizabeth Islands, Nantucket, and Martha's Vineyard. The islands developed as the ice moved in lobes—two lobes coming together, piling up rocks and gravel, to form each island.

The melting ice carried off any rich soil, and the residual sandy soil does not hold enough moisture to nourish most plants. The scrub pine is everywhere, and heath foliage—huckleberry, sheep laurel, blueberry, and bearberry—grows where nothing else will. In low areas cranberry flourishes, providing an important seasonal industry for the region. And azalea, rhododendron, and holly, which were planted later, add color to the landscape.

Some historians believe the Cape was discovered in A.D. 1004 by Thorvald the Viking. We know that Bartholomew Gosnold arrived in his ship, the *Concord*, in 1602. He caught many codfish while anchored here, and the name *Cape Cod* may have been derived from entries in his log. It's also probable that the Pilgrims made a stop at the end of the Cape before landing in Plymouth—a controversy yet to be resolved between Plymouth and Provincetown.

The seafaring heritage of the Cape began in the seventeenth century, when many towns became whaling centers and home ports for the square-riggers that set out to bring native products to the world. A sense of daily life during the seventeenth and eigthteenth centuries has been preserved for us in the stately mansions owned by sea captains, in the cottages patterned after the homes settlers had left behind in Devon and Cornwall, in churches and windmills, and in the recorded heritage of journals, logs, and letters.

The weather on Cape Cod is mild for much of the year. Although you may find heat and humidity in July and August, sea breezes usually cool the land. In summer the average high temperature is in the 70s; the low, around 60 degrees.

The Cape and the islands are ringed with magnificent beaches. Those along the south coast enjoy warmer water (influenced by the Gulf Stream); those on the north side, along Cape Cod Bay, are cooler, sometimes even cold. In the National Seashore area on the Atlantic you'll find heavy surf and an occasional undertow.

Today visitors can hike along sand dunes; swim, fish, or boat on the ocean, bays, and interior lakes; and explore the lighthouses and coves, rich with the legends and lore of shipwrecks.

Before you go, write for maps and information to the Cape and island chambers of commerce. Specific information about tours is available from the **Cape Cod National Seashore** and the **Massachusetts Audubon Society**. For a calendar of current events, "Happenings Along the Americana Trail," contact the **Bristol County Development Council**.

Cape Cod Chamber of Commerce
Mid-Cape Highway
Hyannis
617-362-3225

You'll find summer theater in Chatham, Dennis, Falmouth, Harwich, Hyannis, Orleans, and Provincetown. For performance schedules, write to the Cape Cod Chamber of Commerce or to the tourist information office in the individual town. These are also your sources for the *Sportsman's Guide to Cape Cod*, a pamphlet that lists information about deep-sea fishing, surfing, surf-casting, sailing, scuba diving, swimming, bicycling, hiking, tennis, and golf.

Cape Cod National Seashore
South Wellfleet
617-349-3785

Massachusetts Audubon Society
Ashumet Road
Hatchville
617-563-6390

I-495, which goes directly to the Bourne Bridge, bypassing the congestion of old Route 6 between Wareham and Buzzards Bay, is slightly longer than Route 3 to the Sagamore Bridge and the Mid-Cape Highway, but should be faster during the summer and congested weekends.

Bristol County Development Council
Box 976
New Bedford, 02741
617-997-1250

Once you get on the Cape, travel can be either easy and pleasant or difficult and frustrating, depending on the season. There are three major highways on the Cape. The fastest and most direct route is the Mid-Cape Highway (Route 6), although it changes from four to two lanes as one gets farther out on the Cape. But you see neither towns nor water from this highway until you reach the tip of the Cape. The south shore is served by Route 28, which, apart from a few sections (Bourne to Falmouth, which is four-laned), is slow and congested. A few parts like that between Cotuit and Centerville are pleasant enough to reward the traveler, but others are overdeveloped with shopping centers and condominium development. On the other hand, Route 6A winds along the north shore through beautiful villages and fully repays the traveler for the extra time spent. We suggest using the small roads to dip south from Route 6 as the local inhabitants do.

There are three information booths for on-site visits: at the Bourne traffic circle in Buzzards Bay, at the Sagamore rotary, and on the Mid-Cape Highway at the junction of Routes 6 and 132 (617-362-3225). These centers can advise you on nearby campgrounds as well as other tourist accommodations.

One logical way to explore the Cape and the islands is to head south on the fast and efficient section of Route 28 to Falmouth and then Woods Hole, the best year-round jumping-off place for Martha's Vineyard and Nantucket.

FALMOUTH

Falmouth Historical Society Museum
Palmer Avenue
Falmouth
617-548-4857

First Congregational Church
Main Street
Falmouth

From the Bourne Bridge follow Route 28 south to Falmouth, once a major whaling and fishing port. Surrounding the village green are the stately foursquare homes of sea captains, whose wives watched for their return from widow's walks atop the roofs. The **Falmouth Historical Society Museum**, built in 1790 by Dr. Francis Wicks, has a widow's walk; collections of Sandwich glass, period furniture, and whaling memorabilia; and a colonial garden. In the **First Congregational Church** hangs an original Paul Revere bell, one of the few still being used.

Nearby, the **Market Bookshop** (617-548-5636) has a fine collection of books about the Cape. Behind the bookstore is the **Market Barn Gallery**, which is open from June through September. Here you'll find unusual and distinctive oils, watercolors, sculpture, jewelry, and prints.

Falmouth has twenty-five public parks, many beaches, and several bicycle paths, including the **Shining Sea Bikeway**, a 3-mile track over an abandoned railroad bed from the Falmouth Station to the ferry terminal in Woods Hole. We especially enjoy the **Nobska Lighthouse** area and **Quisset Harbor**. The former has a good beach; the latter, both a beach and bird refuge.

In East Falmouth the Massachusetts Audubon Society maintains the **Ashumet Holly Reservation**. This 45-acre park was given to the society to preserve the famed holly collection of Wilfred Wheeler. Besides holly you'll see dogwood, magnolias, viburnums, rhododendrons, and wildflowers in spring; oriental lotus blossoms in summer; and Franklinia blooms, an unusual fall-flowering shrub, in autumn. There are several nature trails through the groves of trees and shrubs.

Ashumet Holly Reservation Route 151 East Falmouth 617-563-6390

Food in Falmouth? There are lots of good restaurants in the area including: the **Regatta** (617-548-5400) on Scranton Avenue, **Coonamesset Inn** (617-548-2300) on Jones Road, and **The Nimrod** (617-548-5500) on Dillingham Avenue. Less formal are **Country Fare** (617-548-9020) and **Golden Swan** (617-540-6580), both on Main Street. Not far away, in East Falmouth, is a popular, family-run, inexpensive restaurant, **The Big Fishermen** (617-548-4266) on Route 28.

If you're taking Route 28 to Hyannis you'll be glad to know that the Regatta opened another restaurant in Cotuit (617-428-5715), the **Regatta of Cotuit**.

A trip to Cape Cod means beaches, and beaches mean beachcombing. Shells, beach or sea glass, driftwood, and interesting stones are all here for the taking. Or you can join an ecologist at work on the sand. We spent a few days at a conference on Martha's Vineyard where one of the sessions was held on the beach in a pouring rain. The professor who led us there had us entranced with the different life forms at different levels under the sand. And we learned about the composition of the sand, worn from crushed quartz, feldspar, and garnets; the effects of tide and wind; the single-celled plankton, food for larger sea beings; jellyfish, sand hoppers (or beach fleas), clams, snails, oysters, mussels, scallops, starfish, and mole crabs; and the plant life—the seaweed, eelgrass, moss, kelp, and flotsam and jetsam that appear with each tide. Sound interesting? Two excellent books by Dorothy Sterling and Donald Zinn about the hidden life of beaches are available.

Continue for several miles along Route 28 to Woods Hole. A principal port of the Cape, the town is the base for ferry service to Martha's Vineyard and Nantucket. It is also a major center for marine research, home to the **Marine Biological Laboratory** and the **Woods Hole Oceanographic Institute**. The institute, founded in 1930 as a private nonprofit organization for ocean research, is now a world center for oceanography. If you want to know more about the work done here, contact the public information office for a tour of the facilities and research vessels in port. That office is also the place to pick up a weekly calendar of maritime lectures and other scientific programs at the institute.

The aquarium of the **National Marine Fisheries Service** is part of a research project to study fish and invertebrates. It's well organized, and worth a tour both for adults and for children. The service also offers lectures and programs by scientists and technicians from its research groups.

Woods Hole is also the home of the **Sea Education Association**, a year-round school offering students college credit for a twelve-week program that includes six weeks of classes on

WOODS HOLE

Marine Biological Laboratory
167 Water Street
Woods Hole
617-548-3705 Ext. 423

Woods Hole Oceanographic Institute
Water Street
Woods Hole
617-548-1400

National Marine Fisheries Service
Albatross Street
Woods Hole
617-548-5123

shore and then a six-week voyage on board one of two large research schooners, the *Westward* or the new *Corwith Cramer*, named after the founder of the school.

Imagine yourself, a seabag on your shoulder, embarking on a beautiful sunny day. Watch your head as you clamber down the almost-vertical gangway. You share your cabin with anywhere from two to four shipmates; but you might be lucky enough to have a bunk built into the curve of the ship's topsides, with the privacy of a curtain, a shelf for books, and your own porthole! You've brought a minimum of clothing (most of it warm) but remembered your foul-weather gear and sea boots; and all of this resides in your bunk with you.

Research activity goes on day and night, and everyone is eager to share findings. Faculty, students, and ship's officers get to know each other well, eating together, hoisting and striking sails, sharing thoughts through long watches at night, and working together on research projects. Life at sea replaces normal routine with a new one that focuses on the needs of the ship and the shipmates who share this tiny society in the midst of a restless sea.

For a meal out in Woods Hole, try **Landfall** (617-548-1758) on Woods Hole Harbor. The **Black Duck** (617-548-9165) on Water Street is a good spot for lunch, as is **Fishmonger's Cafe** (617-548-9148), also on Water Street.

Sea Education Association
171 Woods Hole Road
Woods Hole
617-540-3954

Take the ferry to Martha's Vineyard. The **Steamship Authority** offers year-round service—for cars too—from Woods Hole. (During summer months, make reservations for your car well in advance.) **Hy-Line**, carrying passengers only, leaves from Hyannis on a seasonal basis.

The island, barely 20 miles long and 10 miles wide, attracts thousands of visitors each year to its splendid colored cliffs, beaches, coves, dunes,

MARTHA'S VINEYARD

Hy-Line Hyannis Harbor Tours
Ocean Street Dock
Hyannis
617-775-7185
617-778-2602
  (reservations)

**Steamship
Authority**
Box 284
Woods Hole
617-540-2022

rolling moors, and salt marshes. The sea spreads its scent everywhere.

You can explore the island in your car or on a bike (rent one or bring your own). More than 20 miles of bike paths leading all over the island have been developed. The Vineyard's roads wind through all kinds of terrain—some flat areas, some hilly ones. The major roads are paved and smooth but with no shoulders. Some have an extra lane for cyclists.

Here's a list for cyclists of several routes to follow, with descriptions and mileage, adapted from Polly Burroughs's *Guide to Martha's Vineyard.*

**Martha's Vineyard
Chamber of
Commerce**
Beach Road
Vineyard Haven
617-693-0085

Vineyard Haven to Oak Bluffs to Edgartown along the shore road: flat, 7½ miles.

Edgartown to Felix Neck Wildlife Sanctuary: hilly, 2 miles.

Chappaquiddick ferry dock to Dyke Bridge: one hill, 3 miles.

Edgartown to South Beach at Katama: flat, 3 miles.

Edgartown to West Tisbury: hilly, 9 miles.

West Tisbury to Beetlebung Corner, Chilmark: hilly, about 5 miles.

Beetlebung Corner to Gay Head: very steep hills, 6 miles.

Menemsha to North Tisbury on North Road: hilly, 5½ miles.

North Tisbury to Vineyard Haven: partly hilly, 5 miles.

Lambert's Cove Road: hilly, 4½ miles.

Vineyard Haven to Edgartown on the inland road: hilly, 6½ miles.

Edgartown to the airport: hilly, 4½ miles.

Oak Bluff to the airport: partly hilly, 7 miles.

Vineyard Haven to the airport: partly hilly, 5 miles.

The ferry from the Woods Hole docks in Vineyard Haven, the major port of the island. Much of Vineyard Haven was destroyed by the Great Fire of 1883. The rebuilt town now houses a substantial winter community. There are shops along Main Street, including the **Bunch of Grapes** bookstore (617-693-2291) and several bike rental stores. When you are ready to eat, try **Le Grenier** (Upper Main Street, 617-693-4906) or the **Tisbury Inn Cafe** (Main Street, 617-693-3416).

From Vineyard Haven take Beach Road to Oak Bluffs, earlier called Cottage City, a cluster of Victorian cottages with gingerbread scrollwork. The cottages were built on tent sites, with each family trying to outdo the next in color and ornateness. The town was settled in 1642, but didn't become popular until 1835, when it was first used for a Methodist camp meeting by "Reformation" John Adams, whose passionate sermons and tearful praying won converts away from the Congregationalists on the island. The conical open Tabernacle, with its lovely stained-glass windows, was built in 1870. As you walk around you'll hear the tinkle of windchimes and see colorful hanging flower baskets.

In the center of town, kids have a chance to catch the brass ring for a free ride on the **Flying Horses,** one of the oldest carousels in the country. And in July there's a craft fair at **Wesley House.** Locals eat at **Linda Jean's** (617-693-4093) on Circuit Avenue. The crab rolls and Greek salads are wonderful and very inexpensive.

Wesley House
Lake Avenue
Oak Bluffs
617-693-0135

From Oak Bluffs take Beach Road around Sengekontacket Pond and then take a sharp right on Vineyard Haven Road. Watch closely for a small stone post on your right, discreetly lettered

**Felix-Neck Wildlife
Sanctuary
Edgartown Road
Vineyard Haven
617-627-4850**

**Christiantown
Cemetery
Christiantown Road
Vineyard Haven**

Felix–Neck Wildlife Sanctuary. The one-laned sandy road leads visitors to a barn containing exhibits and a gift shop. The Massachusetts Audubon Society owns and protects this sanctuary. Pick up a trail guide and head out to see the turkeys and Canada geese wandering around the barn, the Rehabilitation Building that is used for oiled birds and rearing young waterfowl, the Raptor Barn that houses birds of prey, the waterfowl pond, and a network of trails.

Continue on Vineyard Haven Road and take a sharp left onto State Road past fieldstone walls and scrub oak and pine. Watch for a sign to **Christiantown Cemetery.** The cemetery contains fieldstone-marked graves. A large plaque announces that the "Ancient township of the praying Indians" was set apart in 1660 by Josias, the sachem of Takemmy, which was later called Christiantown. **Mayhew Chapel** was built as an Indian chapel in 1910.

At North Tisbury take North Road toward Menemsha. You'll pass Tea Lane, named after smuggled tea that delighted the patriots who refused to pay tax to King George. The dredged harbor along the cut into Menemsha Pond is the home port of an active fishing fleet.

Menemsha's harbor—you'll recognize it if you've seen the movie *Jaws*—is popular with sports fishermen (bluefish and striped bass) and yachtsmen. Menemsha Pond is a beautiful anchorage. Be careful: The entrance is constantly shoaling up and being dredged so the underwater terrain may not be what your chart indicates.

Drive on to Chilmark and follow South Road around Nashaquit Pond to Gay Head. Gay Head, on the southwest tip of the island, is marked by varicolored cliffs, a national monument. Each colored layer records a part of history that took place before the Ice Age. The layer of black at the bottom indicates buried forests; red and yellow layers are clay; a layer of green sand that turns red when exposed to the air contains fossils of crabs and clams; the gravel-like layers contain sharks' teeth, whale bones, and animal skeletons. Sorry, no climbing on the cliffs. Erosion is doing enough damage without visitors' help. The cliffs are just one of Gay Head's claims to fame; its harpooners are another. In *Moby Dick*, Melville wrote that Gay Head had produced the most daring harpooners in the world. (Moby Dick was patterned after a ferocious white whale, Mocha Dick, who caused the death of thirty men before he was killed in 1859.)

Many of the inhabitants of Gay Head are of Indian descent. In September 1981, after four years of negotiations, the town agreed to return 238 acres of shorefront property to the three hundred-member Wampanoag tribe. The land, which is worth close to $3 million, will be kept in its natural state. Part of the agreement allows the Indians to apply for federal funds to buy 175 acres of land to use for housing.

Moshop, a mythical hero to the Indians, was said to have built the Devil's Bridge, a reef of glacial boulders reaching out from the Gay Head cliffs toward Cuttyhunk. On January 18, 1884, the steamship *City of Columbus* crashed into the reef; 121 passengers and crew lost their lives that night. The English thought of Moshop as the devil. You can drive along Moshop's Trail with its windbattered vegetation, but you can't stop to swim or walk on the dunes.

From Chilmark head east on South Road to the town of West Tisbury—a lovely section of road to cycle or drive. Captain Joshua Slocum, the first man to sail around the world single-handed, once lived there. Nancy, Lule, a home-spun poet who wrote about such subjects as her hens in the 1860s and 1870s, lived there in Tiah's Cove.

Follow Edgartown-West Tisbury Road into

Edgartown, one of our favorite places. A famous whaling port, the town retains its colonial charm with the elegant homes built from whale oil fortunes. The harbor is nearly always packed with visiting yachts, but it's especially busy one week in July, during the **Edgartown Regatta**, one of the major sailing events in southern Massachusetts.

The **Thomas Cooke House** has an extensive collection of scrimshaw, ship models, whaling gear, costumes, and antique furniture.

Stop for lunch at **Martha's Restaurant** (617-627-8316) on Main Street. The **Kelley House** (617-627-4394), an Edgartown tradition since 1742, has kept the cozy atmosphere of colonial times. Try a meal in the attractive dining room. **Navigator Restaurant** (617-627-4321), right on the water, features nautical decor and seafood.

Fishermen call it the World Series of Fishing. What is it? It's the annual **Striped Bass and Bluefish Derby**, and it's held in Edgartown between September 15 and October 15. Fishermen from all over the country look on the derby as a test of skill, endurance, and know-how. Although at least a thousand people enter the contest each year, only a small number of them—the hard-core group—spend every waking hour fishing. These are the people who can "smell" the fish; who know to look for an oil slick on the water (a sign of fish secretions). These are the people who suffer long hours of cold, wet, and dark as they watch through the night for striped bass; or who get up in the middle of the night to fish just before high tide, when the fish are running. And these are the people who zealously guard the best fishing spots, passing down secret locations from father to son.

We happened to walk by the headquarters and weigh-in station in the harbor and were entranced by the excitement, activity, and camarad-

NANTUCKET

The center of town is full of visitors all summer long who travel by path and cobbled lane enjoying all the island has to offer.

EASTHAM

The grey shingled octagonal windmill which one ground grain for the residents of this Cape Cod community, was restored by the Works Progress Administration in 1936.

HERITAGE PLANTATION

A diversified museum of Americana including exhibits of military history, horticulture, antique autos, and folk art.

erie among the participants, their families, their friends, and anyone who just came along to check on the latest news.

For derby details—regulations, weigh-in procedures, and the long list of awards—write to the Vineyard's chamber of commerce (page 100).

Three miles south is **South Beach**, one of the finest of the many beaches on the Vineyard.

From Edgartown, you can take the ferry to Chappaquiddick. This island is steeped in the lore of shipwrecks. A terrible one took place in January 1866, during the worst blizzard in many years, when the *Christina*, a two-masted schooner, ran aground on Hawes Shoal. The lighthousekeeper saw the wreck, but couldn't rescue the crew until the storm ended. He watched as the vessel settled lower and lower in the water, the men clinging to the rigging. One by one they froze, until just a single man was left alive; he was eventually rescued by a whaleboat from Edgartown.

NANTUCKET

The Steamship Authority (617-540-2022) takes passengers and cars to Nantucket in 2½ hours from Hyannis during the spring, summer, and fall. During the summer, service is available from Woods Hole to Nantucket. If you are in Martha's Vineyard, you can sail from Vineyard Haven during the spring, summer, and fall, and in the summer from Oak Bluffs.

There are several legends describing the birth of Nantucket, but our favorite is the story of Moshop, the first inhabitant of Martha's Vineyard. One day an Indian maiden came to him. She was from a poor family, and the parents of the boy who wanted to marry her would not allow it. Moshop promised to meet the young lovers on Sampson's Hill, on Chappaquiddick. As they were trying to think of some way to marry, he took out his pipe and began to smoke.

Nantucket Island
Chamber of
Commerce
Pacific Club
Building
Nantucket
617-228-1700

Because he was a giant, his pipe was filled with many bales of tobacco. When he knocked the ashes out into the sea, clouds of smoke and vapor filled the air. The fog lifted to reveal an island gilded by the rising sun. With the island as a dowry, the young couple were allowed to marry.

Moshop's island—stretching 15 miles long and 4 miles wide—sits 30 miles off the mainland. You can get here by ferry from Martha's Vineyard and Woods Hole and from Hyannis.

For information about the island's historical sites and a season pass for most of them, contact the **Nantucket Historical Association.**

Nantucket Historical Association Union Street Nantucket 617-228-1894

The old town is much the same as it was in the early nineteenth century, with beautiful homes built from the proceeds of whaling. Begin your tour at the **Whaling Museum,** up the street from Steamboat Wharf, where the ferries dock. Here you'll find an outstanding collection of whaling gear, a whaleboat, and some fine examples of scrimshaw. You'll also learn about the "Nantucket sleigh ride"—the endurance contest between whale and men in the whaleboat as the whale dove and plunged madly after being harpooned, towing the whaleboat behind it. Our guide related the tale of one such trip: While traveling rapidly to leeward on a "sleigh ride" the crew looked back and saw an empty whaleboat following in their wake. A wave eventually smashed her to pieces, but the crew was still curious, wondering where she had come from. When they arrived back on board their ship and hoisted up their own whaleboat, the mystery was solved. The whale they'd been chasing had traveled so fast that the paint stripped off the whaleboat. What they had seen was their own shell of paint following them!

Whaling Museum Broad Street Nantucket 617-228-1736

Head up Broad Street, turn right on Centre Street, and follow it to **Oldest House,** the home of Jethro Coffin. It was built in 1686. Look for

Oldest House Sunset Hill Nantucket

Hadwen House-Satler Memorial Main Street Nantucket

1800 House Mill Street Nantucket

Old Mill Prospect Street Nantucket

Straight Wharf Nantucket

Maria Mitchell Association 1 Vestal Street Nantucket 617-228-5387

the secret hiding place in the closet, and the horseshoe chimney. Follow Centre Street back to Main Street, turn right to the **Hadwen House-Satler Memorial**, a large, comfortable home built in 1845 for a wealthy whale oil merchant. Turn left on Pleasant to Mill Street, to the **1800 House**, which is furnished as a Nantucket home during the great whaling era. Continue on Pleasant Street to South Mill Street, and the **Old Mill**, which is made of wood salvaged from shipwrecks.

Straight Wharf, once the waterfront home of the *Lightship Nantucket*, has been fully restored, the new cobblestone paths leading past displays of weaving, scrimshaw, jewelry, pottery, leather goods, wood carvings, lightship baskets, and a sidewalk art show in August. Before you leave, stop at Al Hartig's kite shop, **Nantucket Kiteman** (617-228-2297). Al is an expert kite builder and flyer, and he's always willing to share his know-how. And for real aficionados, there's a kite-flying contest at the **Miacomet Fair**, in late July.

The **Maria Mitchel Association** operates an aquarium, an observatory, and a natural science museum, and offers a wonderful series of lectures on astronomy.

The **Jared Coffin House** (617-228-2400), an inn built in 1845 by a successful shipowner, features antiques in the living room and library, and canopy beds in some of the guest rooms. Come for the night or just a meal. Lunch is served in the cozy taproom or on the patio.

From town there are several beaches you can bike to, including two excellent beaches for surfing: **Surfside** (out Atlantic Avenue to the south) and **Siasconset** (out Milestone Road to the east). Notice the wind direction as you set out. The afternoon southwesterly often reaches 25 miles an hour by three or four, just about the time you'll be heading back. Nonbikers can cover the distance by bus—either on a shuttle bus from point to point or on a tour.

Scuba divers have discovered the remains of some 750 wrecks around the island. In the blizzard of 1886 the 117-foot three-masted schooner *T. B. Witherspoon* crashed into Little Mioxe Rip Shoal. As the waves hurtled through portholes flooding the cabin, the sailors took to the ratlines. The mate, his wife, and his five-year-old son, who cried "Papa, won't God save us?" remained in the cabin. Only after the boy and his mother died, did the mate leave them to find all but one of the sailors who had climbed aloft frozen or drowned. He helped rescuers save the surviving sailor, and remained the last man on board who lived to tell the story.

In 1918 the lightship *Cross Rip*, anchored off the northern shore of the island, disappeared in the midst of an ice floe. She drifted away from Nantucket, and was found thirty-nine years later near West Dennis. Scientists used an alarm clock on board to establish her age and identity.

Linguists are fascinated by the speech patterns of native Nantucketers, the heritage of their strong sea background. You "see if the coast is clear," "keep your weather eye peeled," "look out for squalls," and "keep an eye to the windward." If you're reckless you're "sailing too close to the wind." If you get the better of someone you've "taken the wind out of his sails." If you're ready you're "on deck." And if you're experienced you "know the ropes." Most of these nautical expressions, and many more, have crept into the general speech of Americans.

When you've finished exploring the island, take the ferry back to the mainland, where the itinerary continues in Hyannis.

HYANNIS

Hyannis is the center of transportation, shopping, and vacation facilities for the south shore of the Cape. It's often very crowded in summer, but you can find almost anything you need here. For a special meal try **Asa Bearse House** (617-771-4131) on Main Street or the **Paddock** (617-775-7677) on West Main Street.

John Fitzgerald Kennedy Memorial Ocean Street Hyannis

Hyannisport was the summer home of President Kennedy. The **John Fitzgerald Kennedy Memorial**, a 12-foot fieldstone wall with the presidential seal, a fountain, and a pool, is next to the town park. Come for a fine view of the outer harbor.

Did you know that you can go by train from Hyannis to Sandwich, Buzzards Bay, and even Boston? Cape Cod & Hyannis Railroad offers a variety of trips. Call (617-771-1145) in Hyannis, or (617-848-7336) in Boston.

CHATHAM

From Hyannis drive east on Route 28 through West Yarmouth, West Dennis, Dennis Port, and Harwich Port, to Chatham. Or, for less plowing through bumper-to-bumper traffic, take the Mid-Cape Highway to exit 11 and follow Route 137 south to Route 28 into Chatham.

Located on the elbow of the Cape, Chatham is surrounded on three sides by the sea. Once busy with shipbuilding, whaling, saltworks, and shoemaking, residents now support themselves with fishing and tourism. Yet the town has retained many lovely colonial homes and traditional Cape Cod beach homes with exteriors of weathered cedar shingles.

Harwich and Chatham, though geographically close, have had a running rivalry for years. One tall tale about a Harwich ship that foundered says the crew paddled toward shore on planks and hatch-covers. As they got near land, one of them asked the crowd on shore where they were. When someone yelled, "Chatham," the sailor turned around and headed back out to sea.

One of the first spots to visit in Chatham is the **Chatham Lighthouse** on Shore Road. Built in 1828 and rebuilt in 1876, the building houses a 24,000 candle power light that flashes four times every thirty seconds. It is visible for 15 miles on a clear night.

As you stand by the lighthouse you will see one of the ravages of the sea—there is a break in the barrier beach protecting Chatham Harbor that has grown to three-quarters of a mile in width. Where surf was once stopped by the beach, there is now open water with ocean swells breaking over the sandbar. On January 2, 1987, 20-foot waves, during a northeasterly storm, ate through the sand barrier. Now, breakers cascade into the once protected bay, high tides are a foot higher, and up to 50 feet of sand has washed away in some places. Homeowners on the inner beach are now in real danger of losing their land to wave erosion. We saw rows of sandbags lining the beach where owners are struggling to inhibit wave action.

At the top of the wooden steps leading down to the beach is a written warning to mariners. It states the changing nature of new channel patterns and warns that the currents are ferocious and extremely dangerous. Although local fishermen go through the break, there is no stable channel; others are advised of the danger. No one knows what the elements will do to the break. Storms in 1846 created a break that later resealed itself.

If you'd like some exercise you can cycle along a 7-mile bike path. Green signs mark the way all along the trail; you can pick it up anywhere. If you begin at the Lighthouse, head north to Fish Pier. From a balcony there, you can watch fishermen unloading their catch. Then cycle to North Chatham, cross Main Street, go by Oyster Pond, out on the neck to Stage Harbor, and back to the Lighthouse.

Chatham Lighthouse Shore Road Chatham

Stop for a very special dinner at **The Queen Anne Inn** (617-945-0394) at 70 Queen Anne Road. Compliments to the Queen Anne's Austrian chef. Also try **The Impudent Oyster** (617-945-3545) at 15 Chatham Bars Avenue; **Chatham Square** (617-945-0945) at 487 Main Street, and **Chatham Wayside Inn** (617-945-1800) at 512 Main Street.

Old Atwood House
Stage Harbor Road
Chatham
617-945-2493

The **Old Atwood House** was built before the Revolution by Joseph C. Atwood, a sea captain. The Chatham Historical Society maintains the house and has its offices here. Rooms are furnished with period pieces, and there are collections of Sandwich glass, seashells, and china. From the front lawn look for the turret of an old Chatham lighthouse.

Old Grist Mill
Shattuck Place
Chatham
617-945-3163

The windmill at the **Old Grist Mill** still grinds corn when there's enough wind. Bring a picnic to eat here or at nearby **Chase Park**.

Chatham Railroad
Museum
Depot Road
Chatham
617-945-3132

A restored train depot houses the **Chatham Railroad Museum**. On display are photographs, models, and a 1910 caboose. **Sylvan Gardens**, a horticulturist's private garden, is a delight. Come enjoy the plantings and the fine view of the sea—all free.

Sylvan Gardens
Old Main Road
Chatham

On summertime Fridays the Chatham Band gives a concert at **Kate Gould Park** on Main Street. Families can sing together, and children can buy balloons from American Field Service students.

Chatham Chamber
of Commerce
Main Street
Chatham
617-945-0342

For information about the town stop at the chamber of commerce information booth on Main Street, next to the town offices. The booth is also the place for information about gravestone rubbing at **Union Cemetery** and **Old Cemetery**. Gravestone rubbing, in Europe a hobby for years, is growing more and more popular here. Your best source of information about permits and stones is usually the town hall; for supplies (rice or tableau paper, hard wax, masking tape, scissors, and an eraser) try a rubbing center or an art store.

With permit and materials in hand, head for the cemetery. Choose a stone that has a flat raised design. Slate is usually smooth; sandstone, rough. Once you've looked over the stone, keeping pattern and indentations in mind, place your paper over it, tape it securely on all sides to the back of the stone, trace the edges with your fingers, color the boundaries lightly, and finally rub with more pressure. Use short strokes in the same direction, and darken the paper evenly. Polish the rubbing, while it's still taped, with a piece of nylon stocking. You can leave the rubbing just as it is, with weather cracks and chips showing, or you can touch up these marks by laying the paper on a flat surface. When you leave be sure to take all scraps of tape, paper, and crayons with you. At home, glue a small dowel at the top and bottom of your masterpiece and hang it with a cord, or frame it. Happy rubbing!

MONOMOY ISLAND

Monomoy Island, off the coast of Chatham, is now part of a national wildlife refuge. The long sandspit stretches 10 miles to the south, creating problems for mariners. Pollock Rip Passage off Monomoy Point, tricky with riptides and shoals, is the only way to get into Nantucket Sound from the east. A *Cruising Guide to the New England Coast* recommends navigating with extreme caution when the weather is foggy. Even with today's accurate charts and instruments, sailors continue to run aground. In fact, the Coast Gaurd advises that the direction and velocity of the current cannot be predicted accurately off Monomoy.

The island's treacherous shoals have played a part in the history of our country, forcing the *Mayflower* to change course. A sign at Chatham Lighthouse reads:

> About nine miles SE of this place are the shoals of Pollock Rip which turned the Mayflower back to Provincetown Harbor and caused the Pilgrim Fathers to settle in Plymouth instead of on the Jersey Coast, their original destination.

In October 1770 a number of ships foundered during a violent storm: A sloop returning from a whaling trip was wrecked near Eastham, another at Race Point; and a whaling schooner foundered in Chatham.

In 1778 the *Somerset*, a sixty-four-gun British man-of-war, was caught in the area between the Highlands in Chatham and Pollock Rip Shoals, and crashed onto a reef. (Longfellow wrote about the *Somerset* and her captain, George Curry, in the third verse of "Paul Revere's Ride.") The captain surrendered himself and his crew to men from Provincetown who had come to salvage the wreck. Revolutionary history recalls the winter-long march of the five hundred prisoners across the Cape to Boston. Over a hundred years later the *Somerset*'s timbers appeared in the sands of Peaked Hill Bars in Provincetown. And in June 1973 her bones appeared again.

The outer beaches of the Cape between Monomoy and Provincetown—great for swimming and surfing on fine summer days—have been one of the Atlantic's most fearsome graveyards. In 1898 a side-wheeler, the *Portland*, sank with close to two hundred people on board, 7 miles northeast of Highland Lighthouse. The same storm sank ten large vessels and several smaller ones, and blew down nine wharves and twenty-one buildings. Old-timers claimed this particular storm was the most vicious they'd ever experienced. The keeper of the Wood End Light and several other men were able to save survivors from one of two sinking schooners. The men on the *Jordan L. Mott* clung to the rigging for fifteen hours before help came; the men on the *Lester A. Lewis*, also standing in the rigging, were not as lucky.

The dramatic shipwrecks off Monomoy gave rise to dramatic rescues. A local favorite starred a man called "Crazy George" (he was the only one crazy enough to attempt hazardous rescues). It happened in November 1815, in a gale off the island. On his third try—his first two rescue boats were smashed on the rocks—George carefully rode the crest of each wave, jumped over the bar between the inner and outer beach, and then made two passes alongside the stranded ship to pick up survivors!

There was a lifesaving service in operation, even in Crazy George's time. In 1786 the Massachusetts Humane Society had been formed to help seamen in distress. By 1850 the government had begun building lifeboat stations, and the United States Life Saving Service was created by Congress in 1871.

There were thirteen lifesaving stations along the perilous section of Atlantic coast from Wood End and Race Point, at the tip of the Cape, to Monomoy Point. During bad weather this long stretch of beach was patrolled night and day. Each patrol walked anywhere from 2 to 4 miles to a halfway house, where he met the patrol from the next station, and then turned back to his home station. Red flares were used to warn ships away from shoals and to signal that help was on the way. Rescue operations included firing a line to the stricken vessel and sending a breeches buoy to transport the crew to shore. The last time a breeches buoy was used was in January 1962 to save men from the *Margaret Rose*; now helicopters perform the same function.

Although weather and shoals claimed many ships, local history tells too of the mooncussers—salvage pirates who would lead ships to their doom with false lights.

Mooncussers

Would you walk with me there over hallowed soil,
   Would you tread the shores that the Pilgrim
      has trod,
Would you dwell on the way-worn veteran's toil,
   Then haste to the highlands of stormy Cape Cod.

For I've heard there the moon-cusser telling his story
   To the foam of the billows that rolled on the shore,
And I knew as he mumbled the deeds of his glory
   That he thought of the friends that would meet
      no more.

And at last when he finished these sayings of wonder,
   While the winds and the waves were repeating
      the tale,
He exclaimed in a voice that seemed louder
      than thunder,
   "I see in the distance my fortune—a sail!"

Then he lighted his lantern and rapidly flew to
      the beach,
   To the beach that was white with the mariner's
      bones,
But the air that was wet with the evening dew
   Had too often echoed the sufferer's groans.

And the sailor steered boldly his bark o'er the ocean,
   For he well knew the spot where the traveller stood,
And he saw from the dim lamp's tremulous motion
   It was not a light-house of dreary Cape Cod.

But as lately I wandered along on its banks
   And the rough rocks ascended to breathe the sea air,
Oh my heart beat to heaven a tribute of thanks,
   For the robber of midnight no longer was there.

For no more shall be seen there the moon-cusser's
      light;
   No longer to plunder the shores shall he roam,
For the horse and the rider have taken their flight,
   And the lantern they carried shall lighten
      them home.

But I saw in the darkness a white form walking
Around on the sand of the sea-beaten shore,
And he seemed with the spirits of H--l to be talking
And telling the stories of days gone o'er.

A dozen miles north of Chatham on Route 28 is Orleans. Stop at the **Orleans Information Center** or the **Orleans Historical Society** for information about the town.

Orleans is the only town on the Cape with a French name (for Louis-Phillipe de Bourbon, Duke of Orleans, who visited in the 1790s); the others all have English or Indian names. In 1717 the first Cape Cod Canal was dug here. It was large enough to accommodate whaleboats, and its ruins are still visible on Bridge Street. Nearby **Rock Harbor** is a center for fishing boats of all kinds.

Off Orleans, in Cape Cod Bay, sits the **"Target Ship"**—its hull a mass of holes. The *James Longstreet*, a Liberty ship built during World War II, ran aground in a storm. Repairs would have been very expensive, so the ship was towed to her present location and has been used for target practice ever since. (Each attack provides fireworks for miles around.) Sailors take note: Stay clear. There are unexploded shells in the area.

In early July and again in early August the town hosts the **Artists and Craftsmen's Guild Art and Craft Shows** at Nauset Regional Middle School. The school is also the site of the **Antique Exposition** in mid-August. **Peacock Alley**, on Route 28 in the former home of Peter Hunt, houses an interesting potpourri of shops that sell yarn, leather goods, sweaters, stained glass, paintings, and antiques.

Love seafood? You'll enjoy the **Lobster Claw** (617-255-1800) on Route 6. The informal atmosphere, complete with fishnets, makes this a

ORLEANS

Orleans Information Center
Route 6A and Eldredge Parkway
Orleans
617-255-1386

Orleans Historical Society
River and School Roads
Orleans

great place for lunch. For more formal fare try the **Captain Linnell House** (617-255-3400) on Skaket Road. The house, built in 1840, was once a sea captain's mansion. Today the restaurant specializes in seafood and continental cuisine.

EASTHAM

Eastham is the gateway to the National Seashore. The ocean beaches here are among the finest in New England, and aficionados of surfing gather at **Nauset Light Beach** off Route 6 for some of the best conditions in the Northeast. The five beaches on the bay offer warmer water and may appeal more to families with young children. The whole area abounds with sand dunes, lightly traveled roads (good for cycling), and nature trails. Thoreau's walking tour of the Cape began in Eastham. He described the breakers as "wild horses of Neptune" on an ocean where "man's works are wrecks."

Henry Beston, the author of *The Outermost House*, lived on the beach in Fo'castle, once the only house south of Nauset Light. Fo'castle was moved twice when erosion threatened it, and finally was placed on the other side of the dunes for protection from the surf. In the blizzard of February 1978, wild seas destroyed the house, and now even the land on which it stood is under water.

The pride and joy of Eastham, a two hundred-year-old windmill, is the spark each fall for **Windmill Weekend**. Come for kite flying, family volleyball, children's games, a 3- and a 5½-mile road race, square dancing, a parade, a band concert, and a cookout. The windmill is located on Samoset Road and Route 6. Although it isn't operating any longer, you can still see the old handmade machinery—wooden gears, a 7-foot peg wheel, and a full set of sails. And a guide is on hand to give you a full description and answer questions.

Eastham Historical Society
Nauset Road
Eastham
617-255-3380

Stop at the **Eastern Historical Society** for information about other sites in town. You can't miss the entrance, it's made from a whale's jawbones.

Before you leave enjoy a lobster roll, filled with large luscious chunks of meat, at the **Eastham Lobster Pool** (617-255-9706) on Route 6 in North Eastham. You know it's fresh because the pool and the restaurant are in the same building.

The Cape Cod National Seashore was developed in 1961 and is managed by the National Park Service. The 27,000-acre preserve is separated into four major areas, the Nauset area, Marconi Station, Pilgrim Heights, and Province Lands.

CAPE COD NATIONAL SEASHORE

In the Nauset area, at the **Salt Pond Visitor Center**, you'll find exhibits on the natural history of the area; four ten-minute orientation films, descriptions of walks, beaches, and picnic areas; and a schedule of evening programs in the amphitheater.

Salt Pond Visitor Center
Route 6
Eastham
617-235-3421

The **Fort Hill Trail** is a 1½-mile self-guided walk that begins a mile south of the visitors' center at the lovely mansard-roofed home built on Fort Hill by whaleship captain Edward Penniman in 1867. The **Buttonbush Trail** is a ¼-mile long with a guide rope for the blind. Signs, signaled by plastic disks along the rope, are written in braille and large print. The **Nauset Marsh Trail**, one mile long, winds around Salt Pond and Nauset Marsh.

In 1903 the first wireless message was sent to Europe from the Marconi Station in South Wellfleet. The site is marked by an interpretive shelter with exhibits about Marconi Station. The **Atlantic White Cedar Swamp Trail**, a 1-mile inland walk, begins here. The trail winds through thick bushes and tall cedars, and into a swamp, a

MARCONI STATION AREA

remnant of a glacier. (Part of the trail is on a boardwalk through the swamp, so bring insect repellent.)

Wellfleet Bay Wildlife Sanctuary
South Wellfleet
617-349-2615

The **Wellfleet Bay Wildlife Sanctuary** is located nearby. The 600 acres of beach, woods, moor, and salt marsh are maintained by the Massachusetts Audubon Society. The wildlife tour—in a beach buggy—takes at least an hour.

In the Pilgrim Heights area, the interpretive shelter in North Truro has exhibits on Indians and Pilgrims. The **Pilgrim Spring Trail** (leading to a spring where the Pilgrims first drank water) and the **Small Swamp Trail** (a look at the effects of glaciers on the area), each a half mile long, begin here. Nearby **Highland Light** has a collection of materials on shipwrecks, and other historical information.

Province Lands Visitor Center
Race Point Road
Provincetown
617-487-1256

The **Providence Lands Visitor Center** has exhibits and an orientation program on the natural history of the area. And you can pick up information on activities and schedules for evening programs in the amphitheater. The **Beech Forest Nature Trail** begins a mile from the visitors' center and provides water views of inland ponds and a walk through a beech forest.

Part of the function of the National Seashore is to preserve the land. The Cape is vulnerable to erosion by windswept sand and to damage by salt spray. A survey several years ago showed a loss of 105 feet of coastline in just one area since 1973. The staff is constantly struggling to determine the probable course of erosion and to guard against it. At times sand dunes are allowed to shift or migrate in order to form a shield; at others beachgrass is planted to stabilize them.

PROVINCETOWN

Continue on Route 6 to Provincetown. Provincetown has long been a summer colony for painters and writers; exhibits and theater are available all summer. Eugene O'Neill did much of his early experimental work here with the Provincetown Players.

"P-town" is a walking town, with narrow interesting streets. Come early and park your car at **MacMillan Wharf**; then tackle the town on foot.

The waterfront has its own fascination: A large fishing fleet and visiting yachts keep the harbor busy all summer long. Come the last Sunday in June for the **Blessing of the Fleet**—a colorful local ceremony right on MacMillan Wharf.

Pepe's Wharf (617-487-0670), at 371 Commercial Street, offers seafood and Portuguese specialties with the view, in a building that's partially over the water. **The Red Inn** (617-487-0050), at 15 Commercial Street, overlooks the ocean and offers New England country cooking.

Off Bradford Street, which runs parallel to Commercial, is the **Pilgrim Memorial Monument**. The 255-foot granite tower was built in 1910. From the top there's a marvelous view of the area. The **Provincetown Museum**, right next to the monument, displays early firefighting equipment, a dollhouse, a collection of ship figureheads, whaling equipment, scrimshaw, a diorama of the *Mayflower*, and Sandwich glass.

Head out Conwell Street to **Race Point Beach**. Here you can try your hand at hang gliding from the dunes, keep your eyes peeled for whales (they come quite close to the beach), or just enjoy the beautiful clear water.

For more information about the town and local activities, contact the chamber of commerce.

When you leave Provincetown follow Route 6A and then Route 6 back through North Truro (where you can check in the town hall about

Pilgrim Memorial Monument
Monument Hill
Provincetown

Provincetown Museum
Monument Hill
Provincetown
617-487-1310

Provincetown Chamber of Commerce
MacMillan Wharf
Provincetown
617-487-3424

BREWSTER

New England Fire and History Museum
Route 6A
Brewster
617-896-5711

Cape Cod Museum of Natural History
Main Street
Brewster
617-896-3867

Drummer Boy Museum
Route 6A
Brewster
617-896-3823

Sealand of Cape Cod
Route 6A
Brewster
617-385-9252

gravestone rubbing in **North Cemetery**), Wellfleet, Eastham, and Orleans, to Brewster, once home to many sea captains.

Here, start your explorations at the **New England Fire and History Museum**, the **Cape Cod Museum of Natural History**, and the **Drummer Boy Museum** (twenty-one life-size scenes of the American Revolution). Then, farther up Route 6A, stop at **Sealand of Cape Cod**, where you can watch a forty-minute dolphin show, and then stroll through the other buildings to see all sorts of fish and a large loggerhead turtle. Outside there are ducks, penguins, seals, and otters.

Stony Brook Mill, a working gristmill originally built in 1663, was rebuilt in 1873. It's located in an area called Factory Village, where a tannery and cloth mill once stood. If you come in the spring, walk along Stony Brook and watch the herring (or alewives) swim upstream to spawn.

Hungry? Try **Chillingsworth's** (617-896-3640) on Route 6A.

DENNIS

Scargo Hill Tower
Scargo Hill Road
Dennis

Farther west on Route 6A is Dennis, a group of villages made up of Dennis Port, East Dennis, South Dennis, and West Dennis. Henry Hall began the first commercial farming of cranberries here in 1816.

Climb **Scargo Hill Tower** for a fine view of the ocean and bay; on a clear day you see the monument in Provincetown. Gravestone rubbing is allowed behind the town offices (485 Main Street) in South Dennis.

BARNSTABLE

Old Crocker Tavern
Route 6A
Barnstable

Stay on Route 6A heading west, to Barnstable, where the Society for the Preservation of New England Antiquities maintains the **Old Crocker Tavern**. Once known as Aunt Lydia's Tavern, then Sturgis Tavern, it was built in 1754 by Cornelius Crocker; Lydia Sturgis was his daughter. The house contains eighteenth-century furnishings and exhibits. **Sturgis Library**, nearby, is the oldest library in the United States. The rooms in the front are furnished as nineteenth-century sitting rooms and contain old books and records. The rest of the library is modern. Ask about the lectures on Cape Cod. The **Donald G. Trayser Museum** in the old brick Custom House displays Indian relics, old records from the post office, dolls, toys, silver, period furniture, and carriages.

Continue west on Route 6A past Barnstable Harbor and Sandy Neck Beach, to Sandwich. Settled in 1639, it's the oldest town on the Cape. From 1825 to 1888, until a strike forced the factory's closing, it was the home of the Sandwich Glass Company. Many think the factory was built here for the supply of sand needed in processing glass, but the sand used was brought in from the Berkshires. Actually the factory was located in Sandwich because the local scrub pine forests provided cheap fuel for the furnaces.

During the nineteenth century pressed table glassware was inexpensive, and there were dozens of patterns available. But some Sandwich glass is rare and very valuable. The glassmakers often created special designs and blew unusual pieces, many of which are in the superb collection at the **Sandwich Glass Museum**.

If Sandwich whets your appetite for the glassblower's skill, you'll enjoy a visit to **Pairpoint Glass Works** on Sandwich Road in nearby Sagamore. Here you'll see modern-day craftsmen at work.

Other highlights in town: **Dexter's Grist Mill**, built in 1654, has been restored and is working, grinding corn. **Hoxie House**, a restored saltbox overlooking Shawme Lake, dates from 1637 and contains period furnishings. **Heritage**

Sturgis Library
Route 6A
Barnstable
617-362-6636

Donald G. Trayser
  Museum
Route 6A
Barnstable
617-362-2092

SANDWICH

Sandwich Glass
  Museum
Town Hall Square
Sandwich
617-888-0251

Hoxie House
Water Street
Sandwich

**Heritage Plantation
Pine and Grove
  Streets
Sandwich
617-888-3300**

**Dexter's Grist Mill
Town Hall Square
Sandwich**

**Yesteryear's
  Museum
Main and River
  Streets
Sandwich
617-888-1711**

Plantation has a collection of antique automobiles, a military museum, a working windmill, a carousel, Currier and Ives prints, and a collection of folk art. The grounds—76 acres—are a horticulturist's dream. Come in July when the **Arts and Crafts Fair** is held. **Yesteryear's Museum** is filled with dolls and dollhouses from all over the world—a treat for kids of all ages.

Before you leave town, make a stop at **Quail Hollow Farm** (617-888-0438) on Route 130 for delectable blueberry and lemon breads.

Continue along Route 6A to the **Sagamore Bridge**, at the east end of the canal. In 1918 the war department bought the Cape Cod Canal from August Belmont, who had built a narrow canal that would not handle freighters. After reconstruction the canal became a major artery for marine traffic.

Sailors beware: There are very strong currents running through the canal (sailboats must use auxiliary power), and extreme wind shifts from one end of the canal to the other. (A strong afternoon southwesterly against that current can kick up one of the nastiest seas imaginable at the Buzzards Bay entrance.)

After you cross the bridge, follow the west (land) side of the canal on Route 6 and stop at the **Herring Run Diner** (617-888-0084) for one last lobster roll. Then it's into Boston town by way of Plymouth and the towns along the South Shore (Itinerary F).

ITINERARY F: HISTORIC BOSTON

OLD NORTH CHURCH

ITINERARY F

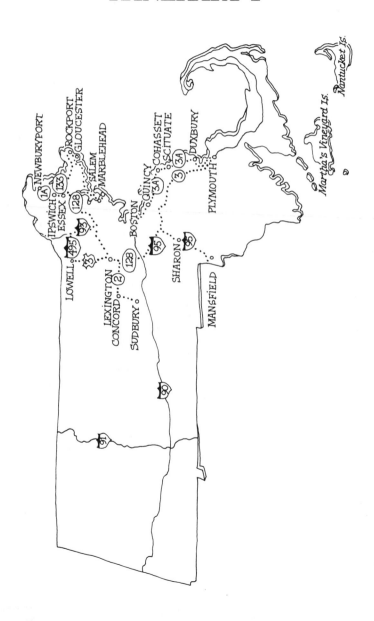

Historic Boston
and the Bay Colonies

The Pine-Tree
John Greenleaf Whittier

Lift again the stately emblem on the Bay State's
    rusted shield
Give to Northern winds the Pine-Tree on our banner's
    tattered field.
Sons of men who sat in council with their Bibles round
    the board
Answering England's royal missive with a firm, "THUS
    SAITH THE LORD!"
Rise again for home and freedom!—set the battle in
    array!—
What the fathers did of old time we their sons must
    do today.

Tell us not of banks and tariffs,—cease your paltry
    pedler cries,—
Shall the good State sink her honor that your gambling
    stocks may rise?
Would ye barter man for cotton?—that your gains may
    sum up higher,
Must we kiss the feet of Moloch, pass our children
    through the fire?
Is the dollar only real?—God and truth and right a
    dream?
Weighed against your lying ledgers must our manhood
    kick the beam?

O my God!—for that free spirit, which of old in
    Boston town
Smote the Province House with terror, struck the crest
    of Andros down!—
For another strong-voiced Adams in the city's streets
    to cry,
"Up for God and Massachusetts!—Set your feet on
    Mammon'e lie!
Perish banks and perish traffic,—spin your cotton's
    latest pound,—
But in Heaven's name keep your honor,—keep the heart
    o' the Bay State sound!"

Where's the MAN for Massachusetts!—Where's the
    voice to speak her free?—

Where's the hand to light up bonfires from her
   mountains to the sea?
Beats her Pilgrim pulse no longer!—Sits she dumb in
   her despair?—
Has she none to break the silence?—Has she none to
   do and dare?
O my God! for one right worthy to lift up her rusted
   shield,
And to plant again the Pine-Tree in her banner's
   tattered field!

Whittier's words capture the sense of oppression felt by colonial settlers throughout the Revolutionary War period. Again and again they struggled for freedom—"What the fathers did of old time we their sons must do today."

The Pilgrims came to American in 1620 to seek freedom from religious persecution—the freedom to believe in and practice their theocratic ideals. They were determined to institutionalize this freedom, as they did in their very first charter, the Mayflower Compact. That agreement encouraged all citizens to abide by the will of the majority, a principle that led to the eventual success of the Revolution, but not without cost. For in some settlements religious zeal recreated the intolerance of England, forcing those of different beliefs to seek out again the freedom they thought they had found.

The success of the Plymouth colony—in contrast to the dismal failures at Jamestown and nearby Weymouth—depended on knowledge that the Pilgrims did not bring with them from Europe. It was the Indians who taught them how to fish for cod and mackerel, how to rotate their crops, how to build canoes, how to make clothing from leather, and how to mold pots from local clay. The Pilgrims survived because they had the Indians, and the Indian lifestyle, to guide them.

If their religious ideals led the early settlers to seek their freedom, their commercial success allowed them to achieve it. As the shipping industry prospered, the colonists quite naturally resisted the British control imposed by the Acts of Trade and Navigation (beginning in 1650), the Stamp Act (1765), and the Tea Act (1773). Battles at Lexington, Concord, and Bunker Hill precipitated the Revolution and the eventual defeat of the British overlords. The freedom sought by the Pilgrims in 1620 was finally achieved a century and a half later.

Itinerary F is long because there is so much to see in this area. The first part covers the South Shore, beginning in Plymouth and ending just south of Boston. The second section includes Boston and Cambridge, as well as side trips to Sharon, Mansfield, and Lowell. The third section features the Lexington and Concord area. And the fourth section begins in the North Shore, north of Boston, in Marblehead, and continues to Newburyport.

The South Shore

The South Shore stretches from Plymouth, at the edge of the Cape, along the coast to Quincy, right outside Boston. Although it adjoins the metropolitan area, this region has the air of being off the mainline of suburban or exurban development, with very attractive old shore towns that maintain their own integrity. You can take yourself back to the year 1620 by visiting Plymouth Rock and a replica of the *Mayflower*; relive the lives of our first settlers at Plimoth Plantation; spend time on quiet, sandy beaches; visit a church built like a ship; and follow the Patriot's Trail through twenty-seven South Shore towns.

PLYMOUTH

Plymouth County Development Council
Box 1620
Pembroke 02359
617-826-3131

Plymouth Town Information Booth
South Park Avenue
Plymouth
617-746-4799

Mayflower II
Water Street
Plymouth
617-746-1622

The itinerary begins in Plymouth, where the spirit of religious freedom led to the settlement of a new country.

Contact the **Plymouth County Development Council** before you go, or stop in at the **Plymouth Town Information Booth** (it's open mid-April through November), for maps and information.

Start your tour of the area where the Pilgrims did, at the harbor. The **Mayflower II**, a replica of the Pilgrim's *Mayflower*, was built in England in 1955, and sailed two years later for Plymouth under the command of Alan Villiers. The bark is only 106 feet long, 25 feet wide—a very small area for a hundred people and their baggage on a two-and-a-half-month trip. And the ship was even more cramped than it seems now: The replica has a foot more headroom than the original.

Cranberries—probably named for the cranes who enjoyed them in the bogs—are a regional industry. The Pilgrims began using the tart berries for food because the Indians told them that the berries tasted good and had the power to heal wounds. Soon the berries were being carried aboard ships to supplement salt pork diets and prevent scurvy. An industry was born!

For a close-up look at that industry, stop in at **Cranberry World** on Water Street (617-747-1000). Here you'll find working bogs, antique harvesting tools, a scale model of a cranberry farm, and daily cooking demonstrations—all free!

Plymouth Rock is right down the street from *Mayflower II*. The symbolic birthplace of this vast nation is actually quite small. It sits under a granite portico, protected from weather and souvenir hunters by a fence. On it is engraved the date—December 21, 1620—when seventeen men waded ashore on the desolate coast.

Plymouth Rock
Water Street
Plymouth

There are other sights to see right in town: **Pilgrim Hall** is filled with things the Pilgrims used—furniture, paintings, pewter, textiles, even Peregrine White's cradle. There's also an extensive library of rare manuscripts and books. **Jenney Grist Mill** is a replica of a mill the Pilgrims built in 1636. Corn, wheat, and rye are still ground by waterpower, and old crafts demonstrations take place daily.

Pilgrim Hall
75 Court Street
Plymouth
617-746-1620

Jenney Grist Mill
8 Spring Lane
Plymouth
617-747-0811

Thanksgiving is a special time to be in Plymouth. Many of the townspeople dress in period clothes, a small group representing those who survived the first winter in America. And there's Thanksgiving dinner in Memorial Hall. Tickets can be purchased at the door by the first two thousand people to arrive. Call the Plymouth Chamber of Commerce (617-746-3377) for information.

Plimoth Plantation is about 3 miles from the center, on Route 3A. Nowhere else can you so clearly sense the hardship of life in those early years or appreciate the courage of those who survived it.

Plimoth Plantation
Rt 3A/Warren
  Avenue
Plymouth
617-746-1622

Pilgrim Village has been recreated according to the descriptions of Governor William Bradford and Edward Winslow, archaeological research, and other records. In 1627 fifty families lived here, with the cattle, poultry, pigs, goats, sheep, and horses necessary for farming. Costumed guides create a living folk-museum, performing everyday tasks as they were done in the seventeenth century. Inside some are cooking in large open fireplaces, sewing, or making barrels; outside others are thatching roofs, chopping wood, or firing their muskets in a twice-daily militia drill. And there's more: an orientation program, movies, and exhibits.

Commonwealth Winery is in an old hemp factory on Court Street, the remnant of a once prosperous industry. You can tour the working winery, learn how wines are made, and taste a selection of current production. For information call 617-746-4138.

DUXBURY

Old Burying Ground
Chestnut Street
Duxbury

Alden House
Alden Road
Duxbury
617-934-6001

Miles Standish Monument
Crescent Street
Duxbury

Duxbury Beach
Route 139
Duxbury

From Plymouth take Route 3A north to Duxbury. In the village visit the **Old Burying Ground**, where you'll find the graves of Captain Myles Standish, John and Priscilla Alden, and their son, Colonel John Alden. Longfellow, a descendant of John Alden, often walked through this cemetery. And he wrote about John and Priscilla in *The Courtship of Miles Standish*. Nearby is **Alden House**, with gunstock beams and clamshell ceilings. A couple of miles away, the **Miles Standish Monument** offers a lovely view of the bay and Plymouth.

Most of the beaches along the South Shore are reserved for residents of the towns. However **Duxbury Beach** is open to the public. **Powder Point Bridge**, the longest wooden bridge in the country, is the gateway to this beautiful 9-mile stretch of sand.

SCITUATE

Continue north along Route 3A to Scituate. The harbor is the most protected deep-water harbor on the South Shore, and yachts of all sizes and commercial fishing boats create a constantly changing scene here.

The story of Scituate's "Army of Two" was told in the *Boston Evening Transcript* in 1879 by Farnham Smith, who heard it from two ladies who were young girls during the War of 1812. It seems Rebecca and Abby saw boats being lowered from two British ships in the harbor. They knew that the British were on their way to ravage flour-laden American ships. So the two girls stood behind a barn and played a fife and drum with such vigor that the British thought a group of settlers was about to attack them. As the British retreated in haste to their ships, the girls gave them a parting tune: "Yankee Doodle." Wonderful!

On March 16, 1956, the 7,000-ton *Etrusco* ran aground on Cedar Point outside Scituate during a northeaster. Everyone said she would be there until she rusted away, but a retired admiral who'd been involved in the salvage work at Pearl Harbor worked out a scheme using dynamite and bulldozers to free her. She floated off in high water and was towed to Boston for repairs and a new life at sea.

Try **Barker Tavern** (617-545-6533), a marvelous restaurant on Barker Road. The building was constructed in 1634, and has wide floorboards and low wooden beams. Paintings of ships line the walls.

COHASSET

A few miles north on Hatherly Road you come to the edge of Cohasset, which was settled in the seventeenth century. Perched high on one side of the town common is **Saint Stephen's Episcopal Church**; the fifty-one bell carillon rings every Sunday. The **First Parish Church**, built in 1745, the town hall, and lovely old homes lines the other sides of the common.

The **Cohasset Historical Society** at the Lothrop House maintains several museums:

Cohasset Historical Society
Lothrop House
14 Summer Street
Cohasset
617-383-6930

Maritime Museum (ship models, scrimshaw, models of Minots Light, relics of shipwrecks, and area artifacts dating back to 1700) on Elm Street; and **Captain John Wilson House** (early Cohasset home furnishings).

If you're in the mood for seafood, try **Hugo's Lighthouse** (617-383-1700) on Border Street in Cohasset Harbor.

Follow Atlantic Avenue to Jerusalem Road, out of town. **Moore's Rocks Reservation**, an untouched stretch of granite ledge on the ocean side of the road, offers a view of the surf pounding on massive rocks below. Look toward the east, where **Minots Ledge Lighthouse**, a 114-foot tower built in 1860, sits in the Atlantic.

HINGHAM
Old Ship Church
90 Main Street
Hingham
617-749-1679

Jerusalem Road leads right into Hingham. Your first stop: the **Old Ship Church** on Main Street. Go inside and look up from the box pews. The ceiling is built of oak beams in the shape of an upside-down ship's hull. The church was built in 1681 by ship's carpenters, and is the only seventeenth-century church still standing in Massachusetts. Since 1825 it's been owned and used by the American Unitarian Association.

Old Ordinary
21 Lincoln Avenue
Hingham
617-749-0013

Old Ordinary is the home of the Hingham Historical Society. Enjoy furnishings, a tool collection, the taproom, and the garden. The historical society and the chamber of commerce both offer more information about the town.

World's End
  Reservation
Martin's Lane
Hingham
617-749-8956

For a great view of the harbor islands and Boston, head for **World's End Reservation**. The 200-acre preserve on an ancient drumlin has wide gravel trails, perfect for hiking.

QUINCY

From Hingham it's just a few miles north on Route 3A to Quincy, where your first stop should be the chamber of commerce or city hall, for maps and information.

Two presidents were born in Quincy—John Adams and John Quincy Adams—and the **Adams National Historic Site** centers on their lives. Begin your tour on Franklin Street, at the two seventeenth-century saltboxes where the presidents were born. John Adams was born at Number 133 in 1735; his son, at Number 141 in 1767. There's a hiding place in the chimney (in case of attack by Indians) at Number 141.

About a mile away, on Adams Street, is the home for four generations of the Adams family. Furnishing shows the development of styles from 1788 to 1927. Look for the John Singleton Copley painting of John Adams, the Trumbull engraving, the three-hundred-year-old grandfather clock, the Louis XV safe, and the high-cushion chairs, specially designed for the hoopskirts of the day.

End your tour of the national historic site in Quincy Square, at the church where the presidents and their families worshipped and are buried.

While you're here, stop across the street at the **Hancock Cemetery**, there sixty-nine veterans of the Revolutionary War are buried. You'll enjoy reading the amusing and unusual poetry on the grave markers. Then head out Hancock Street to the **Dorothy Quincy Homestead**, the home of Dorothy Quincy, who later married John Hancock. The house was built in the seventeenth century, enlarged in the eighteenth. There's a secret chamber here too, where American patriots hid during the Revolution.

The **Patriot's Trail** takes you through twenty-seven towns, most of them along the South Shore, stopping at cultural, historical, and recreational sites. For information and a map contact the Norfolk County Tourist Council, 357 West Squantum Street, North Quincy, 617-328-1776.

Quincy-South Shore Chamber of Commerce
36 Miller Stile Road
Quincy
617-479-1111

Adams National Historic Site
135 Adams Street
Quincy
617-773-1177

Hancock Cemetery
Hancock Street
Quincy

Dorothy Quincy Homestead
34 Butler Road
Quincy
617-472-5117

Boston

Boston is a complex city. We could try to categorize it for you by its history, literature, education, culture, architecture, even geography. Instead we offer a composite itinerary, a cross-section of possibilities drawn from our many discoveries in this fascinating city.

Boston Convention
& Tourist Bureau
Prudential Plaza
Boston
617-536-4100

National Historical
Park Visitor
Center
15 State Street
Boston
617-242-5642

Boston Common
Information
Booth
Tremont Street
Boston

Prudential Tower
800 Boylston Street
Boston
617-236-3318

For information before you go and while you're here, contact the **Boston Convention & Tourist Bureau** or the **National Historical Park Visitor Center**. The **Boston Common Information Booth** is open for on-site visits only. You can pick up a copy of "Boston Byweek"—a monthly calendar of current activities—at any of these visitors' centers or at most hotels.

There's entertainment for everyone in Boston, much more than you'll have time to enjoy. Try the Boston Symphony Orchestra or the Boston Pops, the Opera Company of Boston, or the Boston Ballet. Pick up tickets for a Broadway-bound show at the Colonial, Shubert, or Wilbur theaters. Or catch a professional production at the Boston Shakespeare Company, the Charles Playhouse, or the Next Move. Need more? Colleges and universities, museums, and churches around the area offer a nonstop schedule of concerts, theater, and lectures.

For even more ideas and information, pick up a copy of the *Boston Globe*'s Thursday edition, and look through Calendar, a weekly listing of entertainment in the Hub.

Whenever we travel in Europe, we always head first for the tallest church, winding up worn stone steps to the top for a view of the city. With map in hand, we identify landmarks to fix our visual perspective before choosing our route for the day. In Boston you can enjoy an overview of the city and harbor from several spots. The **Sky Walk** in the fifty-two-story-high Prudential Tower offers a restaurant and shops along with the scenery. There's also a narrated description of local history. The **John Hancock Observatory** provides a panoramic view, exhibits of Boston past and present, a topographical model, and *Cityflight*, a seven-minute film tour of the city from a helicopter. A great introduction to the city: *Where's Boston?* is a montage of the voices, pictures, music, and sounds of the city today. The music track combines eighteenth-century hymns with the twentieth-century theme. You'll find the show at Copley Place, 100 Huntington Avenue. Phone 617-267-4949 for information.

Old Town Trolley (617-269-7010) offers a couple of routes around Boston. You can get off and on as you wish.

John Hancock Observatory
John Hancock Tower
Clarendon Street
Boston
617-247-1977

Unless you're already familiar with historic Boston, start your tour with the **Freedom Trail**. You can pick up a map at any visitors' center, and then walk along the red-signed path.

Hardy souls cover the whole trail—from downtown Boston across the river to Charlestown. But with children try a shorter loop. You could visit the North End and stop at the four sites there: Paul Revere House, Paul Revere Mall, Old North Church, and Copp's Hill Burying Ground. Another short tour begins at the State House, and stops at Park Street Church, Granary Burying Ground, King's Chapel, the Benjamin Franklin Statue, the Old Corner Bookstore, and the Old South Meeting House. Faneuil Hall, Quincy Market, and the Old State House are grouped together in a third tour.

There isn't a single sequence of sites along the trail. We like to explore it slowly, stopping when the spirit moves us. Usually we begin at **Faneuil Hall**, the "Cradle of Liberty." The building, topped with a grasshopper weathervane, was given to the city in 1742. Through the years it's been the site of hundreds of open meetings. On

THE FREEDOM TRAIL

Faneuil Hall
Merchants Row
Boston
617-242-5642

the top (third) floor you'll find the Ancient and Honorable Artillery Company and exhibits.

Quincy Market, a low granite building in Greek Revival style, is a shopper's paradise. So is **Marketplace Center**, adjacent to Faneuil Hall Marketplace. Set a time limit, or you may spend the day in the tantalizing maze of specialty shops here and in the many markets nearby.

Old State House
206 Washington
Street
Boston
617-242-5619

From the Marketplace, walk up State Street to the **Old State House**. The Declaration of Independence was read from a balcony here on July 18, 1776. The building now houses a museum filled with ship models, revolutionary relics, and other memorabilia. Outside, at the intersection below the Old State House, the **Boston Massacre** site is marked by a ring of cobblestones. Here, on March 5, 1770, nine British soldiers were confronted by a crowd of angry Bostonians, throwing rocks. The Redcoats fired into the crowd, killing five men.

Old South Meeting
House
310 Washington
Street at Milk
Street
Boston
617-482-6439

Up Washington Street is the **Old South Meeting House**, where plans were laid in 1773 for the Boston Tea Party. In the museum are a model of the city in 1775 and copies of historic documents. Benjamin Franklin's birthplace is marked by a plaque just around the corner, on Milk Street. The **Old Corner Bookstore**, across Washington Street, was once a gathering place for Longfellow, Lowell, Whittier, Hawthorne, Thoreau, Stowe, Howe, and Holmes. Today, amongst the first editions and period furnishings, you'll find a bookstore filled with New England titles.

Old Corner
Bookstore
Washington and
School Streets
Boston
617-523-6658

Benjamin Franklin
Statue
School Street
Boston

Up School Street, four bronze panels at the base of the **Benjamin Franklin Statue** depict him signing the Declaration of Independence and a peace treaty with France, working as a printer, and experimenting with lightning and electricity. Look carefully: One side of Franklin's face is smiling; the other, sober.

Early settlers believed that free public education was a citizen's right. And the people in Massachusetts were largely responsible for the early development of education in this country. The first public school in the country was built in Boston in 1635. You can read about it on the plaque outside Old City Hall, on School Street, right near the Franklin statue. And Harvard was founded in nearby Cambridge one year later.

At the corner of Tremont and School sits **King's Chapel**, the oldest stone church in Boston. In its steeple hangs a bell made by Paul Revere. The graves of Governor Winthrop and William Dawes are in the **Burying Ground** outside. In *The Scarlet Letter* Nathaniel Hawthorne, who often walked here, wrote about the small gravestone of Elizabeth Paine, which is on the southern edge of the cemetery. In 1683 she was tried for the murder of her child and acquitted, but some people say they can see the letter A on her gravestone. In *The Scarlet Letter* Hester, who's forced to wear a red letter A embroidered on her dress, imagines an angel writing an A on the stone.

King's Chapel and Burying Ground
54 Tremont Street
Boston
617-227-2155

In the **Granary Burying Ground** across the street are the graves of John Hancock, Robert Treat Paine, Samuel Adams, Paul Revere, Benjamin Franklin's parents, the victims of the Boston Massacre, and Mary Goose (the creator of Mother Goose).

Granary Burying Ground
Tremont Street
Boston

You may hear the bells of the **Park Street Church**, around the corner, before you see the building. They chime every day at noon. The sails for the USS *Constitution* were made here, and brimstone for gunpowder was stored in the cellar during the War of 1812. Over the years **Boston Common** has been used for hanging criminals, grazing cows, and training militia. Today the criminals, cows, and militia are gone, but soapbox orators and sidewalk musicians are here

Park Street Church
Tremont and Park Streets
Boston
617-523-3383

in force. Come in the summer to wade in Frog Pond, hear a band concert, or feed the pigeons; in winter, to skate. People watching, we're happy to report, is available year-round.

The **Boston Public Garden**, across Charles Street, is a lovely spot. You can feed the ducks, ride the swan boats, or find a bench and just watch the world go by.

State House
Beacon Street
Boston
617-727-3676

Walk up Park Street to the gold-domed **State House.** Meetings of the legislature are open to the public. In the **Archives Museum** are modern documents and proclamations, as well as famous written records from our colonial past.

From the State House cross over Beacon Hill, through Government Center, under the expressway, to the North End. This area has been the first home for different groups of immigrants. Now an Italian-American neighborhood, its narrow streets are lined with grocery stores, vegetable stands, and cafes serving espresso and cappuccino. There are four Freedom Trail stops in the area.

Paul Revere House
19 North Square
Boston
617-523-2338

Paul Revere Mall
Hanover Street
Boston

Old North Church
193 Salem Street
Boston
617-523-6676

The first, **Paul Revere House,** was purchased by Revere in 1770 when it was already a hundred years old. There are four rooms (and he lived here with his sixteen children!) filled with seventeenth- and eighteenth-century furnishings. From here head up Hanover Street to **Paul Revere Mall.** Look for the equestrian statue of Revere. **Old North Church**, on the back side of the mall, was the site of the historic lantern signal—"one if by land, two if by sea"—that set off the midnight ride of Paul Revere. The church was built in 1723. The bells in the steeple, rung by Revere when he was a fifteen-year-old member of the Bell Ringers' Guild, are still rung every Sunday morning. Cross Salem Street to Hull Street, to Snowhill, where you'll find **Copp's Hill Burying Ground**. Some of the stones still display bullet marks made by the Redcoats, who used them for target practice.

Copp's Hill
  Burying Ground
Snowhill and
  Charter Streets
Boston

Paul Revere's Ride

Henry Wadsworth Longfellow

Listen, my children, and you shall hear,
    Of the midnight ride of Paul Revere,
On the eighteenth of April, in '75;
    Hardly a man is now alive
Who remembers that famous day and year.
    He said to his friend, "If the British march
By land or sea from the town tonight,
    Hang a lantern aloft in the belfry arch
Of the North Church tower as a signal light—
    One, if by land, and two, if by sea;
And I on the opposite shore will be,
    Ready to ride and spread the alarm
Through every Middlesex village and farm,
    For the country folk to be up and to arm."
Then he said, "Good night!" and with muffled oar
    Silently rowed to the Charlestown shore . . .
Meanwhile, his friend, through alley and street,
    Wanders and watches with eager ears,
Till in the silence around him he hears
    The muster of men at the barrack door,
The sound of arms, and the tramp of feet,
    And the measured tred of the grenadiers,
Marching down to their boats on the shore.
    Then he climbed the tower of the Old North Church
By the wooden stairs, with stealthy tread,
    To the belfry chamber overhead, . . .
By the trembling ladder, steep and tall,
    To the highest window in the wall,
Where he paused to listen and look down
    A moment on the roofs of the town,
And the moonlight flowing over all . . .
    A moment only he feels the spell
Of the place and the hour, and the secret dread
    Of the lonely belfry and the dead;
For suddenly all his thoughts are bent
    On a shadowy something far away,
Where the river widens to meet the bay—
    A line of black that bends and floats
On the rising tide, like a bridge of boats.
    Meanwhile, impatient to mount and ride,
Booted and spurred, with a heavy stride
    On the opposite shore walked Paul Revere.

Now he patted his horse's side,
    Now gazed at the landscape far and near,
Then, impetuous, stamped the earth,
    And turned and tightened his saddle girth;
But mostly he watched with eager search
    The belfry tower of the Old North Church,
As it rose above the graves on the hill,
    Lonely and spectral and somber and still.
And lo! as he looks, on the belfry's height
    A glimmer, and then a gleam of light!
He springs to the saddle, the bridle he turns,
    But lingers and gazes, till full on his sight
A second lamp in the belfry burns! . . .

There are several Freedom Trail sites across the river in Charlestown. You can walk across Charlestown Bridge, or pick up your car and follow the signs to Charlestown City Square and Constitution Road off I-93.

**USS *Constitution*
Charlestown Navy
  Yard
Charlestown
617-242-5670**

The **USS *Constitution*** is at the Charlestown Navy Yard. The forty-four gun frigate was launched in 1797 and was never defeated in its 24 battles. The flavor of sea life is everywhere: from the camboose (galley stove), the scuttlebutt, and the grog tub, to the bilge pumps and the anchor capstan, to the captain's cabin, officers' quarters, and crew's hammocks. Look up and you will see on each mast a fighting top—a platform where marines stood to fire muskets at the decks of enemy ships. And all around are guides in 1812 naval uniforms ready to answer questions and share the ship's history.

The USS *Constitution* took part in a number of memorable battles, including two with the British frigate *Guerrière* in 1812. In the first, Captain Isaac Hull, caught in a calm amongst a squadron of British ships, used his kedge anchors to escape. A boat went ahead, perhaps a half mile, and dropped the kedges; the men hauled on the long hawsers, drawing the ship up to the point where the anchors lay. Then the whole process was repeated. In two days, the *Constitution* had outdistanced the enemy; when the wind came, it sailed for Boston.

In the second adventure with the *Guerrière* patience was the byword. The men held their fire until the ships were abreast, close aboard. Then Captain Hull ordered, "Now, boys, pour it on them!" and the *Guerrière*'s mizzenmast and rigging crashed down. She was helpless. It was during this battle that one of the British sailors pointed to the undamaged *Constitution*, and shouted, "Huzza! Her sides are made of iron!" "Old Ironsides" was born.

In 1830, her battles long over, the *Constitution* was scheduled to be destroyed. Oliver Wendel Holmes wrote a poem about the ship that moved the public to save her.

The **USS Constitution Museum**, across the drydock, has a number of exhibits and hands-on displays, including knot tying, swinging in a sailor's hammock, raising a sail, and turning the wheel. You can also walk around on a platform that used to be 90 feet above the deck on the mizzenmast—close your eyes and imagine what it must have been like up there on a windy day!

USS Constitution Museum
Charlestown Navy Yard
Charlestown
617-426-1812

Nearby you can see the **USS *Cassin Young***. This ship, launched in September 1943, saw action in the Philippines and Japan, and sank four Japanese carriers in the battle at Cape Engano. She represents all of the many ships built at the navy yard that served the country during World War II. Across the water from the USS *Constitution*, in the Bunker Hill Pavilion, is **The Whites of Their Eyes**—a sound-and-light show that recreates the Battle of Bunker Hill. Call 617-241-7575 for information.

USS *Cassin Young*
Charlestown Navy Yard
Charlestown
617-269-0419

Old Ironsides
Oliver Wendell Holmes

Ay, tear her tattered ensign down!
Long has it waved on high,
And many an eye has danced to see
That banner in the sky;
Beneath it rung the battle shout,
And burst the cannon's roar;—
The meteor of the ocean air
Shall sweep the clouds no more.

Her deck, once red with heroes' blood,
Where knelt the vanquished foe,
When winds were hurrying o'er the flood,
And waves were white below,
No more shall feel the victor's tread,
Or know the conquered knee;—
The harpies of the shore shall pluck
The eagle of the sea!

Oh, better that her shattered hulk
Should sink beneath the wave;
Her thunders shook the mighty deep,
And there should be her grave;
Nail to the mast her holy flag,
Set every threadbare sail,
And give her to the god of storms,
The lightening and the gale!

**Bunker Hill
Monument
Breed's Hill
Charlestown**

The **Bunker Hill Monument** is just a few blocks north of the navy yard in a section of Charlestown that is being restored. (Ask for direction at the yard.) The monument commemorates the battle of June 17, 1775. The British lost 1,054 men that day; the American, 450.

OFF THE TRAIL

**New England
Aquarium
Central Wharf
Boston
617-742-8870**

From Charlestown, take I-93 south to the Dock Square-Callahan Tunnel exit; then follow the signs to the **New England Aquarium.** You can't miss the giant orange mobile sculpture, "Echoes of the Wave," on the plaza. Here you'll find the world's largest circular glass tank. A highlight: watching divers in the tank feed the sharks and giant sea turtles. When you've finished exploring the multilevel exhibit galleries (and the more than seven thousand fish they display), head next door to the *Discovery* to watch otters, seals, sea lions, and dolphins performing in a large pool.

From the aquarium drive south on Atlantic Avenue to Purchase Street, where you'll bear right (Atlantic Avenue becomes one way the wrong way); turn left on Congress Street and follow the signs to the **Boston Tea Party Ship and Museum**. Here you can explore the brig *Beaver II*, a full-sized replica of one of the three original Tea Party ships. Audiovisual programs tell about the original Tea Party and the replica's voyage from Denmark. (The *Beaver II* was built in Denmark, and sailed to Boston in 1973.) There's also a model of eighteenth-century Boston, which traces the route of the Tea Party participants.

Boston Tea Party Ship and Museum Congress Street Bridge Boston 617-338-1773

The next wharf off Congress Street, Museum Wharf, houses the **Children's Museum**. Children can climb through City Slice, a three-story section of a house and street; dress up in Grandmother's Attic; explore the Giant's Desk Top, where everything is twelve times normal size; learn about another culture in the Japanese House; and stop at the Resource Center to ask questions. It's a marvelous, noisy, try-your-hand-at-everything place.

Children's Museum Museum Wharf 300 Congress Street Boston 617-426-6500

Also on Museum Wharf the **Computer Museum,** beside the giant milkbottle, offers more than your children ever dreamed of knowing about computers. Exhibits range from the vacuum tube, the transistor, and the integrated circuit to modern-day computers. Lots of hands-on fun.

Computer Museum Museum Wharf Boston 617-426-2800

The **Museum of Science** is on the Charles River Dam Bridge between Leverett Circle and Lechmere Square. The museum is filled with exhibits about space, technology, and biology.

Museum of Science Science Park Boston 617-742-6088

Among them are many push-a-button-and-do-it-yourself exhibits, including one that reveals your skeleton and a generator that you operate to produce electric lighting. A new $24-million wing has opened, containing on IMAX theater. You'll think you're floating in space if you are there for "The Dream is Alive" show. Visit **Hayden Planetarium** for a forty-five minute program about the stars. Then head for the cafeteria or sandwich shop for a snack.

Museum of Fine Arts
465 Huntington Avenue
Boston
617-267-9300

Boston's **Museum of Fine Arts** is one of the most comprehensive museums in the Western Hemisphere. Enjoy the vast collections and the library, research laboratory, restaurant, children's programs, gallery talks, and special lectures and films. The I. M. Pei–restored Evans Wing has reopened. The museum is on Huntington Avenue, which you can pick up at Copley Square.

Gardner Museum
280 the Fenway
Boston
617-566-1401

Around the corner is the **Gardner Museum**, Isabella Stewart Gardner's home until she died in 1924. The building is of Italian design and is filled with Mrs. Gardner's eclectic collection of paintings, tapestries, stained glass, and furniture. The enclosed central courtyard, filled with flowers year-round, is used for chamber music concerts.

John F. Kennedy Library
Columbia Point
Dorchester
617-929-4523

From downtown, take I-93 south to exit 17, and follow the signs to the **John F. Kennedy Library**. After seeing an excellent introductory film, walk through exhibits depicting Kennedy's childhood, war experiences, Senate term, and days as president. There's a small exhibit, too, about Robert Kennedy. The library itself—which most visitors don't go into—contains films and documents from the Kennedy administration, and other materials (including a fine collection on Ernest Hemingway).

Franklin Park Zoo
Franklin Park
Dorchester
617-442-0991

A few miles away is the **Franklin Park Zoo**. We especially enjoy the Bird's World, a walk-in aviary.

The Boston Harbor Islands, low and sandy, stand in marked contrast to the city's sky-scrapers. The more than thirty islands offer eighteenth-century forts and ruins to explore, and picnicking, fishing, boating, swimming, camping, and hiking. Pick up a copy of the *AMC Guide to Country Walks Near Boston*, which describes several walks on the islands.

Ferry schedules are available from **Bay State Spray & Provincetown Steamship Company** (617-723-7800), **Boston Harbor Cruises** (617-227-4321), and **Massachusetts Bay Line** (617-749-4500). All stop at Georges Island, where you board a free water taxi to the other islands.

Eighteen of the islands now make up the Boston Harbor Island State Park. For complete information, contact the **Department of Environmental Affairs**.

BOSTON HARBOR ISLANDS

Department of Environmental Affairs
100 Cambridge Street
Boston
617-727-3180

The problem isn't finding good restaurants in Boston; it's choosing one. Our favorites: For first-rate seafood try **Legal Seafoods** (617-426-4444) at the Boston Park Plaza Hotel. **Davio's** at 269 Newbury Street (617-262-4810) is famous for wonderful Italian fare. The upstairs cafe offers gourmet pizza and more. **Durgin Park** (617-227-2038) has been open in the Marketplace for over 140 years. Come for New England boiled dinners, Boston baked beans, and Indian pudding. On nearby Union Street, the **Union Oyster House** (617-227-2750) features shore dinners, lobster, and an oyster bar. **Maison Robert** (617-227-3370) on School Street serves both lunch and dinner on the patio behind the Franklin statue.

Across the Charles from Boston sits Cambridge, a city rich in historical and cultural traditions. The city boasts two of the nation's finest universities—Harvard, the first college founded in America, and MIT, a leading research center in science and technology.

CAMBRIDGE

Harvard
  Information
  Center
1353 Massachusetts
  Avenue
Cambridge
617-495-1573

Harvard University
  Museums of
  Natural History
24 Oxford Street
Cambridge
617-495-1910 or
  617-495-3045

Arthur M. Sackler
  Museum
485 Broadway
Cambridge
617-495-2397

Busch-Reisinger
  Museum
29 Kirkland Street
Cambridge
617-495-2317

Fogg Art Museum
32 Quincy Street
Cambridge
617-495-7768

MIT
Massachusetts
  Avenue
Cambridge
617-253-4795

Frances Russell
  Hart Nautical
  Galleries
77 Massachusetts
  Avenue
Cambridge
617-253-5942

Harvard University opened in 1636. It was originally funded by John Harvard, who donated his library, farm, and money to begin the school. Today the campus sprawls from the river through Harvard Square, and beyond.

Start your explorations in the square, at the **Harvard Information Center.** This is the place for area maps and activity schedules. Then walk through **Harvard Yard**, past **Widener Library** and a fine collection of eighteenth-century buildings, to the **Harvard University Museum.** Actually the building houses four different museums: the **Botanical Museum** (look for the glass flowers), the **Mineralogical Museum,** the **Museum of Comparative Zoology,** and the **Peabody Museum of Archaeology.**

There are now three university art museums. The newest is the **Arthur M. Sackler Museum;** the collection includes Oriental, Ancient, and Islamic art. The **Busch-Reisinger Museum** houses a fine collection of sculpture, paintings, drawings, and prints. The **Fogg Art Museum** has one of the richest university collections in the world. Here you'll see paintings, sculpture, prints, and silver.

The **Massachusetts Institute of Technology** was chartered in 1861 and moved to its present location on Massachusetts Avenue in 1916. Eero Saarinen designed the cylindrical **MIT Chapel;** its aluminum bell tower was sculpted by Theodore Roszak. The lighting inside is reflected from the surrounding moat through high arches.

Across the street, in the **Frances Russell Hart Nautical Galleries,** are ship and engine models that trace the development of marine engineering. Around the corner, in the **Charles Hayden Memorial Library,** is the **Hayden Gallery** and its exhibits of contemporary art.

Most college campuses are not also art museums—here's one that is! The **List Visual Art Center** collection includes exhibits inside (the

Wiesner Building, Hayden Gallery, and Bakalar Sculpture Gallery) as well as outside. One of the most striking sculptures is made of steel, "The Big Sail" by Alexander Calder. As you walk around the campus, look for works by Henry Moore, Louise Nevelson, Jacques Lipchitz, and Picasso.

There is life in Cambridge beyond the universities. **Cambridge Discovery, Inc.** (Box 1987, Cambridge, MA 02238; 617-491-6278) is a non-profit visitor and information center. Look for the booth in Harvard Square. You will find it very helpful in planning your visit to Cambridge. Contact the **Cambridge Historical Commission** for the "Old Cambridge Walking Guide," a brochure that describes thirty sites in the area. Among them is the **Longfellow National Historic Site**, once lived in by George and Martha Washington. Henry Wadsworth Longfellow later lived here for forty-five years. He was married to Fanny Appleton in the house. Most of his furnishings and belongings are still here. In the library are several paintings of Minnehaha Falls (Yes, there is a Minnehaha Falls. It's in Minneapolis), the setting of *The Song of Hiawatha.*

**Cambridge
Historical
Commission
57 Inman Street
Cambridge
617-498-9040**

**Longfellow
National Historic
Site
105 Brattle Street
Cambridge
617-876-4491**

Longfellow wasn't the only literary figure to make Cambridge home. At one time or another Oliver Wendell Holmes, Margaret Fuller, James Russell Lowell, Robert Frost, E. E. Cummings, and Thomas Wolfe all lived here too.

There are many places in Cambridge to stop for a meal. One of them is the **Blacksmith House** (56 Brattle Street; 617-354-3036) where Longfellow's village blacksmith lived. It offers "old world" pastries and tortes to take out as well as lunch or high tea served in the cafe. **Dolphin Seafood** (1105 Massachusetts Avenue, 617-354-9332 or 661-2937) is a good place for seafood. For a special night out, try **Michela's** (254 First

Street, 617-494-5419); there is also a takeout shop next to the restaurant for all sorts of cheese, desserts, and lunch to eat in the atrium; you can also browse through an assortment of cookbooks. **Lai Lai** (700 Massachusetts Avenue, 617-876-7000) offers a complete Chinese menu.

There are a number of interesting side trips in the greater Boston area. We mention several that you might miss because they are out of the way: Sharon, Mansfield, and Lowell.

SHARON

**Kendall Whaling
Museum
27 Everett Street
Sharon
617-784-5642**

From Boston take I-93 south to I-95 south to Route 27 east into Sharon. Turn onto Moose Hill Parkway and follow the signs to the **Kendall Whaling Museum**. This unique museum has a fine collection of whaling objects from all different times and places. You can see a whaleboat from the last New Bedford whaler, the *John R. Manta*, and whaling tools, figureheads, harpoons and lances, logbooks, and journals.

We were especially entranced by the Reddick mural rendering of a killer whale. Head downstairs and you'll meet the snout painted on the wall. Walk past the barnacles on the whale's head, watch the eye that watches you, continue on down the hall past its body, and end up with the tail in the Reception Room (sometimes known as the Printz of whales). Don't miss seeing the stuffed sea lion, its brown fur reminiscent of koala bears; if you're a child you can face him eyeball to eyeball and not feel afraid. Other special exhibits include the 12-foot jawbone of a finback whale, a kayak made of seal skin, a Chinese map of the world from 1598–1630, and wonderful figureheads.

In addition the museum has remarkable collections of paintings depicting the inauguration and development of worldwide whaling—seventeenth-century Dutch paintings of the Greenland arctic whale fishery, Japanese village whaling portrayed on long scrolls, and the American industry at its peak in the nineteenth century. It continues to acquire new paintings and artifacts of historic interest, like the Van de Velde oil of a whale beached near Sheveningen, Holland, in 1617.

Not far from Sharon is Mansfield. From Boston or Sharon take I-95 south to Route 40 and drive into Mansfield. There you will find the **Fisher-Richardson House,** which has also been known as "The Worn Doorstep," "Seven Pines Farm," and "Independence Hall." Dating from 1704, the house was expanded in 1800 to allow for a growing family with nine children. This house is especially interesting because it portrays the lives of families who did not live in mansions, but instead in dwellings like those inhabited by much of the population. The house is furnished, and there is an especially poignant doll collection, reminding us of the dolls our mothers and grandmothers played with. For information call the **Mansfield Historical Society** (617-339-8739).

Also in Mansfield, the **Great Woods Center for the Performing Arts** (P.O. Box 810, Mansfield, MA 02048; 617-339-2331) offers a variety of performances. There are 5,000 seats in the shed and room for 10,000 more on the lawn. Concerts and performances have been put on by the Pittsburgh symphony, Willie Nelson, Bill Cosby, Bob Dylan, Joan Baez, Beach Boys, and Rudolf Nureyev, to name a few.

From Boston take I-93 north to I-495 south; then follow the signs to Lowell, a center of the state's industrial development. From 1821, when the potential power of the Merrimack River was first realized, through the beginnings of the Industrial Revolution, men and women left their New England farms to work in the city's mills.

MANSFIELD

Fisher-Richardson House
Willow Street
Mansfield

LOWELL

After World War I, labor troubles and later the depression slowly led to the eventual shutdown of those mills. But today, Lowell is coming back to life.

Lowell National Historical Park
Market Mills
Market Street
Lowell
617-459-1000

The **Lowell National Historical Park**, established in 1978, commemorates the significance of the Industrial Revolution in shaping our modern industrial society. Exhibits portray the lives of ordinary working people—from the factory girls working fourteen-hour days, six days a week, to today's unionized workers—during 150 years of economic and social change. And there are canal trips and river walks, and mills, boardinghouses, and museums to visit.

Lowell's ethnic neighborhoods add the story of immigrant workers to the era's history. Jack Kerouac grew up in Lowell and wrote about those workers and the city in several of his novels. Look for *The Town and the City*, *Vanity of Duloz*, *Maggie Cassidy*, *Visions of Gerard*, *Dr. Saw*, and *Book of Dreams*.

Museum of American Textile History
800 Massachusetts Avenue
North Andover
617-686-0191

To follow the story of one of Lowell's basic industries, visit the **Museum of American Textile History**. Exhibits include hand-powered tools, powered tools, machines, and equipment used in the preparation of fibers and finishing of textiles. Colorful linens, carpets, and coverlets are on display.

The Trail of the Minutemen

In the spring of 1775 Massachusetts was "a bonfire waiting for a match." The Continental Congress had authorized an army of 18,000 men, but only 4,000 had been collected. England decided to take advantage: General Thomas Gage was ordered to subdue the provincials while they were still "a rude rabble." But, the "rude rabble" pieced together the British plans on April 15, 1775, when General Gage relieved his best troops of their routine duties. Paul Revere rode to Lexington to warn John Hancock and Samuel Adams, then went to Boston to arrange a special signal from the steeple of Old North Church. Meanwhile Adams and Hancock began moving supplies and arms to new hiding places. Three nights later, as seven hundred Redcoats boarded boats on the Charles River, two lanterns glowed in the Old North's steeple, and Revere and William Dawes rode off to warn the Minutemen.

The Minutemen, led by Captain John Parker, gathered on the green in Lexington. As the British marched onto the green someone fired a shot—no one knows from where—and in just a few minutes eight Minutemen had been killed, shot in the back. The Redcoats marched on to Concord and took the town, then moved on to North Bridge. There "the shot heard round the world" set them on their heels. They panicked and ran.

As the defeated troops marched back to Boston along Battle Road, local patriots fired at them from behind trees, Indian style. A thousand reinforcements arrived, allowing the Redcoats time to rest and treat their wounded, but still the provincials harassed them. The British, angry at this method of fighting, began killing any civilian unlucky enough to be in the way, even innocent men sitting in a tavern. Forty-nine Americans died that day, forty-one were wounded, and five were reported missing; the British lost seventy-three dead, close to two hundred wounded, and twenty-six missing. This was the beginning of the American Revolution.

LEXINGTON

From Boston take Route 2 west to Waltham Street; then follow the signs into Lexington Center. Stop at the chamber of commerce for maps and information, and to see a diorama of the battle, which should help you get the historical pattern into focus.

Then walk out onto **Battle Green**, where it began early in the morning of April 19, 1775. In summer you'll find young the eager to share the story. The **Minutemen Statue** of Captain John Parker was designed by Henry Hudson Kitson.

The **Lexington Historical Society** operates a visitors' center just off Massachusetts Avenue. Here you'll find another diorama of the clash on the green, pamphlets about local shops, and information about bike and walking trails to Concord. And guides are on hand to help you chart your course.

Lexington Chamber of Commerce
1875 Massachusetts Avenue
Lexington
617-862-1450

Lexington Historical Society
Meriam Street
Lexington
617-861-0928

Buckman Tavern
1 Bedford Street
Lexington
617-861-0928

Hancock-Clarke
House
36 Hancock Street
Lexington
617-862-5598

Munroe Tavern
1332 Massachusetts
Avenue
Lexington
617-862-1703

Museum of Our
National Heritage
33 Marrett Road
Lexington
617-861-6559

The society maintains three historic houses. **Buckman Tavern,** on the green, was where the Minutemen gathered before the early-morning skirmish. It's been restored with eighteenth-century furniture, mugs for making "hot flip," signs limiting travelers to four in a bed, and a display of colonial clothing. A few minutes away is the **Hancock-Clarke House,** where Paul Revere rode to warn John Hancock and Samuel Adams that the British were coming. **Munroe Tavern,** back out Massachusetts Avenue toward Arlington, was used by Earl Percy as his headquarters and a as refuge for wounded British soldiers.

Nearby, off Route 2A, is the **Museum of Our National Heritage.** There are four galleries here, each with a changing display about the growth and development of the United States.

Minuteman National Historical Park sprawls across three towns: Lexington, Lincoln, and Concord. There are several visitors' centers in the park, each with informed staff, maps, and pamphlets. The first center you come to as you drive along Battle Road (Route 2A) is the **Battle Road Visitor Center** in Lexington (617-862-7753). Follow signs to the parking lot; then walk along the winding path through the woods to the striking modern cedar building nestled in the pines. There are exhibits, a movie, an electric map, and a bookstore.

CONCORD

Grapevine Cottage
491 Lexington
Road
Concord

The Wayside
Lexington Road
Concord
617-369-6975

From Lexington Center follow Battle Road (Route 2A) into Concord. On your right, before you come into the center of town, are several historical houses.

Grapevine Cottage is one of the oldest houses in town. In the yard is the original Concord grapevine, still bearing fruit in late summer. **The Wayside** was the home of Nathaniel Hawthorne, the Alcotts, and Margaret Sidney, who wrote the "Five Little Peppers" series. And beyond Alcott Road, you come to **Orchard**

House, where Louisa May Alcott wrote *Little Women*. Look for her "mood pillow." When she set it on end, pointed up, she was in a good mood; but when she laid it flat, watch out!

**Orchard House
399 Lexington Road
Concord
617-369-4118**

Beyond Orchard House, on the left, is the **Concord Museum**. Here are fifteen rooms with furniture dating from the seventeenth to the mid-nineteenth century. Also here: one of the two lanterns that hung in Old North Church, Emerson's study recreated with its original furnishings, a copper kettle used by Louisa May Alcott during the Civil War, and a diorama of the fight at North Bridge.

**Concord Museum
200 Lexington Road
Concord
617-369-9606**

Continue on Route 2A to the rotary, and take a right onto Route 62 (Bedford Street). In **Sleepy Hollow Cemetery**, on the left, look for **Author's Ridge**, where Hawthorne, Emerson, Thoreau, and the Alcotts are buried. Gravestone rubbing is allowed.

**Sleepy Hollow Cemetery
Bedford Street
Concord
Old North Bridge
Monument Street
Concord**

Turn back on Bedford Street and follow it straight out onto Monument Street. Park on the right, then cross the street to **Old North Bridge**, where the "shot heard round the world" was fired. Standing nearby is Daniel Chester French's famous statue of the Minuteman.

**North Bridge Visitor Center
174 Liberty Street
Concord
617-369-6993 or
617-484-6156**

Most people see Old North Bridge from land; but you can also see it from water. The **South Bridge Boat House**, on Route 62 a mile west of Concord Center, rents canoes and runs guided boat tours to historic sites along the Concord River. Phone 617-369-9438 for information.

From the bridge it's a short walk up to the Buttrick mansion, where you'll find the **North Bridge Visitor Center**. There are exhibits, a room where children can try on colonial clothing, and a fully stocked bookstore. Outside you may see a colonial regiment recreating a battle.

On your way out, stop at the **Old Manse**, just to the right of the bridge. Reverend William Emerson, Ralph Waldo Emerson's grandfather, and Nathaniel Hawthorne both lived here at different times.

**Old Manse
Monument Street
Concord
617-369-3909**

Concord Hymn
Ralph Waldo Emerson

By the rude bridge that arched the flood,
  Their flag to April's breeze unfurled,
Here once the embattled farmers stood
  And fired the shot heard round the world.

The foe long since in silence slept;
  Alike the conqueror silent sleeps;
And Time the ruined bridge has swept
  Down the dark stream which seaward creeps.

On this green bank, by this soft stream,
  We set to-day a votive stone;
That memory may their deed redeem
  When, like our sires, our sons are gone.

Spirit that made those heroes dare
  To die, and leave their children free,
Bid Time and Nature gentle spare
  The shaft we raise to them and thee.

**Concord Chamber
of Commerce
½ Main Street
Concord
617-369-3120**

**Thoreau Lyceum
156 Belknap Street
Concord
617-369-5912**

**Walden Pond State
 Reservation
Route 126
Concord
617-369-3254**

Follow Monument Street back into Concord Center. You can stop at the chamber of commerce in Monument Square or the information booth on Haywood Street (open summers only) for more information about the area. When you're ready for lunch, try **The Colonial Inn on the Green** (617-369-9200) or **Walden Station** (24 Walden Street, 617-371-2233). Then finish up at the **Thoreau Lyceum**, where you'll find exhibits about Concord's history and Thoreau memorabilia. There's even a replica of his cabin at Walden Pond.

The site of that original cabin is a couple of miles away, at **Walden Pond State Reservation**. Thoreau, having taken Emerson's essay "Nature" to heart, believed that every person should have an original relationship with the natural world. When Emerson offered him the use of the land around the pond for his own "original relationship," Thoreau jumped at the chance. The cabin he built in 1845 cost $28.12½ (12½ cents!), and measured 10 by 15 feet. Thoreau lived here for two years, writing in his journal:

> It will be a success if I shall have left myself behind. But my friends ask me what will I do when I get there. Will it not be employment enough to watch the progress of the seasons? . . . I have, as it were, my own sun and moon and stars, and a little world all to myself.

Thoreau on the changing seasons at Walden: "At the approach of spring the red-squirrels got under my house, two at a time, directly under my feet as I sat reading or writing, and kept up the queerest chuckling and chirruping and vocal pirouetting and gurgling sounds that ever were heard. . . . When the warmer days come, they who dwell near the river hear the ice crack at night with a startling whoop as loud as artillery. . . . When the frogs dream, and the grass waves, and the buttercups toss their heads, and the heat disposes to bathe in the ponds and streams, then is summer begun. . . . October is the month of painted leaves, of ripe leaves, when all the earth, not merely flowers, but fruits and leaves are ripe. With respect to its colors and its seasons, it is the sunset month of the year."

The pond itself is interesting: Its water level does not rise and fall rapidly with wet and dry spells as it does in other ponds nearby; also it remains pure and clear while the quality of the water changes in other ponds. The reasons are geological: The other ponds in the area are made up of nonporous clay; Walden was formed from a glacial remnant that remained stationary as sand and gravel built up around it. When the ice melted, a glacial kettle hole resulted. Rainwater quickly fills up clay-bottomed ponds, while the sand and gravel sides around Walden absorb much of the moisture. And this debris forms a natural underground reservoir that supplies the pond with water in times of drought. The sand and gravel play a part in the water quality too, acting as a filter.

The woods around the pond are filled with hickory, red and black oak, red maple, birch, white pine, hemlock, black chokeberry, sumac, and blueberry. In this varied woodland Thoreau would have seen loons, deer, gray squirrels, chipmunks, rabbits, skunks, raccoons, red fox, kingfishers, blackbirds, bluejays, chickadees, and thrush, ducks, and Canada geese.

Today the pond is busy year-round. Come for swimming, hiking, canoeing, fishing, picnicking, ski touring, and snowshoeing.

Drumlin Farm
Lincoln
617-259-9005

From the pond head south on Route 126 to Route 117. Turn east and look for signs to **Drumlin Farm**, an Education Center and Wildlife Sanctuary operated by the Massachusetts Audubon Society. Drumlin Farm offers a full program for adults and children, including visits with the animals in residence, sleigh rides, hayrides, Indian life and lore, backwoods tracking, maple sugaring, planting vegetable gardens, barn dance, and hiking.

DeCordova and
Dana Museum
and Park
Sandy Pond Road
Lincoln
617-259-8355

Not far away, on Sandy Pond Road, is **DeCordova and Dana Museum and Park**. As a center for visual and performing arts, the museum offers a collection of 1500 paintings, sculptures, prints, and photographs featuring New England artists. You can't miss the large sculptures outside on the lawns. A concert series is held during the summer; other performances are held inside during the rest of the year.

SUDBURY

Longfellow's
Wayside Inn
Wayside Inn Road
Sudbury
617-443-8846

Follow Route 126 south to Route 20 in Wayland; follow Route 20 west about 6 miles to Wayside Inn Road, on the right.

Longfellow's Wayside Inn was called How's Black Horse Tavern when it was licensed in 1661. Travel was slow, uncomfortable, and difficult in those days, and the inn offered a welcome respite for travelers from Boston to Worcester or Hartford. The original building had two rooms, one above the other; in 1716 another section of two rooms was added to the left of the entrance, and the name was changed to the Red Horse Tavern. More rooms and the west wing were added later, In 1897 the name was changed to the Wayside Inn by owner Edward Rivers Lemon.

Longfellow visited the inn with a group of professors who encouraged him to write *Tales of a Wayside Inn*. He used his own memories as well as those of his friends to create a poet, a musician, a student, a theologian, a Spanish Jew, and a Sicilian; Lyman Howe (over the years the spelling changed) was the landlord-narrator.

A turning point in the evolution of the old hostelry came in 1923, when Henry Ford began collecting articles that originally belonged to the inn as well as old stagecoaches, fire engines, and other historic memorabilia. In 1926 he brought the **Redstone School**, the setting for "Mary Had a Little Lamb," from Sterling to Sudbury. (Mary was Mary Elizabeth Sawyer; John Roulston wrote the poem.) He built the **Martha-Mary Chapel** in honor of his and his wife's mothers. In 1929 the **Gristmill** was added. The mill operates today as it would have long ago: You can see the water wheel, the gears on the first floor of the three-story structure, and the grinding stones. There's even a miller filling bags with flour.

Tales of a Wayside Inn
Henry Wadsworth Longfellow

One Autumn night, in Sudbury town,
　　Across the meadows bare and brown,
The windows of the Wayside Inn
　　Gleamed red with fire-light through the leaves
Of woodbine, hanging from the eaves
　　Their crimson curtains rent and thin.

As ancient is this hostelry
    As any in the land may be,
Built in the old Colonial day,
    When men lived in a grander way,
With ampler hospitality;
    A kind of old Hobgoblin Hall,
Now somewhat fallen to decay,
    With weather-stains upon the wall,
And stairways worn, and crazy doors,
    And creaking and uneven floors,
And chimneys huge, and tiled and tall. . . .

A fire in 1955 destroyed a great deal of the inn, but it has been restored, with interior and furnishing as they were. Come for traditional colonial fare, and a tour of the inn and the lovely grounds.

To get back to Boston, follow Route 20 to I-95 (Route 128) south, to I-90 (the Massachusetts Turnpike) east. Or you can take Route 128 and I-95 from the Concord/Lexington area to Marblehead.

The North Shore

The North Shore winds along the coast from Marblehead, a lovely sailing center, through Salem and Cape Ann, to Newburyport, a town steeped in seafaring tradition.

MARBLEHEAD
From Boston take the Callahan Tunnel to Route 1A north, to Route 129 east. (For one last look at Boston's skyline, take Route 1A into Lynn and follow Nahant Road to the ocean.) Continue on Route 129 through Swampscott, past the lovely homes on Atlantic Avenue, into Marblehead.

Old Marblehead—it was called Marble Harbor then—was settled in 1629 by fishermen from Cornwall and the Channel Islands; it remained a part of nearby Salem until 1649. In the late 1600s the town was the scene of some verbal and physical sparring. The issue? Whether or not to celebrate Christmas. Dr. Pigot, who had recently arrived as vicar of the Episcopal church, planned to hold a Christmas service; the Puritans, not to be outdone, scheduled a lecture at the same time. Dr. John Barnard, parson of the Puritan church, argued against the celebration. He maintained that Christ was born in October and that Christmas was merely a pagan custom. Dr. Pigot replied in a paper entitled "A Vindication of the Practice of the Ancient Christian as well as the Church of England, and other Reformed Churches in the Observation of Christmas-Day; in answer to the uncharitable reflections of Thomas de Laune, Mr. Whiston and Mr. John Barnard of Marblehead." Universalists and Catholics, as well as Episcopalians, fought for the observance of Christmas. Gradually, the Puritans weakened, and in 1681 the law against Christmas was repealed. That year "December Relaxation" brought a polar bear to Boston Common; the following year, a pair of camels, a sea lion, and a leopard were on display in Dock Square. Salem's celebrations centered around a "sapient dog" who could read, write, and fire a gun!

The best way to see **Marblehead** is on foot. Antique shops, boutiques, and historical houses fill the narrow winding streets. Visit **Abbot Hall** to see the *Spirit of '76*. The painting by Archibald Willard was given to the town by General John Devereux, whose son was the model for the drummer boy. You'll also see the deed to the town, written in 1684, that transferred the land from the Nanepashemet Indians to the settlers for $80. And there's an information booth here too.

Abbot Hall
Washington and
Lee Streets
Marblehead

The Marblehead Historical Society owns and maintains the **Jeremiah Lee Mansion**, near the intersection of Washington and Hooper streets. This home is a fine example of Georgian

Jeremiah Lee
Mansion
161 Washington
Street
Marblehead
617-631-1069

architecture, with beautiful furniture from all over the world. It is unusual because it is the only house in the country that still has the original hand-painted tempura paper on the walls in several rooms. In the State Drawing Room the panels feature classical ruins, with each panel designed to fit the wall. Look for the pianoforte that was made in England and shipped here legless, ready for a local cabinetmaker to design its underpinnings. In 1789 and 1794, Washington and Lafayette were guests in the Great Room, which is elegant indeed with its elaborately carved chimney piece and marble fireplace.

Don't miss the "Museum Rooms" on the top floor, which are filled with colorful paintings of Marblehead by J.O.J. Frost, carefully stitched samplers, portraits by William T. Bartoll, a collection of dolls, and a wooden codfish hanging to portray the early industry of the town.

St. Michael's
Church
13 Summer Street
Marblehead
617-631-2242

St. Michael's Church is one of the oldest Episcopal churches in the country. Its bell is especially meaningful because it was rung so hard and long after the news of the signing of the Declaration of Independence that it cracked and had to be recast by Paul Revere.

You can enjoy wonderful harbor views from **Crocker Park** and **State Street Landing**, both on Front Street. The harbor of this sailing center is so packed with fine boats that you can practically walk across it! Farther up Front Street is **Fort Sewall**. It was built in the seventeenth century and "modernized" in 1742; only half-buried buildings remain today. During the War of 1812 guns from the fort saved the USS *Constitution*. The view from here is great too. Bring a picnic lunch and enjoy it.

Speaking of food, try "Top Side" on the second floor of the **Sail Loft** (State Street, 617-631-9824) for great seafood. If you have a sweet tooth, head for **Macaw's** (70 Atlantic Avenue, 617-639-1786) and ask for "Death by Chocolate," or try **Stowaway Sweets** (154 Atlantic Avenue, 617-631-0303) for wonderful chocolate.

Heading out of town on Atlantic Avenue, take a left onto Ocean Avenue and continue out the causeway to **Marblehead Neck**. There's a marked bicycle path (you can drive it too) around the peninsula, past beautiful homes. Watch for the signs to the Massachusetts Audubon Society's **Marblehead Neck Sanctuary**. Farther out, at the very end of the neck, are **Marblehead Light** and **Chandler Hovey Park**—the best vantage point for watching the sailing competition during Marblehead's Race Week during the last week in July.

Marblehead Neck Sanctuary Risley Road Marblehead

SALEM

From Marblehead take Route 114 into Salem—the city of the witch trials, of a long marine tradition, and of Hawthorne.

In 1623 Roger Conant and a group of fishermen crossed the Atlantic and settled on Cape Ann. They found the soil there so rocky and the harbors so open and unprotected, that they sailed southwest to a cove they called Naumkeag, later Salem. In 1628 the Dorchester Company was chartered and organized here, with Captain John Endecott as leader, and the settlers began building homes along Washington Street. Two years later Governor Winthrop arrived on the *Arbella* with the charter of the Massachusetts Bay Company.

Although the city is steeped in the lore of witchcraft—much to the dismay of many of its residents—the actual witch hysteria lasted just a little bit over a year. Between February 1692 and May 1693 some four hundred people were accused of the crime of witchcraft; nineteen of them were put to death on Gallows Hill. The executions stopped when the wife of Governor Phipps was accused. He immediately released all suspected witches from jail and stopped the hangings.

Salem's witches were accused of voodoolike powers. It was believed that they made clay or wax images of their victims, and in destroying those images (in fire or water, or with a knife) would kill their victims. People also believed witches could fly, using a magic ointment on themselves and their broomsticks.

Although the hysteria was uncontrolled, the procedure for trying the witches was a specific one. It began with an accusation, a warrant for the suspected witch's arrest and an examination by at least two magistrates. Then came indictment and trial. If found guilty—and only if he or she did not confess—the witch was hung the same day.

Why people did "cry out" against witches remains somewhat mysterious. Perhaps some enjoyed the feeling of importance; others sought revenge for real or imagined slights; still others wanted to divert suspicion away from themselves. Motives for the naming of witches may have been various, but, once started, the hysteria gained its own momentum.

Salem's maritime tradition goes back to the seventeenth century, and began with fishing. Soon sailing vessels were carrying dry cod, whalebone, whale and fish oil, and furs from Salem to the rest of the world, and returning with spices and luxury items.

There are many stories about the men who sailed out from Salem on long voyages and then died at sea; it has been said that their spirits always returned home. In a tale reminiscent of Coleridge's "Rime of the Ancient Mariner," a sailor aboard the *Neptune* reported seeing a ship four times her size bearing down upon her. He threw the wheel over hard to avoid a collision. The other vessel veered slightly and came along the starboard side without a sound. There was no rush of water, no crunch of wood splitting, no straining of lines and canvas—only a glowing

silence. And there wasn't a seaman in sight. As
the ship faded away in the distance the sailor
said, "It's the Ghost Ship. A proper Salem man
has died somewhere and the ship is bringing his
spirit home to Salem, home for Christmas."

The Mermaid

'Twas Friday morn when we set sail,
    And we were not far from the land,
When the captain spied a lovely mermaid,
    With a comb and a glass in her hand.

Oh! the ocean waves may roll,
    And the stormy winds may blow,
While we poor sailors go skipping to the tops,
    And the landlubbers lie down below, below, below,
And the landlubbers lie down below.

Then out spake the captain of our gallant ship,
    And a well-spoken man was he:
"I have married me a wife in Salem town,
    And to-night she a widder will be."

Then out spake the cook of our gallant ship,
    And a fat old cookie was he:
"I care much more for my potties and my kets
    Than I do for the depths of the sea."

Then out spake the boy of our gallant ship,
    And a well-spoken laddie was he:
"I've a father and a mother in Boston city,
    But to-night they childless will be."

"Oh! the moon shines bright and the stars give light;
    Oh! my mammy'll be looking for me;
She may look, she may weep, she may look to the deep,
    She may look to the bottom of the sea."

Then three times around went our gallant ship,
    And three times around went she;
Then three times around went our gallant ship,
    And she sank to the depths of the sea.

Through the eighteenth century the shipyards in Salem were busy producing ships of up to two hundred tons. During the Revolutionary War, when both Boston and New York were occupied by the British, the town's citizens converted existing ships into armed privateers. They also built larger vessels designed to capture prizes from the British. After the war this enterprising spirit was transferred to world trade. Salem's ships traveled to the East Indies, China, Russia, and Japan in a burst of trade that lasted some fifty years. Hurt by the embargo of 1807 and the War of 1812, the final blow came with the newer, larger clipper ships. Salem's harbor was too shallow to handle them.

The chamber of commerce operates two visitors' centers: in the Old Town Hall and at Pickering Wharf. Pick up a copy of the "Best of Salem and the North Shore," published weekly, which lists information about all kinds of entertainment, restaurants, and tourist attractions.

**Peabody Museum
East India Square
Salem
617-745-9500**

Start your tour at the brick mall on Essex Street. In the **Peabody Museum** are many of the articles brought back to Salem from exotic ports by captains and their crews, as well as paintings, figureheads, models, navigational instruments, and a professional library. It is one of the finest maritime museums in America and is responsible for many important publications, including the *American Neptune*, a journal of maritime history.

**Essex Institute
132 Essex Street
Salem
617-744-3390**

The nearby **Essex Institute** is a museum, art gallery, library, and publishing house. Lectures, conferences, and workshops—all about and for the heritage of Essex County—are held in the remarkable main building. On the grounds are several houses that have been restored and opened to the public: the **John Ward House** (1684), the **Crowninshield-Bentley House** (1727), the **Gardner-Pingree House** (1804–1805), and the **Andrew-Safford House** (1818–1819). The **Peirce-**

Nichols House (1782) and **Assembly House** (1782), on Federal Street, are also owned by the institute.

The **Salem Witch Museum** is around the corner from the institute. Here life-size dioramas tell the story of the witchcraft hysteria with sound and light. More witches? Backtrack down Essex Street to the **Witch House,** the site of some of the trials. Once the home of Judge Jonathan Corwin, the house has been restored and furnished with antiques.

From the witch museum cross Salem Common and turn off Essex Street at Turner. The **House of the Seven Gables** was built in 1668 by Captain John Turner, whose family later sold it to the Ingersoll family. In the 1840s Nathaniel Hawthorne visited his cousin Susan Ingersoll and saw the structure in the attic that supports the gables. He was just finishing his novel of the same name and used the house for various scenes: the parlor where Colonel Pyncheon sat dying in the oak chair; the shop where Hepzibah sold scents and candy; the secret staircase that led to Clifford's room.

To preserve its rich heritage in world trade, contemporary Salem has added the **Salem Maritime National Historic Site** to its waterfront. Stop at the visitors' center in the **Custom House**, where Hawthorne was a surveyor from 1846 to 1849. (His description of the building forms the first chapter of *The Scarlet Letter*.) Then walk through **Bonded Warehouse** and **Derby House**.

Right next to the national historic site is **Pickering Wharf**, a reconstructed village filled with shops and restaurants and a theater where you can travel to exotic ports aboard the *India Star*.

A taste treat! Several years ago we received a package of sailboat-shaped almond buttercrunch candies called "sweet sloops." They were delicious, and our first introduction to **Harbor**

Salem Chamber of Commerce
32 Derby Square
Salem
617-744-0004

Salem Witch Museum
19½ Washington Square North
Salem
617-744-1692

Witch House
310½ Essex Street
Salem
617-744-0180

House of the Seven Gables
54 Turner Street
Salem
617-744-0991

Salem Maritime National Historic Site
Derby Street
Salem
617-744-4323

Sweets. Ben Strohecker, the owner, is a candy craftsman. He designs special candy for the Boston Symphony Orchestra, the Museum of Fine Arts, the USS *Constitution* Museum, the Peabody Museum in Salem, the Metropolitan Opera Company, and Saks Fifth Avenue. Stop in at the shop on Leavitt Street in Salem (617-745-7648).

CAPE ANN

Cape Ann, a 55-square-mile peninsula jutting out into the Atlantic, is 30 miles from Boston. The region includes Gloucester and Rockport on the cape proper, and Manchester and Essex at its approaches. Along its 25 mile coastline are six scenic harbors, twenty-four coves, and more than twenty sandy beaches—a natural beauty that has drawn artists and writers to the area.

Small but good beaches are all around Cape Ann. In Gloucester try **Good Harbor Beach**, off Thatcher Road (Route 127A). The drop-off is gradual, but the surf can be heavy. Continue along Route 127A to South Street and Penzance Road, to **Cape Hedge Beach**. At low tide you'll find sand; at high tide, stones. Father on, along Penzance Road, is **Pebbly Beach**, a half mile long. (Parking at both Cape Hedge Beach and Pebbly Beach is by sticker only; you'll have to park along the road and walk in.) Rockport Center boasts **Front Beach** and **Back Beach**, each 150 yards long, clean, and sandy, and a favorite of skindivers.

GLOUCESTER

From Salem take Route 1A to Route 127, the coast road to Gloucester. You'll pass sections of elegant homes, particularly in Manchester. Turn off Route 127, at the sign for Magnolia, onto Hesperus Avenue, and watch for **Rafe's Chasm**. Leave your car and walk through the small shrubs to the 200-foot-long, 60-foot-deep chasm. The granite rocks pounded by the Atlantic make a spectacular setting for lunch.

Continue on Hesperus Avenue, and follow the signs to **Hammond Castle Museum**, on the coast near the reef of Norman's Woe. John Hays Hammond, Jr., an inventor and collector of medieval art, designed the castle for his collections. Throughout this huge replica of a structure never native to America, great care was taken to provide the feeling of authenticity, no matter what the cost. The Great Hall is 100 feet long, 58 feet high, and 25 feet wide. Concerts are held here year-round on the 8,000-pipe organ. The inner courtyard, filled with tropical plants, has its own weather system that can produce a tropical downpour and then turn back to sunlight.

**Hammond Castle Museum
80 Hesperus Avenue
Gloucester
617-283-2080**

Follow Hesperus Avenue out to Route 127 (Western Avenue). As you enter Gloucester, the **Fisherman's Statue** stands facing the harbor. It is a bronze memorial to the ten thousand men lost at sea over the centuries. Every August there's a service in honor of those men, the Gloucestermen who "go down to the sea in ships."

Psalm 107

> They that go down to the sea in ships.
> They that do business in great waters.
> These see the works of the Lord
> And His wonders in the deep.

Longfellow captured the danger of seafaring on this reef-strewn coast in "The Wreck of the Hesperus."

The Wreck of the Hesperus
Henry Wadsworth Longfellow

It was the schooner Hesperus,
That sailed the wintry sea;
And the skipper had taken his little daughter,
To bear him company.

Blue were her eyes as the fairy-flax,
    Her cheeks like the dawn of day,
And her bosom white as the hawthorn buds,
    That ope in the month of May.

The skipper he stood beside the helm,
    His pipe was in his mouth,
And he watched how the veering flaw did blow
    The smoke now West, now South.

Then up and spake an old Sailor,
    Had sailed the Spanish Main,
"I pray thee, put into yonder port,
    For I fear a hurricane.

"Last night the moon had a golden ring,
    And tonight no moon we see!"
The skipper, he blew a whiff from his pipe,
    And a scornful laugh laughed he.

Colder and louder blew the wind,
    A gale from the Northeast,
The snow fell hissing in the brine,
    And the billows frothed like yeast.

Down came the storm, and smote amain
    The vessel in its strength;
She shuddered and paused, like a frighted steed,
    Then leaped her cable's length.

"Come hither! come hither! my little daughter,
    And do not tremble so;
For I can weather the roughest gale
    That ever wind did blow."

He wrapped her warm in his seaman's coat
    Against the stinging blast;
He cut a rope from a broken spar,
    And bound her to the mast.

"O father! I hear the church-bells ring,
    O say, what may it be?"
" 'Tis a fog-bell on the rock-bound coast!"
    And he steered for the open sea.

"O father! I hear the sound of guns,
  O say, what may it be?"
"Some ship in distress, that cannot live
  In such an angry sea!"

"O father! I see a gleaming light,
  O say, what may it be?"
But the father answered never a word,
  A frozen corpse was he.

Lashed to the helm, all stiff and stark,
  With his face turned to the skies,
The lantern gleamed through the gleaming snow,
  On his fixed and glassy eyes.

Then the maiden clasped her hands and prayed
  That saved she might be;
And she thought of Christ who stilled the wave,
  On the Lake of Galilee.

And fast through the midnight dark and drear,
  Through the whistling sleet and snow,
Like the sheeted ghost, the vessel swept
  Tow'rds the reef of Norman's Woe.

And ever the fitful gusts between
  A sound came from the land;
It was the sound of the trampling surf
  On the rocks and the hard sea-sand.

The breakers were right beneath her bows,
  She drifted a dreary wreck,
And a whooping billow swept the crew
  Like icicles from her deck.

She struck where the white and fleecy waves
  Looked soft as carded wool,
But the cruel rocks, they gored her side
  Like the horns of an angry bull.

Her rattling shrouds, all sheathed in ice,
  With the masts went by the board;
Like a vessel of glass, she stove and sank,
  Ho! ho! the breakers roared!

At daybreak, on the bleak sea-beach,
　　A fisherman stood aghast,
To see the form of a maiden fair,
　　Lashed close to a drifting mast.

The salt sea was frozen on her breast,
　　The salt tears in her eyes;
And he saw her hair, like the brown sea-weed,
　　On the billows fall and rise.

Such was the wreck of the Hesperus,
　　In the midnight and the snow!
Christ save us all from a death like this,
　　On the reef of Norman's Woe!

Some say Longfellow wrote the poem after reading a newspaper account of a wreck on Norman's Woe Reef; others say the poet took bits and pieces from many shipwreck legends and used them here. We know there was a real-life parallel some fifty-seven years after Longfellow's poem was published. In February 1898 the *Asia* foundered on Nantucket Shoals with Captain George Dakin, his wife, and their eleven-year-old daughter, Lena, on board. Knowing that Captain Dakin would obey the tradition of the sea and be the last to leave the ship, his chief mate offered to look after Lena. And he did. He lashed himself and the child to the ship. They were found later, not drowned, but frozen to death, still tied together.

Longfellow was not the only writer to set a work in Gloucester. Rudyard Kipling wrote with feeling about the unpretentious heroism of the town's fishermen in *Captains Courageous*. That heroism shows strongly too in Winslow Homer's many paintings of the sea and Gloucester's fishing fleet. And some of the most remarkable sea paintings ever produced are those by Fitz Hugh Lane, particularly in the series called "The Stranded Boat," set on Eastern Point.

Another sea legend involves pirates, not shipwrecks, and has a happier ending. In 1720 pirates boarded a ship off the Massachusetts coast. Their leader, Captain Pedro, intended to kill everyone on board until he heard a baby cry. He went below and found a mother and newborn baby girl. He promised not to harm the ship or passengers if the mother would name her baby after his own mother, Mary. She agreed, and Pedro released the captives. Then he handed the mother a bolt of beautiful silk for "Ocean-born Mary's" wedding gown. The ship landed in Boston, Mary's father died, and the mother and child moved to Henniker, New Hampshire. Mary grew up to be a tall, beautiful woman with red hair and green eyes. She married and had four sons.

Eventually Captain Pedro moved to Henniker, built a lovely colonial home, and asked Mary to live with him. One night the captain returned with a large chest, which he buried in the yard, some say with the body of his pirate helper. When he died a year later Mary buried him, as he had requested, under an 8-foot slab in front of the kitchen hearth. After Mary died the legend tells of strange things happening in the house and orchard, where the chest was buried: It seems Mary's ghost still walks down the stairs inside the house, and into her coach-and-four for drives; and out in the yard the pirate's helper moans as he guards the treasure.

Gloucester's legends also tell of sea monsters. One huge sea serpent was sighted in August 1817. A witness wrote that the serpent had a head as large as a 4-gallon keg and a body as large as a barrel, and was 40 feet long. A watcher on shore fired at the creature, who sank straight down into the sea like a "caterpillar," then reappeared 100 yards away. And one believer later killed a 3-foot snake, thinking it was a baby sea serpent.

Gloucester has its very own ghost town! **Dogtown Commons** sits in the center of the peninsula, accessible from Washington Street or Route 128. The community was settled in the 1600s and thrived until the Revolutionary War. With all the men off fighting, the women were alone with only dogs for protection. Strange derelicts and toothless old crones moved in—and the people who had lived there began moving out.

Today all that remains are ruins of foundations and cellars, and a hearthstone here and there among the blueberry bushes. And the population? Otters, foxes, raccoons, rabbits, pheasants, and all kinds of birds.

The fishing industry has existed longer in Gloucester—since 1623—than anywhere in the United States. (There's a Gloucesterman's saying that if the mackerel are running even a wedding can be postponed.) Gloucester's ships brought in fish, square-riggers came heavily laden with salt, and racks of drying salted fish were everywhere. Today modern plants process more fish here than in any other city in the country. Spend some time on the piers watching the ships unload in the harbor. For more information, stop at the booth on Route 127 near the Fisherman's Statue or contact the chamber of commerce.

The **Gloucester Fishermen's Museum** is a unique "atticy" kind of museum. You can follow a series of numbered hands-on exhibits—tasting, reading, using, and handling artifacts and marine animals. A sign reading "Help us shape this mast" invites you to use old shipwright's tools to shape the wood. You can also try to drill a hole in a block with a hand drill. It's not easy, and it took eleven thousand holes to build a 100-foot schooner. (Electric drills weren't invented until the 1920s.) the museum is the place to sign up for a four-hour whale-watching cruise on Stellwagen Banks. If you can, go on an overcast day, when

Cape Ann
  Chamber of
  Commerce
128 Main Street
Gloucester
617-283-1601

Gloucester
  Fishermen's
  Museum
Rogers and Porter
  Streets
Gloucester
617-283-1940

BOSTON

The restoration of the historic Quincy Market, Faneuil Hall Market Place, attracts millions of people annually with its cosmopolitan melange of boutiques, restaurants, gift shops, and exhibits.

CAMBRIDGE

The USS Constitution, "Old Ironsides," floats quietly at her dock at the entrance to the Boston Navy Yard.

BOSTON

Visitors can trace the Kennedy family story in exhibits and film at the John Fitzgerald Kennedy Memorial Library.

**Cape Ann
Historical
Association
27 Pleasant Street
Gloucester
617-283-0455**

the sea is a little rough and the whales surface often.

The **Cape Ann Historical Association** houses a superb collection of Fitz Hugh Lane paintings and drawings. As a resident of Gloucester, Fitz Hugh Lane provided the town with a unique collection of views from a century ago. Works by Winslow Homer and John Sloane are also on exhibit. Don't miss the collection on the second floor of fishing industry statues, ship models, photographs, a Grand Banks Dory, and scale models of the waterfront.

If you're ready for a night out; call the **Gloucester Stage Company** (267 East Main Street, 617-281-4099) or the **Blackburn Theater Company** (36 Rocky Neck Avenue, 617-283-9410). The **Rockport Chamber Music Festival** (Main Street, 617-546-7391) offers concerts during June.

Hungry? Try **Captain's Courageous** (617-283-0007), **Gloucester on the Waterfront** (617-281-4416), or **Gloucester House Restaurant** (617-283-1812).

Follow signs around Gloucester Harbor to **Rocky Neck**, where there's a small art colony with galleries, a book shop, a restaurant, and several working boatyards—relatively untouched by tourism. Try **The Outrigger** on Rocky Neck Avenue (617-281-4998) for great seafood.

A boat trip? Come aboard the *Dixie Bell* or the *Daunty*, which leave from Rocky Neck, East Gloucester, and the Gloucester House Restaurant downtown. Call 617-283-5110 for information.

A fishing trip? **Yankee Fleet** operates half- or full-day excursions. Call 617-283-0313 for information.

On the other side of Rocky Neck is **Beauport**. The house was built by Henry Davis Sleeper, a Boston architect and interior designer.

He wanted each of the twenty-five rooms in the mansion to reflect a different period, and they do. Each was designed around a particular object or collection of objects, in different styles, colors, and shapes.

From Beauport follow the road to the end of Eastern Point for ocean views, **Eastern Point Light**, and **Dog Bar Breakwater**. Then double back to Farmington Avenue and Atlantic Avenue, and follow the coast into Rockport.

Beauport
Eastern Point
Boulevard
Gloucester
617-283-0800

Rockport, once a fishing village and stone quarry, is now a year-round artists' colony, a town full of shops and galleries. The imposing sea wall of granite blocks makes the harbor one of the loveliest anywhere.

ROCKPORT

On **Bearskin Neck** stands **Motif Number 1**, the red house that's been painted by hundreds of artists, an appropriate symbol of Cape Ann. The original shack was destroyed in a blizzard in 1978, but funds were raised to rebuild it. Many of the other buildings on the neck are now used by artists and craftsmen for shops and studios. The area can be very crowded during the summer.

The **Rockport Art Association** is in an old tavern built in 1770. Here you will find paintings, drawings, and sculptures by more than two hundred artists. The association also offers information about local art galleries and artists' homes that are open to the public.

Rockport Art
Association
12 Main Street
Rockport
617-546-6604

Main Street turns into Granite Street as you continue along to the quarry. Today the workers are gone. In their place: a bird sanctuary and beautiful lake for diving.

In 1710 Joshua Norwood began using pieces of granite for mooring stones. He would drill a hole in the center of a stone, and push an oak tree, roots and all, through the hole. The roots and slab sat at the bottom of the sea, and the boat was moored to the top of the tree! How's that for Yankee ingenuity?

Paper House
Pigeon Hill Street
Rockport

On the hill above town, off Route 127, is the **Paper House**. This unique house, made entirely of newspaper, was built by the Stenman family in 1922. Even the furnishings are made of paper.

Halibut Point
Reservation
Gott Avenue
Rockport

Continue north on Granite Street to Gott Avenue on the right, and **Halibut Point Reservation**. Follow a path through the woods to the rocky point, the outermost tip of Cape Ann. The view is superb. If you come when the fog is in, expect an eerie mist full of the sound of the sea crashing below.

ANNISQUAM

Continue along Route 127 to Annisquam, where you can drive out to **Annisquam Lighthouse** on Wigwam Point. The stark white building with its black top is a welcome beacon to yachtsmen entering Ipswich Bay and the Annisquam Canal, which cuts through the peninsula to Gloucester. This is an area of long tidal inlets that empty out at low tide.

ESSEX

Follow Route 127 to Route 128 south, to Route 133 toward Essex. Stop at **Farnhams** (617-768-6643), or drive on to **Woodman's** (617-768-6451) for clams, lobster, and the world's best fried onions. During the summer Woodman's features a clambake: steamed clams, lobster, corn, watermelon, and a drink, all at a special price.

In 1668 the town set aside an acre of land on the river for shipbuilding, an industry that flourished and is still providing maintenance and repair. Cross the Essex River Bridge and look to the right for the **Arthur D. Story Shipyard**, which has produced over four hundred ships through the years. Farther along Main Street is the **Essex Shipbuilding Museum**. You can see ship models, builders' half-models, shipyard

Essex Shipbuilding
Museum
28 Main Street
Essex
617-768-7451

tools, photographs, and a film. There are more than seventy antique shops in Essex.

From Essex turn off Route 133 at North Gate Road to beautiful **Crane's Beach**, one of the best beaches on the Atlantic seaboard. From the parking lot you can follow **Pine Hollow Trail** through the dunes or walk up to **Castle Hill**. The Georgian-style estate, the second at the site, is a center for performing arts.

From the beach follow Argilla Road to Route 1A, to Ipswich. The town has an historical, industrial, and culinary claim to fame. Here was the first denunciation of taxation without representation; here was the birthplace of the lacemaking and hosiery industries in this country; and here is the home of the famous Ipswich clam.

Visit the **John Whipple House**, built in 1640, which contains a collection of seventeenth- and eighteenth-century furnishings and a lovely seventeenth-century garden. The **Thomas Franklin Waters Memorial** (John Heard House), just across the street, is a large Federal house built in 1795. It's filled with treasures from the Orient and a collection of carriages.

The Ipswich River is a favorite of canoeists. Begin at the bridge on Route 97 in Topsfield and paddle for 7 miles through a marsh sprinkled with gnarled oaks and maples, and grapevines. Around you: the **Ipswich River Wildlife Sanctuary**, a 2,400-acre preserve maintained by the Massachusetts Audubon Society. What's here? Fifteen hundred species of trees and shrubs, over two hundred species of birds, and deer, muskrat, red fox, and otter; miles of hiking trails through woods and marsh, ponds and wildflower gardens; and camping (with advance reservations) on Perkins Island.

IPSWICH

**John Whipple House
53 South Main Street
Ipswich
617-356-2811**

**Thomas Franklin Waters Memorial
40 South Main Street
Ipswich
617-356-2641**

NEWBURYPORT

Newburyport
Chamber of
Commerce
29 State Street
Newburyport
617-462-6680

Cushing Museum
98 High Street
Newburyport
617-462-2681

Custom House
Maritime
Museum
25 Water Street
Newburyport
617-462-8681

Parker River
National Wildlife
Refuge
Plum Island
Newburyport
617-465-5753

Follow Route 1A to Newburyport, at the mouth of the Merrimack River. Stop at the chamber of commerce for information.

Shipowners and captains built a series of Federal-style homes along **High Street,** many of them three stories tall and very elegant. The **Cushing Museum,** once the home of Caleb Cushing, now houses the Historical Society of Old Newbury. Here you'll see collections of paintings, furniture, needlework, clocks, silver, china, and carriages, and a library.

Farther up High Street you come to **Piel Craftsmen** (617-462-7012), where ship models are still made by hand. The expert craftsmen, consultants to several national museums, are happy to answer questions about their work. By the river, on Merrimack Street, the **1690 House** (617-465-8430) displays Towle silver and pewter. (Don't be fooled by the name. The house was built in 1738.) Nearby **Market Square** has been restored; it is filled with shops specializing in antiques and handcrafted products.

Down the street **Custom House Maritime Museum** exhibits tell the story of Newburyport's shipping heritage. Also here: treasures from foreign lands, local artisans' crafts, and a professional library.

Follow Water Street to the causeway to **Plum Island,** a 9-mile strip of sand that acts as a breakwater. Cross the bridge and turn right to the **Parker River National Wildlife Refuge.** Here, along the 7-mile stretch of beach and dunes, is an activity for everyone—swimming, picnicking, hiking, clamming (with a permit), even picking cranberries.

The **Plum Island Lighthouse** is now at the northern tip of the island; it was moved because the ocean eroded the shoreline. This light is crucial to seamen, protecting them from treacherous reefs that have claimed hundreds of ships over the years.

The Wreck
Walter De la Mare

Storm and unconscionable winds once cast
    On grinding shingle, masking gap-toothed rock,
This ancient hulk. Rent hull, and broken mast,
    She sprawls sand-mounded of sea birds the mock.
Her sailors, drowned, forgotten, rot in mould,
    Or hang in stagnant quiet of the deep;
The brave, the afraid into one silence sold;
    Their end a memory fainter than of sleep.
She held good merchandise. She paced in pride
    The uncharted paths men trace in ocean's foam.
Now laps the ripple in her broken side,
    And zephyr in tamarisk softly whispers, Home.
The dreamer scans her in the sea-blue air,
    And sipping of contrast, finds the day more fair.

You can return to Boston on I-95 (pick up Route 113 in Newburyport to I-95), or continue up the coast along Route 1A, into New Hampshire for another coastal itinerary.

The itinerary you've just completed covers very little distance—a mere 150 miles from Plymouth to Newburyport—but this small section of coastline is filled with history. You can sense what it was like to live in the seventeenth and eighteenth centuries. Colonial America reappears here, beneath the overlays of more recent eras, as the fundamental shape of our civilization.

ITINERARY G: THE BERKSHIRES

TANGLEWOOD

ITINERARY G

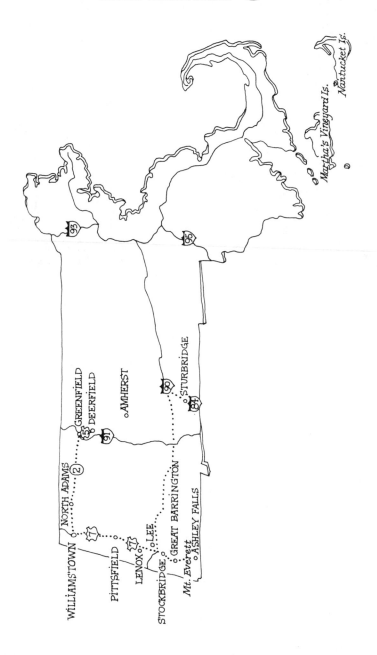

The Berkshires of Massachusetts

The Pesky Sarpent

On Springfield mountain there did dwell,
A comedy youth I knew full well.

Ri tu di nu, ri tu di na,
Ri tu di nu, ri tu di na.

One Monday morning he did go,
Down in the meadow for to mow.

He scarce had mowed half the field,
When a Pesky Sarpent bit his heel.

He took his scythe and with a blow,
He laid the Pesky Sarpent low.

He took the Sarpent in his hand,
And straitway went to Molly Bland.

Oh Molly, Molly, here you see,
The Pesky Sarpent what bit me.

Now Molly had a ruby lip,
With which the pizen she did sip.

But Molly had a rotten tooth,
Which the pizen struck and kill'ed 'em both.

The neighbors found that they were dead,
So laid them both upon one bed.

And all their friends both far and near,
Did cry and howl they were so dear.

Now all you maids a warning take,
From Molly Bland and Tommy Blake.

And mind when you're in love don't pass,
Too near to patches of high grass.

The Berkshire "hills," a north-south spine of rounded mountains located between the Taconic and Hoosac ranges, peacefully blend the natural beauty of forests, orchards, rivers, and waterfalls. This area remained a wilderness long after settlers populated the state farther east. The English chose not to advance over the granite Hoosac Mountains from the east, and the west was protected from the Dutch settlers on the other side by the Taconic Mountains. Theologians such as Jonathan Edwards and the Shakers' Mary Lee looked upon this area as a retreat into the wilderness.

During the nineteenth century the region began to be developed, as iron foundries produced ore for industry and marble was quarried for public buildings. The beauty of the mountains also began to attract vacationers who built summer homes or visited their friends, including Nathaniel Hawthorne, Herman Melville, Edith Wharton, and, later, Norman Rockwell.

From Williamstown near the Vermont border to Ashley Falls near the Connecticut border, the Berkshires are full of special pleasures for vacationers today. There are three major mountains to climb or simply enjoy from a distance; there are lakes and streams to fish and swim in. The towns and villages abound with historic homes, antique shops, and fairs. And the whole region is touched with a rich heritage of literature, drama, art, and music. During each summer music, theater, and dance festivals bring renewed life to the Berkshires, continuing the tradition begun in the nineteenth century.

WILLIAMSTOWN

Williamstown—the home of **Williams College**—is one of the most beautiful college towns in the country. On the campus: **Thompson Memorial Chapel**, a modern Gothic building; **Chapin Library**, with a fine collection of rare books; **Hopkins Observatory**; and the **Williams College Museum of Art**.

When you've finished exploring the college grounds, head for the **Sterling and Francine Clark Art Institute**. The classic white marble building was built in the 1950s to contain the growing collection of Robert and Francine Clark. Mr. Clark started seriously collecting art in 1912 when he lived in Paris. He married Francine in 1919 and they returned to live in the United States in the early 1920s. The collection includes Renoir's *The Bay of Naples with Vesuvius in the Background, 1881, Venice, the Doges*

Sterling and Francine Clark Art Institute
South Street
Williamstown
413-458-8109

Palace, 1881, and *L'Ingénue, 1876*; Monet's *The Ducks, 1926, Spring at Giverny, Rouen Cathedral, Bridge at Dolceacqua,* and *Cliffs at Etretat*; Turner's *Rockets and Blue Lights*; Van Gogh's *The Terrace at Tuileries, 1890*; Homer's *Undertow, 1886, Eastern Point, Prout's Neck, 1900, Western Point, Prout's Neck, 1910, Sunset, Saco Bay, 1896,* and *A Summer Squall, 1904.* Don't miss the bronze sculpture, *Little Dancer,* by Degas. There are several Frederic Remington paintings including *Dismounted: the Fourth Troopers Moving the Led Horses, 1890,* and *The Scout: Friends or Enemies, 1890,* and his bronze sculpture, *The Wounded Bunkie, 1896.*

Stop for a meal in **The Williams Inn** (Routes 2 and 7, 413-458-9371) where you can relax in the dining room or have a quick light meal in the Tavern Lounge. Sunday brunch is a specialty. Friends recommend **The Orchards** (222 Adams Road, 413-458-9611), **The River House Restaurant** (Route 43, Water Street, 413-458-4820), **The Captain's Table** (Routes 2 and 7, 413-458-2400, and **Le Jardin** (Route 7, 413-458-8032).

MOHAWK TRAIL

The western end of the Massachusetts section of the Mohawk Trail begins at Route 2 in Williamstown. The trail was first used by the Indians, a path from the villages of central Massachusetts to the Finger Lakes of New York. Later it was used by colonial troops marching to New York during the French and Indian Wars. Still later, settlers followed the trail in their covered wagons and stagecoaches.

Heading eastward, the trail winds through several forests: **Greylock Mountain State Reservation** (south of Route 2), and **Savoy Mountain State Forest** and **Mohawk Trail State Forest** (both along Route 2). There's good hiking and camping here, and the views are spectacular.

Greenfield sits at the eastern end of the trail, in **Pioneer Valley**—an area of tobacco fields, apple orchards, and lovely villages. The Connecticut River formed this rich agricultural region and was the main source of transportation for its early settlers.

If you are interested in following the trail east toward Boston, or east and south toward Connecticut and New York, follow Route 2 east from Williamstown to North Adams. The town has been able to turn the loss of its nineteenth-century industry to advantage: it's now an arts and crafts center. The **Hoosac Community Resources Corporation** was formed in an old mill by weavers, leather workers, potters, and glass-blowers. You can tour the building and buy their products.

North Adams is the site of the only natural **marble bridge** in North America. It's located 1½ miles northeast of the town on Route 8. It was formed by water erosion, and sits over a 60-foot-deep chasm that winds through 475 feet of rock. (That rock is over 550 million years old.) Hawthorne described the bridge in his *American Notebooks.*

In North Adams you need to decide if you want to go to Deerfield or Pittsfield. If you choose to go to Deerfield, continue out Route 2 along the Mohawk Trail to Greenfield. Then take Route 5 and 10 south to Deerfield. The town was settled in 1669 by Samuel Hinsdell, a squatter who began farming the fertile soil. He was soon joined by other settlers, and within six years the population reached 125. The Pocumtuck Indians, who had used the land to raise corn, tobacco, and pumpkins, were enraged. They attacked the settlement and killed or drove away all the white settlers during the Bloody Brook Massacre of 1675. The town stood empty for seven years, but slowly people began to return;

NORTH ADAMS

Hoosac
 Community
 Resources
 Corporation
121 Union Street
North Adams

DEERFIELD

and by 1686 Deerfield had held its first town meeting.

In 1704, during Queen Anne's War, the Indians attacked again. They burned more than half the village, took a hundred people for slaves, and killed the fifty who resisted. Peace finally came in 1735.

Historic Deerfield
Routes 5 and 10
Deerfield
413-773-5581

You can learn more about the town's history in **Historic Deerfield**, where the Flynt family has restored many original homes and buildings. Henry N. Flynt first came to Deerfield in 1936 (he was bringing his son to the academy). He liked the town and bought an inn; then he bought one home, then another, and another, restoring each in turn. Over the next twenty-five years, Flynt and his wife oversaw the restoration and furnishing of twelve buildings, acquiring more than eight thousand antique pieces in the process.

Stop first at **Hall Tavern**, the visitors' center, for tickets and information. Then enjoy the houses—among them a print shop, a tavern, a silver shop, and **Allen House**, the Flynts' own home—spread along one of the most beautiful village streets in New England.

At historic Deerfield there is more than enough to fill a day. We chose to begin with the **Wright House**, a brick house dating from 1824, because it contains a Chippendale and Federal furniture gallery. Visitors can compare furniture from different centuries and look at the underpinnings of a stripped Philadelphia Chippendale camelback sofa to understand its construction. Even the tack marks of generations of upholsterers are in full view. As you walk around the house be sure to look at the exquisite door handles. Large collections of export China reside in several illuminated closets.

Across the street is the **Ashley House**, dating from 1730. The Reverend Jonathan Ashley was the second minister in Deerfield where he became a leader of society at the age of 20. His diploma is on loan from Yale University and hangs in the study. Ashley had six children; his descendants farmed the land until 1946.

The **Parker and Russell Silver Shop**, recently renamed the **Henry Needham Flynt Silver and Metalwork Collection**, is housed in a new, fire-resistant addition to the Joseph Clesson House. There are a number of pieces that will dazzle any visitor including an ornate cruet stand made by Daniel Fueter, a two-handled cup by Gerrit Onckelbag, a tankard by William Vilant, a tea set by John Coburn, and candlesticks by Thomas Dane. The collection of tankards includes those given to the church and those to family members. Each state had different penalties for those who tried to counterfeit silver pieces—offenders could have their ears cropped, be hung, or dragged behind a wagon. We learned for the first time what a "sucket fork" is. The shape is that of a spoon but it has a forked handle—a piece of several uses!

When you've walked through enough houses, head for the **Deerfield Inn** (413-774-5587) for lunch in the dining room (reservations are suggested) or in the coffee shop downstairs.

AMHERST

Head south on Route 116 to Amherst for a visit to the **Emily Dickinson Homestead** (280 Main Street, 413-542-8161). It was built by Samuel Fowler Dickinson, the poet's grandfather and one of the founders of Amherst College, in 1813. She lived in the house as a recluse, withdrew from society, and wrote 1,800 poems. Much of her work was discovered in her bedroom after her death. Furnishings in her room include a sleigh bed, Franklin stove, cane chair, cradle, and a child's chair.

Also in Amherst, on the campus of Amherst

College, is the **Pratt Museum of Geology**. Visitors can see a collection of dinosaur tracks, a mastodon skeleton and fossils.

The Strong House Museum (67 Amity Street, 413-253-2678 or 9695) is maintained by the Historical Society. This 18th century house contains textiles and artifacts of the period. Herb and flower gardens are on the grounds.

STURBRIDGE

Old Sturbridge Village
Route 20
Sturbridge
413-347-3362

Take Routes 9, 202, and 21 to I 90, then head east to signs for Sturbridge. Or for a pleasant drive through the country take Route 9 to Route 49 south to **Old Sturbridge Village.** Spread out in this recreated nineteenth-century New England town you'll find forty buildings and a farm. (There's a horse-drawn cart for the foot-weary.) Guides in period costumes demonstrate their skills at weaving, horseshoeing, shearing, printing, candlemaking, and more. Special programs? There are loads. Come for lectures, sunrise strolls, sleigh rides, family workshops, Militia Training Day, Fourth of July fireworks, even Thanksgiving dinner.

Before you leave the area, head into town for some shopping. The stores are lovely; their products, distinctive. Then stop at the **Publick House** (413-347-3313) for a traditional New England meal. We've been back many times and love it! A special treat: the international dinners on Friday nights during the spring.

If you want to head south through the Berkshires rather than go east, from North Adams follow Route 8 to Pittsfield, the capital of the region. Contact the **Berkshire Visitors' Bureau** or stop at the booth in Park Square for local and regional information.

Herman Melville lived in Pittsfield between 1850 and 1863. He wrote *Moby Dick* at **Arrowhead**, in a study that faced the whalelike Greylock range. In the house are all kinds of Melville memorabilia—his spectacles, his books, genealogical charts of the family, portraits, photographs, even his daughter's toys. Look for the inscription on the fireplace in the Chimney Room from "I and My Chimney."

More Melville lore? Visit the library—the **Berkshire Athenaeum**— to see the **Herman Melville Memorial Room**. Here you'll find the secretary from his New York apartment (on which he wrote *Billy Budd*), manuscripts, first editions of his books, and pictures from his home. Melville brought home lots of mementoes such as an olive-wood blotter holder, a thimble in a wicker basket (made from a whale tooth), a tobacco box with a compass set in the cover, and many scrimshaw pieces. They're all on display.

The **Berkshire Museum**, on South Street, has ethnological, geological, and zoological displays, in addition to its collection of paintings and sculpture.

Follow Route 20 west about 5 miles to **Hancock Shaker Village**, a restored Shaker settlement dating from 1790. Highlights: The 1826 **Red Stone Barn**, the five-story **Brick Dwelling** (the kitchen dates from 1830), craft shops, and the herb garden. Come in early August for the **Shaker Kitchen Festival.** You'll see cooking demonstrations and may take part in a Shaker meal.

Every summer the Berkshires come alive with music, theater, and dance. For performance schedules, contact the Berkshire Visitors' Bureau or stop at an information booth. You'll find one

PITTSFIELD

Berkshire Visitors'
Bureau
20 Elm Street
Pittsfield
413-443-9186

Arrowhead
780 Holmes Road
Pittsfield
413-442-1793

Berkshire
Athenaeum
1 Wendall Avenue
Pittsfield
413-499-9480

Berkshire Museum
39 South Street
Pittsfield
413-443-7171

Hancock Shaker
Village
Route 20
Pittsfield
413-443-0188

in Williamstown (at the junction of Routes 2 and 7), North Adams (at 69 Main Street), Pittsfield (at Park Square), Lenox (at 75 Main Street), Lee (in the park on Main Street), Stockbridge (on Main Street), and Great Barrington (at 362 Main Street).

If there's something you're anxious to see, don't wait for tickets. You can order in advance for performances:

- **Berkshire Theatre Festival**, Main Street, Stockbridge, MA 01262, 413-298-5576 (summer), 413-298-5536 (winter).

- **Jacob's Pillow Dance Festival**, Box 287, Lee, MA 01238, 413-243-0745.

- **Shakespeare & Company at the Mount**, Plunket Street, Lenox, MA 01240, 413-637-3353.

- **Tanglewood**, West Street, Lenox, MA 01240, 413-637-1940 (summer); Boston Symphony Orchestra, Symphony Hall, Boston, MA 02115, 617-266-1492 (winter).

- **Williamstown Theatre Festival**, Box 517, Williamstown, MA 01267, 413-597-3400.

LENOX

From Pittsfield follow Routes 20 and 7 into Lenox, once "America's Lake District." In the nineteenth century, literary figures gathered here, among them Edith Wharton, Henry Wadsworth Longfellow, Nathaniel Hawthorne, Herman Melville, and Henry Adams. Around the turn of the century several large mansions were built as summer homes. You can catch glimpses of them and a few small castles, half hidden by trees and set behind long green lawns. Most are still owned privately.

The Mount was the summer estate of Edith Wharton, built in 1901. She felt that the Mount was her first real home and enjoyed living there for six or seven months a year. Wharton tended to write early in the day, then work in her garden and visit with friends. Although she wrote both *Ethan Frome* and *Summer* while living in France, the characters and environment belong to Lenox. Henry James called the Mount "a delicate French chateau mirrored in a Massachusetts pond." Wharton and her niece, landscape architect Beatrix Farrand, planned the grounds.

The Mount
Plunkett Street
Lenox
413-637-1899

Both the mansion and the grounds are undergoing restoration but tours are given and the bookshop is open. Matinee plays are performed during the summer as well as Shakespeare under the stars, and there are other programs throughout the year.

The best known treasure in Lenox is **Tanglewood**—the summer home of the Boston Symphony Orchestra. The concerts featuring the BSO, the Boston Pops, and other noted musicians draw more than a quarter of a million people each summer. Join them in the music shed or bring a picnic supper and find a spot on the lawn. Both the setting and the music are magnificent.

Tanglewood
West Street
Lenox
413-637-1940

If you're a cheesecake aficionado stop in **Cheesecake Charlies** (83 Church Street, 413-637-9779) for breakfast or lunch.

Continue south on Route 7 to Stockbridge. You may recognize the wide main street lined with classic New England homes—a setting Norman Rockwell used often in his paintings.

STOCKBRIDGE

Another Rockwell favorite was the **Red Lion Inn** (413-298-5545). This large white building on Main Street looks like a New England inn should. You can wander around inside (there's a nice gift shop), then have a meal in the **Widow Bingham's Tavern** or on the patio ablaze with impatiens in the summer.

**Old Corner House
Main Street
Stockbridge
413-298-3822**

The **Old Corner House**, next door to the library, contains a permanent collection of Rockwell's paintings. Here you'll see the originals of the magazine covers, posters, and prints we all know. The guide who takes you through is eager to share background information and to point out the humor inherent in the artist's work.

**Naumkeag
Prospect Street
Stockbridge
413-298-3239**

Turn off Main Street onto Pine Street, to Shamrock Street, to Prospect. **Naumkeag** was once the estate of Joseph Choate, an ambassador to England in the late nineteenth century. The twenty-six-room Norman mansion, built by Stanford White in 1885, is filled with beautiful antiques. In the gardens are fountains, a sculpted topiary, and a Chinese pagoda.

**Chesterwood
Route 183
Stockbridge
413-298-3579**

Chesterwood was the summer estate of Daniel Chester French, who sculpted the *Seated Lincoln* in the Lincoln Memorial and the *Minuteman* at Old North Bridge. You can visit the mansion, the studio, and the nineteenth-century barn (now a gallery); walk along a nature trail; and enjoy the gardens and the views of Monument Mountain. The sculptor once said: "I live here six months of the year—in Heaven. The other six months I live, well—in New York." To get to French's heaven take Route 102 west to Route 183. Turn left and follow the signs.

A few miles up Route 102, in West Stockbridge, is the **Old Yankee Marketplace**, a restored New England village filled with shops.

**MOUNT
WASHINGTON**

From Stockbridge follow Route 7 south through Great Barrington to Route 41. Continue on Route 41 through South Egremont to Mount Washington. This small town—a population of fifty—is on a hill near the summit of **Mount Everett,** one of the highest peaks in the state. The area is beautiful; the scenery, spectacular.

STOCKBRIDGE

The Old Corner House, an 18th century landmark, displays delightful original paintings by Norman Rockwell and revolving exhibits from the Stockbridge Public Library's fine historic collection.

OLD STURBRIDGE VILLAGE

Men and oxen handle the plowing at Old Sturbridge Village. Plowing can be observed on most good weather days in April.

DEERFIELD

The tri-colored Dwight Barnard House was given its red and blue trim in the 1750s. The original paint colors were determined through microscopic analysis of paint layers remaining on the building.

There are several good hiking trails nearby. You can follow the **Elbow Trail**, which begins off Route 41 near the Berkshire School, to **Guilder Pond**, the highest natural body of water in Massachusetts. Another, steeper trail takes you to **Bash Bish Falls**, a 50-foot waterfall in **Mount Washington State Forest**. Turn right south of Smiley's Pond at the Mount Everett–Bash Bish Falls sign, and follow the road west to the foot of the mountain. (There's a longer but easier path off Route 22 in New York, from a parking lot below the falls.) Legend tells of an Indian maiden, saddened when her husband took another wife, who jumped from the cliff here into the water. It seems she heard her mother (a witch who lived underneath the falls) calling to her. Her husband jumped in to save her, and died. His body was found, but the maiden lives on with her mother behind the falls. You can still see her profile in the pool on moonlit nights.

Wherever you're hiking, be sure to bring a bucket or pail along. You're in blueberry country!

Mount Washington State Forest
East Street
Mount Washington
413-528-0330

ASHLEY FALLS

Bartholomew's Cobble
Weatogue Road
Ashley Falls
413-229-8600

Colonel John Ashley House
Cooper Hill Road
Ashley Falls
413-229-8600

From Route 41 follow the road into Sheffield; then take Route 7A into Ashley Falls. Watch for the signs along Weatogue Road for **Bartholomew's Cobble**. *Bartholomew* is a George Bartholomew who lived here in the late nineteenth century; *cobble* is a local term for a rock outcropping. This particular outcropping—a gigantic natural rock garden—was formed by glaciers. It's filled with over five hundred species of wildflowers, forty species of ferns, and a hundred species of trees and shrubs. Stop at the museum on the hill for a map before you set out. If you come in late June you'll find special programs and walks on **Annual Cobble Day**.

In town stop at the **Colonel John Ashley House**. The house, dating from 1735, is the oldest in the Berkshires. The Sheffield Declaration of Independence was drafted here in 1773.

If you're heading south to Connecticut take Route 7 to Caanan, where you will join the northernmost swing of Itinerary A, or continue on Route 63 to its beginning in Litchfield. For itineraries in eastern Massachusetts head back north to I-90, if you want to get there in a hurry, or wander eastward through the countryside on local roads if you have more time. To join the itinerary in southern Vermont, head north on Route 7 from Williamstown to Bennington.

ITINERARY H: THE NEW HAMPSHIRE SHORE

FORT POINT LIGHTHOUSE

ITINERARY H

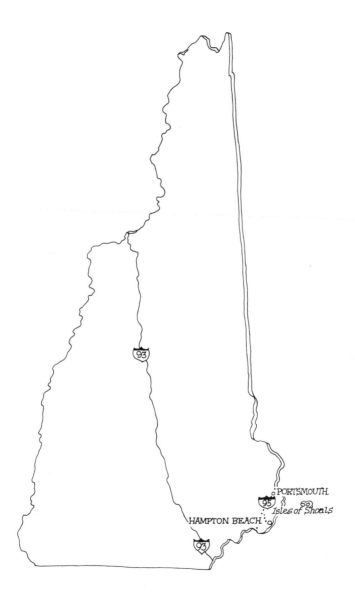

The New Hampshire Shore

The first permanent settlement in New Hampshire was established in 1623 on Odiorne Point in Rye. Dover, Portsmouth, Exeter, and Hampton were settled soon after, and the five were the only towns in the area for years. Their isolation did not create good feelings among the settlements: Bitter arguments arose over land deeds and religion. And infighting was not their only problem. At one point Massachusetts tried to take over the New Hampshire villages—a dispute that was settled by the crown in 1629.

People who chose to settle in New Hampshire had to be persistent in their struggle to tame the rocky soil, clear forests, and cope with long winters. Although they had a good relationship with the Indians in the beginning, eventually their lumbering and construction encroached upon the rights the Indians thought they should have. Finally, in 1675, King Philip's War was begun as a protest against the settlers. The Wampanoags, Narragansetts, and Nipmucks joined forces under the chief of the Wampanoags, Philip. For one year they raided settlements with great loss of life on both sides.

As time passed, fisheries grew up along the shore, including the processing of salt cod, among others. The tall pines of New Hampshire, some rising to 200 feet, were harvested and used as masts for English ships. The settlers were not happy to see the very best of the lot shipped off to the king.

John Wentworth, chosen by the king in 1717 to govern New Hampshire, was a capable leader who provided stability for the settlers. Benning Wentworth, who was appointed governor of New Hampshire in 1741, granted tracts of land to people, allowing five hundred acres from each tract for himself. His nephew, John Wentworth II, carried on the family leadership as a royal governor, until 1775 when he fled from a threatening mob in Portsmouth. New Hampshire was the first of the colonies to declare its independence from England with its own government taking power on January 5, 1776. "Live free or die," words written by General John Stark, New Hampshire's Revolutionary War hero, is now the state motto.

HAMPTON BEACH   New Hampshire's shape is close to triangular, with the inverted apex taking up little space along the shoreline. This itinerary is short because the area is condensed. If you come across the border from Massachusetts follow Route 1A along the coast to Hampton Beach. Here you can stop for a swim in the ocean, a stroll along the boardwalk, or a ride at the amusement park. More activity? There's often a talent show or a fishing derby going on in this busy resort town.

Continue up Route 1A into Portsmouth, New Hampshire's only seaport. The city is also a service center for the naval base across the river in Kittery. Your first stop in Portsmouth should be the chamber of commerce for a map of the city and brochures on its many sights.

Imagine the delight of the first settlers when they disembarked the *Pied Cow* and found wild strawberries growing in great profusion along the banks of the Piscataqua River. They named their settlement "Strawbery Banke," which it was called until 1653 when it was renamed Portsmouth. Strawbery Banke prospered as a deepwater seaport, fishing center, shipbuilding site for clippers, and lumber depot.

You might begin your visit at Portsmouth's major historical museum, **Strawbery Banke,** which is located in the "Puddle Dock" section of town. Rather than allowing their many surviving historical buildings to be razed, determined inhabitants began a major restoration in the late 1950s. Put on your walking shoes and pick up a map at the entrance that will introduce you to thirty-five historic buildings. You can wander in and out of a wide range of buildings including the elegant Governor Goodwin Mansion, the Dinsmore Shop where the museum's cooper makes barrels, the Goodwin Garden with its Victorian flair, and the Joshua Jones House, dating from 1790, which contains an archaeological laboratory from the "digs" on the grounds of the museum. Part of the fun is seeing restoration still going on as building after building are readied for visitors. One of the most recent to open was the Pitt Tavern. Built in 1766, the tavern was visited by George Washington, Lafayette, and John Hancock, among others. It was also a stage

PORTSMOUTH

**Portsmouth
Chamber of
Commerce
500 Market Street
Portsmouth
603-436-1118**

**Strawbery Banke
Marcy Street
Portsmouth
603-433-1100**

stop with a constant flow of travelers arriving with fresh news.

Did you know that the Grand Banks Dory is still made here? The **Strawbery Banke Boat Shop** is itself a replica of the Hiram Lowell Boat Shop in Amesbury, Massachusetts. Original tools used by the Lowell family for seven generations were given to the museum. Today you can walk into the boat shop and watch the ongoing construction of the 18-foot Grand Banks Dory. At this writing the museum is raffling off a 14-foot dory, built of pine and oak and fastened with copper and bronze. She has a centerboard, rudder, tiller, and a spritsail rig. By the time you read this, some lucky person will be setting sail in this lovely boat.

Across the street on the bank of the river is **Prescott Park**. Come in the summertime to enjoy the beautiful flower gardens, free outdoor concerts, and arts and crafts exhibits.

The Historic Associates of the Greater Portsmouth Chamber of Commerce maintain and keep open old homes in town. Your map will show you the way to all of them along the historic Portsmouth Trail.

Moffatt-Ladd House
154 Market Street
Portsmouth

The **Moffatt-Ladd House** was built in 1763 as a wedding gift for Samuel Moffatt from his father, an English sea captain named John Moffatt. John's son-in-law, William Whipple, a signer of the Declaration of Independence, later lived here. There are three floors of eighteenth-century furnishings, a cellar with a secret passageway to the wharves, and beautiful gardens.

John Paul Jones House
Corner of Middle and State Streets
Portsmouth

The **John Paul Jones House** is where—you guessed it—John Paul Jones stayed while he was supervising the outfitting of the *Ranger* in 1777 and the *America* in 1781. Look for the models of the *Ranger* and the collections of silver, glass, ceramics, portraits, and guns.

ISLE OF SHOALS

The White Island Lighthouse is located on the Isles of Shoals, nine miles off the New Hampshire coast at Portsmouth. An excursion boat makes two trips daily.

PORTSMOUTH

The Steamship Company's Oceanic *gives tourists a constantly changing perspective on the Isles of Shoals.*

PORTSMOUTH

A view down Atkinson Street at Strawbery Banke, a 10 acre neighborhood museum. It features 37 historic homes dating from 1695 to 1945, as well as crafts shops, historic exhibits, archaeology, and a restaurant.

H•207

The **Rundlet-May House** (Middle Street) is unusual because it contains family pieces passed down through the generations, rather than a collection of other people's furniture from one period of time. The **Governor John Langdon House** (Pleasant Street) was built in 1784 and contains beautiful carving. George Washington visited the house in 1789 and wrote about both the house and his host with compliments. The **Wentworth Gardner House** (Mechanic Street) was built in Georgian style in 1760 for Thomas Wentworth, brother of John Wentworth II, the last of the Royal Governors. Look for the windmill spit in the great fireplace in the kitchen and original Dutch tiles around the fireplaces.

The **Warner House** (corner of Daniel and Chapel streets) was built of brick in 1716. There are six mural paintings on the stairway and paneling in some of the rooms. The lightning rod on the west wall may have been installed under the watchful eye of Benjamin Franklin in 1762.

Portsmouth
Submarine
Memorial
Association
Albacore Park
Portsmouth
603-436-1331

If you've never been aboard a submarine before, you can have that chance in Portsmouth. The USS *Albacore*, built in the Portsmouth Naval Shipyard in 1952, was in active service from 1953 to 1972. She is 205 feet long, has a maximum speed of over 20 knots, and carried a crew of fifty men and five officers. Those who thought that she should be returned to her birthport had their work cut out for them during two years of planning and coping with mountains of paperwork. In April 1984 she was towed to Portsmouth, where preparations were made to bring her into drydock. It wasn't easy—a railroad bridge had to be taken apart, a dual highway cut through—and the project came to a standstill while she sat looking "like a beached whale." Finally, creative minds built a series of locks and the 1200-ton sub was floated onto her concrete cradle in Albacore Park. As you walk through, ask yourself if you would have felt claustrophobic while under the sea for long periods of time.

Hungry? There are lots of good restaurants in town. Our favorites: **Dolphin Striker** (15 Bow Street, 603-431-5222), **The Grill** (37 Bow Street, 603-431-6700), and **The Library** (401 State Street, 603-431-5202).

For your first taste of Down East, board the *Thomas Laighton* and cruise to the Isles of Shoals. The islands, which lie 8 miles out of Portsmouth Harbor, were discovered in 1614 by Captain John Smith. They were a prosperous fishing center until the Revolution, when most of the residents moved to the mainland.

Star Island still maintains a little stone chapel that's over 150 years old, and a graveyard that's supposedly hiding pirate treasure. Or is the treasure on **Appledore**? Rumor has it that Captain Kidd killed one of his men here so that he would haunt the spot where the treasure lies. And Old Bab's been seen, with white face and a ghostly light emanating from his body, wearing a red ring around his neck.

ISLES OF SHOALS

Thomas Laighton
Steamship
  Company
Market Street Dock
Portsmouth
603-431-5500

Captain Kidd

Oh! my name was Robert Kidd, as I sailed, as I sailed,
Oh! my name was Robert Kidd, as I sailed,
My name was Robert Kidd, God's laws I did forbid,
And most wickedly I did, as I sailed, as I sailed,
And most wickedly I did, as I sailed.

Oh! my parents taught me well, as I sailed, as I sailed,
Oh! my parents taught me well, as I sailed,
My parents taught me well, to shun the gates of hell,
But against them I rebelled, as I sailed, as I sailed,
But against them I rebelled, as I sailed.

I murdered William Moore, as I sailed, as I sailed,
I murdered William Moore, as I sailed.
I murdered William Moore and left him in his gore,
Not many leagues from shore, as I sailed, as I sailed,
Not many leagues from shore, as I sailed.

And being cruel still, as I sailed, as I sailed,
And being cruel still, as I sailed,
And being cruel still, my gunner I did kill,
And his precious blood did spill, as I sailed, as I sailed,
And his precious blood did spill, as I sailed. . . .

Take warning now by me, for I must die,
Take warning now by me, for I must die,
Take warning now by me, and shun bad company,
Lest you come to hell with me, for I must die, I must die.
Lest you come to hell with me, for I must die.

Old Bab may not be real, but the treasure was. In the early 1800s Captain Haley found silver bars on **Smuttynose Island** while he was digging a well. Haley, who owned a mill and a ropewalk, kept a lighted lamp in the window for ships at sea. In 1813 the *Sagunto* foundered off the island. Three survivors crawled toward his light in vain. They were buried on the island. (Look for the millstones near the mill.)

And Smuttynose saw more tragedy. In 1873 Louis Wagner rowed out to search for treasure and killed two of the three women living on the nearly deserted island. The survivor, Maren Hontvet, escaped to tell the horrible story. The well where Wagner tried to wash the blood from his hands is still here.

From Portsmouth you have a choice of traveling to southern or northern New Hampshire or heading into Maine. If you're going to southern New Hampshire take I-95 to the Exeter Hampton Expressway and Route 101 to Peterborough, or drive north on Route 4, the Spaulding Turnpike, and then Route 11 to Lake Winnipesaukee. The route to northern New Hampshire for Itinerary J from Portsmouth begins on Route 4, the Spaulding Turnpike, and then Route 16 north to Conway. To head into Maine take I-95 toward Kittery.

ITINERARY I: SOUTHERN NEW HAMPSHIRE

MT. MONADNOCK

ITINERARY I

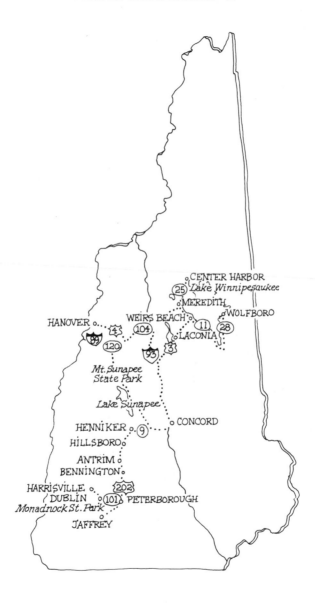

The Lake District and Southern New Hampshire

Apart from the brief coastal plain, so much of New Hampshire is mountainous that small agricultural communities tended to remain isolated and self-sufficient throughout the eighteenth and early nineteenth century. But during the second half of the nineteenth century industry swept into the state. Rivers provided power for mills, and cities like Manchester and Concord grew. Some of these mill towns still flourish; others have turned to different kinds of industries to survive.

As in neighboring Vermont, much of New Hampshire's development in recent years has been built on tourism. Southern New Hampshire is a pleasant vacation area with mountains, lakes, and forests to entice visitors.

This itinerary begins at Lake Winnipesaukee, then heads west either to Hanover for a visit to Dartmouth College, or southwest to Lake Sunapee for more relaxation. From Lake Sunapee you can head south to Hillsboro, Antrim, Hancock, Harrisville and Dublin, to Monadnock State Park for an invigorating hike up to the bald top. Jaffrey and Peterborough are also nearby.

LAKE WINNIPESAUKEE

Lake Winnipesaukee, New Hampshire's largest lake, was given an appropriate name meaning "the smile of the Great Spirit." Formed by glaciers, the lake is dotted with 274 islands and ringed by three mountain ranges.

Located at the southeastern end of the lake, **Wolfeboro** claims to be the oldest summer vacation resort in the country. In 1768 Governor John Wentworth came up from Massachusetts to build a summer home; it burned in 1820, but many more lovely homes have been built since. Stop for a meal at the **Wolfeboro Inn** (603-569-3016) on North Main Street.

On the western side of the lake, **Weirs Beach** offers good swimming, sailing, fishing, and waterskiing and a boardwalk. You can see the lake from a cruise ship such as the **MS *Mount Washington***, which leaves from Weirs Beach on three-hour cruises. Or you can choose to ride with the mail on the *Sophie C* as she makes her way around the lake.

MS *Mount Washington*
Winnipesaukee Flagship
Weirs Beach
603-366-4837

Meredith, located between Lakes Waukewan and a northwestern bay of Winnipesaukee, was in a perfect spot for industry with a waterway between the two lakes providing power for mills. John Jenness bought water rights and land in 1795, and then built a gristmill and a sawmill on the waterway. Later John Bond Swasey channeled the water under the Main Street horse path and over a 40-foot waterfall. He used the power from this source to saw lumber, grind flour, comb cotton flax, and weave cloth. Although fire and bad times took some of the mills, a few buildings remained. The **Mill Falls Marketplace** is housed in one of the old mill buildings, reconstructed and renovated. Stop for lunch at **Mame's** or the **Millworks** (603-279-7006) after shopping.

Center Harbor, at the northern end of the lake, is a resort community located between Lake Winnipesaukee and Squam Lake. If you loved *On Golden Pond* you can visit the actual setting for the film—Squam Lake. Settle yourself on the shore and listen for the mournful call of the loons.

From the Lake Winnipesaukee region take Route 104 west to Route 4 where you have a choice of several attractive destinations.

HANOVER

Route 4 north will take you to Hanover, the home of **Dartmouth College,** founded in 1769 by Reverend Eleazar Wheelock. His mission: to spread Christian education among the Indians. You can join a tour of the campus at the college information booth on the east side of the green during the summer. **Hopkins Center for the Arts** offers concerts, an art gallery, and a theater. The **Baker Memorial Library** contains frescoes by Jose Clemente Orozco. Don't miss **Dartmouth Row**, a series of four classroom buildings dating from 1784. Stop for a meal in the **Hanover Inn** (603-643-4300), which is right on campus.

LAKE SUNAPEE

Route 4 south to Route 11 leads to Lake Sunapee, which has been a favorite vacation area

**Mount Sunapee
State Park
Sunapee
603-763-2356**

since the mid-nineteenth century. You can take a cruise on the lake on one of the tour boats or ride up the mountain in a gondola at **Mount Sunapee State Park** for a lovely view of the lake as a whole.

If you're an aficionado of covered bridges you will be delighted to know that there are eighteen in the Dartmouth–Lake Sunapee Region. Their locations are shown on New Hampshire tourist maps with a little red symbol of a covered bridge. Look for them near the towns of Langdon, Cornish, Plainfield, Enfield, Lyme, Orford, Andover, Webster, Warner, Bradford, and Newport. Look at the variations in truss work on these bridges, ranging from lattice to multiple kingpost designs. We especially like the name of one, "Blow Me Down," which is near Blow-Me-Down Hill.

HENNIKER/ HILLSBORO

**Franklin Pierce
Homestead
Routes 9 and 31
Hillsboro
603-495-3678**

From Lake Sunapee, Routes 103 and 114 will take you to Henniker, home of New England College, and Route 9 to Hillsboro. The **Franklin Pierce Homestead** was built in 1804 by Benjamin Pierce, a general in the American Revolution and two-time governor of New Hampshire. His son, Franklin Pierce, was the fourteenth President of the United States from 1853–1857. This white colonial center chimney home has green shutters and is maintained by the Hillsboro Historical Society.

ANTRIM/ BENNINGTON

**Crotched Mountain
Ski Area
Francestown
603-588-6345**

Continue on Routes 9 and 31 south through rolling hills past Franklin Pierce Lake to Antrim. The town was origianlly settled by Scots who had landed in Ireland in the seventeenth century and then crossed the Atlantic in the early eighteenth century. Routes 31 and 202 continue to Bennington where you can take a side trip to **Crotched Mountain Ski Area.** Or continue on Route 31 to **Greenfield State Park,** a fine place

Squam Lake in the New Hampshire hills gives scenic views to canoeists and backpackers alike.

SQUAM LAKE

Hanover's Dartmouth College was founded in 1769 by Reverend Eleazar Wheelock, who hoped to spread Christian education among the Indians.

HANOVER

All of New Hampshire's lakes provide aquatic recreation for their summer visitors.

SOUTHWESTERN NEW HAMPSHIRE

for picnicking, boating, and swimming. It is located off Route 136.

If you're ready for a gourmet meal, stop in **Petite Maison** in Bennington Square (603-588-3000). The house itself dates from 1788 and its pineapple-stenciled walls, wideboard floors, and print curtains offer welcome to hungry travelers. The menu is reminiscent of "city" menus without city prices—a culinary jewel of a find in these lovely hills.

HANCOCK

Harris Center for Conservation Education King's Highway Hancock 603-525-4073

From Bennington take Route 137 into Hancock, which has an exceptionally attractive Main Street with large homes dating from 1781. The bell in the Town Meeting House was cast by Paul Revere and his son. Look for the **Harris Center for Conservation Education**, which was created to introduce people to the forests, lakes, meadows, monadnocks (hills and mountains of hard rock that resist erosion), and wildlife of the area. The center offers programs to schools and the public; if you're around on Halloween you might learn to carve "mangle-wurzles," the ancient Celtic predecessors of Jack O'Lanterns!

DUBLIN

Continue south on Route 137 to Bonds Corner, then turn right on Route 101 and head for Dublin, a beautiful New England town untouched by industry. Scotch-Irish settlers had arrived by 1753, but the town was not incorporated until 1771. Mark Twain spent time in the summer here, finding it a peaceful place for writing.

Take a side trip to **Harrisville** by turning north on the road near *Yankee Magazine* headquarters called New Harrisville Road. Harrisville is one of the most perfectly preserved New England mill villages to be found anywhere. Brick buildings are grouped along the pond and the river. Look for the series of gates letting water cascade down the millrace all through the town.

Hikers, we're coming to you. From Dublin head south on a road marked for **Monadnock State Park**. The first area you will come to is the Gilson Pond Area, but continue on to the main gate where you can get trail maps. There are many trails up to the top. For a three- or four-hour hike up a reasonably steep trail, take White Dot or White Cross. For an easier five- to seven-hour climb, try Cascade to Pumpelly, which is twice the distance but more gradual. The bald area on the top is a wonderful place to look at the view while you have your picnic lunch. You can also enjoy the network of cross-country ski trails, which are marked according to difficulty for winter use.

From Monadnock continue down into Jaffrey Center, with its lovely large white buildings including a 1775 Meeting House, which was raised on the day of the Battle of Bunker Hill.

From Jaffrey continue east on Route 124 toward New Ipswich, and turn right on Prescott Road just before the Millpore factory. You will come to **Cathedral of the Pines,** which is an outdoor shrine dedicated to the memory of the son of Dr. and Mrs. Douglas Sloane. A bell tower contains carillonic chimes and two large Sheffield bells. The Altar of the Nation has a stone from each of our United States, to honor all of America's war dead. Services are conducted for those of all faiths; there are outdoor chapels and flower gardens to visit. Imagine attending a service under the whispering pines, sitting on benches over a pine-needle floor, and looking out over the hillside and into space beyond.

For a side trip to see the home of Edward MacDowell, take Route 119 west, and north on Route 202, which will bring you to Peterborough, now the home of the MacDowell Colony. Writers, painters, sculptors, composers, and filmmakers come as resident artists to create their

JAFFREY CENTER

Monadnock State Park
Jaffrey Center
603-532-8862

Cathedral of the Pines
Prescott Road
Rindge
603-899-3300

PETERBOROUGH

works, undisturbed by anyone. You can visit MacDowell's grave, the library, and Colony Hall; and you might see someone who has been working hard all day out stretching legs or attending the theater.

Peterborough Players (603-924-7585) offer theater on Middle Hancock Road at the Stearns Farm.

Your itinerary through this section of New Hampshire is complete. If you're heading for northern New Hampshire from Peterborough, take Route 202 to I-89 east to I-93 north to Route 3 north (taking you to Meredith) to Route 25 and Route 16 into Conway. For a tour along the coast head east from Peterborough on Route 101, take the Exeter Hampton Expressway to I-95 and head for the beaches or Portsmouth.

ITINERARY J: THE WHITE MOUNTAINS

MOUNT WASHINGTON

ITINERARY J

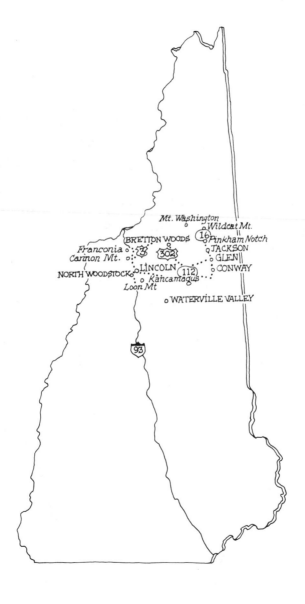

The White Mountains of New Hampshire

New Hampshire's White Mountains are rugged and irregular. Once much taller, these mountains have been ravaged by periods of folding, faulting, and terrific pressure from molten rock within them. What this has done is create a landscape cut by ravines and embellished with unusual contours.

You can make a circuit of the White Mountains, stopping to ski or hike on various peaks. A good place to begin is Conway, where you can head west on the Kancamagus Highway to Loon Mountain. Waterville Valley lies to the south and Franconia Notch to the north. From the natural wonders of the Franconia area, head east to the Mount Washington valley. There you will have access to some of the best hiking in the East on the network of trails through the Presidential Range, good skiing at Wildcat Mountain, and the bowl at Tuckerman's Ravine for hikers and die-hard skiers.

CONWAY

From Conway, head west on Route 112, known as the **Kancamagus Highway**, one of the most scenic drives in the state. You won't be bored as you round each hairpin turn of this 34-mile drive. There are gorges, falls, and overlooks with superb mountain views all along this wilderness highway.

Kancamagus, the "fearless one," was the grandson of Passaconaway and became chief in 1684. Although he tried to encourage harmony between the Indians and the white men, war broke out and his tribe moved away. Chocorua was another brave Indian, probably a chief of the Ossipee tribe, who lived in the area about 1760. Legends suggest that he died on the summit of Mount Chocorua, south of the Kancamagus Highway.

Sabbaday Falls, a five-minute walk each way, shouldn't be missed. It is a series of falls tumbling over ledges, into potholes, and finally through a flume. The **Passaconaway Information Center** (on Route 112 at the foot of Bear Notch Road) offers information, craft demonstrations, and hiking trails.

Just before the end of the Kancamagus Highway you will come to **Loon Mountain** (603-745-8111), where you can ride a four-person gondola up 7000 feet to see the view from the top. Climb up even higher to the observation tower for a panorama of the White Mountains.

For skiers, the vertical drop at Loon Mountain is 2,100 feet and the main exposure is north and northeast. Lifts include the gondola, two triple chairlifts, and five double chairlifts. During the winter Loon follows the policy of limiting the sale of lift tickets to keep lines to a minimum.

Beginning skiers will want to start out on the easiest trails, marked with green circles on the map. Experts will probably prefer the North Peak and East Basin chairlifts. That leaves a lot in the middle for intermediate skiers to sort out. We suggest taking the gondola to the top for an easy run down Upper Bear Claw and Lower Bear Claw. For a second run try Exodus to Upper Picked Rock and Lower Flying Fox, the latter a nice wide cruiser. For something slightly harder but still intermediate we suggest Upper Flying Fox and Seven Brothers. The West basin area has steeper trails, but Rampasture is a pleasant run. Advanced intermediates would enjoy Walking Boss (the upper part has moguls but is not cluttered with them, and the lower part is intermediate). If you want to ski only intermediate trails, from North Peak take Sunset, double back on Haul Back, then rejoin Lower Walking Boss. Those who love moguls and steep slopes will enjoy Flume and all of the trails from the East Basin chair.

Stop for a meal in **The Bear Trap** in The Mountain Club right on the slope (603-745-6222) or even plunge into the pool in the new Health Club. Or drive into town and wander through the shops and restaurants in the **Millfront Mar-**

ketplace. Nearby, in North Woodstock, the **Woodstock Inn** (603-745-3951) is open for all meals. One of their rooms is housed in the Woodstock Station, which was moved from the tracks and placed adjacent to the inn.

KINSMAN NOTCH

Lost River Reservation Route 112 Kinsman Notch 603-745-8031

For an interesting side trip, continue on Route 112 about 6 miles west of North Woodstock to Kinsman Notch and the **Lost River Reservation**. Lost River flows through a glacial gorge that is narrow, steep, and strangely shaped. Years ago boulders broke off and slid down into the gorge to form caverns. The **Giant Pothole** is a pear-shaped bowl, 28 feet across, worn smooth by swirling water. **Paradise Falls** was formed as the river flowed over two dikes and into a basin at the bottom. Also here: a natural history museum, an ecology trail, and a garden.

WATERVILLE VALLEY

Skiers will enjoy another side trip south of Lincoln to Waterville Valley (603-236-8311). This year-round resort offers skiing in the winter and tennis, riding, golf, and swimming in the summer. It is located in a bowl surrounded by 4,000-foot mountains. In the winter there is a special appeal for the "I Don't Ski" population— a spa program as well as the complete facilities of the new Indoor Sports Center.

The vertical drop is 2,020 feet on Mount Tecumseh, serviced by three triple chairlifts, five double chairlifts, and three surface lifts. Snow's Mountain offers a double chairlift and three trails, all rated "more difficult." Waterville Valley limits admission on busy weekends to keep you from being overwhelmed by long lift lines.

Beginning skiers will want to start on the Lower Meadows chairlift, which services two wide slopes. Experts will enjoy Gema, which does not have as many moguls as True Grit. Sel's Choice and the World Cup Slalom Hill offer challenge on the east side. The intermediate skier will find Valley Run pleasant; Stillness is on the same slope and more interesting but without snowmaking facilities at this writing. White Cap leading to Old Tecumseh is nice; the only way down from there is Sel's Choice, which is marked advanced but is not that difficult. Tippecanoe leads into Siegel Street and then to Old Tecumseh, providing another pleasant intermediate run.

One hundred kilometers of cross-country trails are also available, including a challenging 6-kilometer race training course.

Stop for lunch in the **World Cup Bar and Grill** where each menu item sports a name you will recognize from World Cup locations. Or try **O'Keefe's** (603-236-8331) for a special dinner out.

FRANCONIA

Franconia Notch State Park
Route 3
Franconia
603-823-5563

From Lincoln pick up Route 3 north, which takes you right into **Franconia Notch State Park**, a lovely area surrounded by the White Mountains National Forest. Come to swim, to hike, to ski, to camp—or simply to enjoy the extraordinary natural beauty of the place.

Part of that natural beauty is the **Flume**. This narrow gorge has walls of granite rising 70 to 90 feet. The boardwalk along the 800-foot length of the gorge is lined with descriptions of its geological development and leads to the 40-foot **Avalanche Falls**.

Beyond Whitehouse Bridge you come to the **Basin**, a granite glacial pothole 20 feet in diameter, which sits at the base of a waterfall.

The information booth at Lafayette Place is the best place to stop for hiking information. Appalachian Mountain Club staff members are on hand to help you plan your own trail route.

A few miles north of the Flume, on the west side of Route 3, you'll find **Profile Lake**. Look up to see **Old Man of the Mountains** (he's sometimes called Great Stone Face) rising above the gorge. Plaques at the lake tell how the 40-foot-high profile was formed thousands of years ago.

Right beyond the park, you'll find the **Cannon Mountain Aerial Tramway**. Ride up to the top, where gaps and notches give you a view right into the heart of the White Mountains.

**Cannon Mountain
Echo Lake Road
Franconia
603-823-5563 or
603-823-7751**

If you're there in the winter try skiing **Cannon Mountain,** advertised as "the mountain that'll burn your boots off!" Experts will head off the top of the mountain on Taft Slalom, Skylight, or Upper Hardscrabble. Beginners will enjoy the ski school slope and Toss-up or Gremlin on the lower mountain.

Intermediates may want to warm up by taking the double chairlift that serves the lower mountain, skiing Lower Cannon leading into Toss-Up. Or take the longer double chairlift on the right and ski Lower Ravine leading into Gremlin. Turnpike and Red Ball are nice but use the "C" double chairlift and cut across, as it is steep heading out from "D" in that direction. If you take the tramway to the top, try Tramway or Upper Cannon, avoiding the steeper By Pass, and feed into Lower Cannon or Lower Ravine. To get back to the tramway take Lower Cannon and turn off to the right on Gary's, then follow signs to the tram station. Some intermediate trails have rather narrow expert sections on the upper mountain—so don't feel bad about sidestepping down those sections.

**Franconia Inn
Cross-Country
Ski Center
Route 116
Franconia
603-823-5542**

If you're a cross-country skier, try the Franconia Notch State Park Trail System. Begin from the parking lot at Echo Lake on Route 18 and enjoy over five miles of trails along old logging roads and old Route 3. Also, try the system of **Franconia Inn Cross-Country Ski Center.**

**New England Ski
Museum
Franconia Notch
603-823-7177**

While you're at Cannon be sure to stop in the **New England Ski Museum,** which is located right next to the tramway base. There are nineteenth-century handcrafted wood skis, a variety of old-time bindings, a collection of ski clothes from the past, lots of photographs, films, and audio-visual exhibits.

Robert Frost spent summers and vacations from 1915 to 1920 in Franconia, a few miles north of the park. His home—**Robert Frost Place**—has been restored, and mementos and photographs depict the poet's life here. The house is now an arts center, where a summer program of readings and lectures is conducted by a visiting poet in residence. To get there, take Route 116 (exit 38) off I-93 to Bickford Hill Road; turn right over the ridge, then left onto Ridge Road.

Robert Frost Place
Ridge Road
Franconia
603-823-5510 or
603-823-8038

Routes 3 and 302 will take you east to the Mount Washington area; which is also known as the Presidential Range because most of the important peaks are named after presidents.

MOUNT WASHINGTON VALLEY

Facing Mount Washington on Route 302 is **Bretton Woods**, which was the site of the United Nations Monetary and Financial Conference in 1944. Representatives of forty-four nations met here at that conference. The foundations of the International Monetary Fund and World Bank were developed at the conference, as well as the gold standard. This conference set the pattern for the worldwide financial interdependence after World War II.

Bretton Woods Ski Area
Route 302
Bretton Woods
603-278-5000

Today, Bretton Woods is one of the very best ski areas for novices and intermediates anywhere. No trails are too difficult, and the area gets twice as much snow as other ski areas in the vicinity. The area was built in 1972, the base lodge is attractive, and the slopes are lined with pines to look through as the snowflakes fall. A few more expert runs have been created to broaden the appeal of the resort. Across the road you can't miss the Mount Washington Valley Hotel, not yet open in the winter. However, there is a cross-country trail system at the hotel. Call **Bretton Woods Ski Touring Center** (603-278-5181).

**Mount Washington
Cog Railway
Route 302
Bretton Woods
603-846-2256**

Nearby, the **Mount Washington Cog Railway** has its base station at Marshfield. You can leave the driving to them and have fun chugging up and down the mountain for an hour and a half each way in a railway dating from 1869. The passenger cars are pushed up hill by a locomotive for 3½ miles. If you go, watch for the very steep section known as Jacob's Ladder, where the grade is 37.4 percent; usually the grade is only 25 percent!

Mount Washington, at 6,288 feet, is the highest mountain in New England. It is also one of the coldest places in the United States, with much higher winds and lower temperatures than the surrounding region. It has what is considered an arctic climate, and the winds once reached 231 miles per hour in April 1934. Any flora and fauna that can exist up there are seen nowhere else but in arctic regions.

At the top you will see radio and TV towers and the **Sherman Adams Summit Building**. If the weather is behaving the rooftop deck provides nice views up to 50 miles in all directions. The Mount Washington Weather Observatory is perched up there too, recording the most extreme weather conditions in the East and studying various problems of arctic survival and aeronautics.

BARTLETT

Continue south on Route 302. Just after passing through Bartlett you'll come to the **Attitash Alpine Slide and Ski Area** (603-374-2369). The alpine slide dives downward for three-quarters of a mile, and the two waterslides add to the fun.

JACKSON

Continue south on Route 302, curving around to meet Route 16 heading north to Jackson. There's a lovely covered bridge to go through leading into this pretty New England village. Right in the center you will see cross-country trails branching out across the golf

MOUNT WASHINGTON

Mount Washington, one of the Eastern Seabord's highest peaks, commands a spectacular view from its watch tower.

FRANCONIA

Franconia Notch State Park's Rim Trail provides a prime opportunity for hikers to tour the scenic park.

FRANCONIA

For those not afraid of heights, the Aerial Tram at Franconia Notch State Park gives sightseers a bird's-eye view of this unspoiled region.

course during the winter. The **Jackson Ski Touring Foundation** (603-383-9355) also maintains an extensive network of more demanding cross-country trails in mountainous terrain. Downhill skiers also have a choice of three areas nearby—Black Mountain above Jackson, Attitash, and Mount Cranmore.

PINKHAM NOTCH

Wildcat Mountain Ski Area
Route 16
Jackson
603-466-3326

From Jackson continue north on Route 16 through Pinkham Notch to the **Mount Washington Auto Road**. If your car can take eight miles of mountain driving with a lot of braking on the way down, check it for gas, and off you go. You can also ride up in a van, leaving your mind free to enjoy the views.

In the winter, **Wildcat Mountain Ski Area** is there as well, with a 2,100 vertical drop to please skiers, and a gondola to provide some shelter from Mount Washington winds. Beginners will enjoy the Snowcat Novice Area, which has its own triple chairlift as well as the long winding Polecat from the top. Expert skiers are off on their own runs, so you won't have to keep looking over your shoulder. Intermediates will enjoy most of the trails on the lower mountain and the upper sections of Catapult and Wildcat (but be sure to get off before the expert sections start!)

Tuckerman's Ravine at Pinkham Notch is the scene of a spring ritual for slightly crazy skiers and their only-a-bit-more-sane camp followers. The skiers carry skis and poles up the steep trail to the base of the ravine; the followers bring cameras, lunch, and the yen to watch. And what a show! A few skiers making it down the very steep bowl with style, the rest tumbling down the hill—all to the cheers and boos of the crowd.

At Pinkham Notch you'll see people doing just that—getting ready to climb one of the ravines on the east face of the mountain. Of course hiking is the best way to discover the beauty of the Presidential Range. The whole of the White

Mountain National Forest is interlaced with well-marked hiking trails, lean-tos, and huts where you can get a bunk or a meal or both (reservations are a must in season). This network allows you to travel light even on an extended hiking trip. For information, guidebooks, and maps before you go, write to the chamber of commerce or the **Appalachian Mountain Club**. The AMC also has a store in the camp at Pinkham Notch.

Whether you're hiking or driving or riding the rails to the top, dress warmly. Mount Washington records the highest wind velocities in the country, often well over a 100 miles an hour during the winter. And the weather on top is changeable. The average temperature at any time of the year is below 30 degrees, and there's snow every month of the year. Always carry sweaters and jackets.

NORTH CONWAY

To complete your White Mountain circuit, drive back south a few miles beyond Jackson to pick up Route 302 south to North Conway, a busy place all year round.

The **Conway Scenic Railroad** leaves from the century-old restored train station in town for an hour trip on an 11-mile track. There's also a railroad museum and a roundhouse on the grounds.

Just east of town, the **Mount Cranmore Skimobile** has been operating since 1938. Watch for hang gliders preparing for takeoff at the top.

To the west of town you'll find **Echo Lake State Park**. (Follow the signs from the railroad station.) Come for a swim and a picnic, and two dramatic rock formations—**White Horse Ledge** and **Cathedral Ledge**. You can drive to the top (some 700 feet) for a beautiful view of the valley.

Drive south on Route 302 to Route 16 to Conway, where you began this itinerary. You are not very far from Maine's Sebago Lake, the beginning of Itinerary L.

PEMAQUID POINT

ITINERARY K

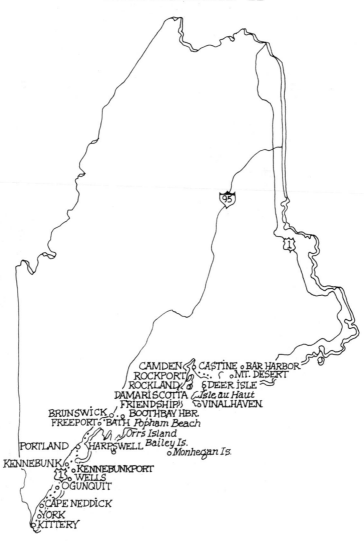

CAMDEN CASTINE ○ BAR HARBOR
ROCKPORT ○ MT. DESERT
ROCKLAND ○ DEER ISLE
DAMARISCOTTA *Isle au Haut*
FRIENDSHIP ○ VINALHAVEN
BRUNSWICK ○ BOOTHBAY HBR.
FREEPORT ○ BATH *Popham Beach*
Orrs Island
PORTLAND ○ HARPSWELL *Bailey Is.*
○ *Monhegan Is.*
KENNEBUNK ○ KENNEBUNKPORT
WELLS
○ OGUNQUIT
CAPE NEDDICK
YORK
KITTERY

Down East Along the Coast of Maine

Maine: waves crashing on rocky shores, crisp mornings licked by wisps of fog, huge jumbled rock formations. The bedrock of the state was formed during the Precambrian era, which produced weathered formations from sandstone and limestone; other sections with rich beds of fossils date from the Paleozoic era. During the Ice Age the weight of the icecap caused the land to sink below sea level. Water flooded into long valleys, creating fjords and coves, and leaving clay as much as 75 miles away from the modern shoreline. Some clay deposits, exposed by running streams and excavations, are now 500 feet above sea level. As the glacier dissolved, mountains that were near the shore became islands, and those that were farther inland became headlands jutting into the sea, creating a drowned coastline that's one of the most fascinating anywhere in the world.

The first inhabitants of Maine were roving hunters, Indian descendants of Asian immigrants who crossed the land bridge when the Bering Strait was dry. Their graves, found in more than fifty tribal cemeteries, contain red ochre (powdered hematite), which gave them the name Red Paint People. Heavy stone tools were found in the same graves. Later Indians called themselves Wabanackis, which means "easterners" or "dawnlanders"; their language was that of the Algonquian tribes. Today there are two tribes left: the Passamaquoddies and the Penobscots.

The first Europeans to arrive in Maine were probably the Vikings, who had occupied islands and coastal towns in the North Sea from the late eighth to the late twelfth century, then pushed west to colonize first Iceland and Greenland, then Newfoundland and Nova Scotia. Leif Erikson sailed to Newfoundland in 1003, and continued past Maine to Cape Cod. Several years later his brother Thorvald landed in Maine, probably at Somes Sound, a fjord cutting into Mount Desert Island, where he was killed by Indians.

In 1496 John Cabot and his sons Lewis, Sebastian, and Sancius received permission from King Henry VII of England to look for and occupy new lands. Between 1497 and 1499 they made a number of voyages along the Maine coast—voyages that formed the basis of England's claim to Maine and other parts of North America. In 1524 Giovanni da Verrazano, an Italian explorer serving under the French flag, also reached Maine, but he did nothing to establish a settlement. And a year later, Esteban Gomez, a Spanish explorer, left too when he did not find the gold he was looking for. Not until the seventeenth century did the European explorers realize the treasure that was here in fish, fur, and timber.

In 1614 Captain John Smith arrived in Maine and named the coastline from Nova Scotia to Cape Cod, New England. The origin of the state's name isn't clear: Some believe the name was a tribute to Queen Henrietta Marie, because she ruled the French provinces of Meyne or Maine; others believe the name was derived from "mainland." But to sailors none of it mattered. Maine was always Down East. Why? Because you could only get here from other parts of New England by running downwind.

Away Down East

There's a famous fabled country never seen by
    mortal eyes,
Where the punkins are a-grow-in', and the sun is
    said to rise,
Which man doth not inhabit, neither reptile, bird,
    nor beast.
But one thing we're assured of, it's AWAY DOWN EAST!

It is called a land of notions, of applesauce
    and green,
A paradise of punkin pies, a land of pork and
    beans.
But where it is who knoweth? Neither mortal, man,
    nor beast.
But one thing we're assured of, it's AWAY DOWN EAST!

Once a man in Indiana took his bundle in his hand,
And he went to New York City for to find this
    famous land.
But how he stares on learning this curious
    fact at least:
He'd nowhere near begun to get AWAY DOWN EAST!

So he traveled on to Bangor, whereby he soiled
    his drabs,
And the first that greets his vision is a pyra-
    mid of slabs.
Oh, sure this must be Egypt, 'tis a pyramid, at
    least.
And he thought that with a vengeance, he had
    found DOWN EAST.

This itinerary will take visitors "down east" along the coast of Maine. The southwesterly section of this shore begins at Kittery with salt marshes and beaches. Many years ago, saltwater farms provided marsh grass for thatch and fodder. The second section, northeast of Portland, resembles Norwegian fjords with a network of fingers of the sea stretching inland.

KITTERY

Kittery, incorporated in 1647, is the state's oldest town and has long depended on shipbuilding for its major industry. The *Ranger*, which sailed to France under the command of John Paul Jones to announce Burgoyne's surrender, was built here. The John Paul Jones Marker is located at the end of the park on Route 1 at the intersection of Government Street.

Kittery Historical and Naval Museum
Routes 1 and 26
Kittery
207-439-3080

Kittery Historical and Naval Museum features a 13-foot model of the *Ranger*, as well as other models of eighteenth-, nineteenth-, and twentieth-century naval vessels. Exhibits portray the life of those who lived on the Piscataqua River and the story of the development of shipbuilding in Kittery.

Drive along the coastal road toward Kittery Point past several homes dating back to 1690 (not open to the public): the Fernald House on Williams Avenue, the Whipple Garrison House on Whipple Road and Willowbank, and the home of the artist John P. Benson, also on Whipple Road. Look to the right to see the Naval Shipyard located on two islands in the Piscataqua River. Although the shipyard is not open, exhibits may be seen at Kittery Museum.

Kittery Point is the oldest part of town. The **Lady Pepperell House** on Pepperell Road, a striking white Georgian mansion, is a private residence. There is an interesting graveyard beyond the house overlooking the harbor. Look there for Browning's epitaph for the husband of poet Celia Thaxter that is carved on an irregular stone.

The grave of unknown sailors who died when the
Hattie Eaton ran aground on Garrish Island is
also there. Many ships foundered along the
treacherous coastline between Kittery Point,
Boon Island, and Cape Neddick. Read *Boon Island* by Kenneth Roberts to set your spine tin-
gling. Names on other old stones are still well
known in the area.

Farther up the road you come to **Fort Mc-
Clary Memorial Park**. The fort—all that remains
is the hexagonal blockhouse—dates back to
1809. Sit back and enjoy the view of the outer
harbor: hundreds of sailboats bobbing on moorings, fishing boats going in and out, and a maze
of lobster pots everywhere.

Fort Foster sits as a sentinel for Portsmouth
Harbor. Built in 1872, the bunkers now lie idle
among the ducks and other shore birds who pass
through. The park contains picnic facilities,
beaches, and a fishing pier. There are two
beaches there: one 200 feet long and one 400 feet
long. Both are clean and sandy and sprinkled
with rocks. **Sea Point Beach**, off Route 103 on
Cutts Island Road, is also sandy with some
rocks.

York, north of Kittery on Route 1A, is part
of a national historic district. Many of the seven-
teenth- and eighteenth-century homes in the village are open. Turn off Route 1 at Lindsay Road,
and park your car in the lot. Then walk through
the **Old Burying Ground**. Mary Nason's grave is
covered with a giant stone slab. Legend says she
was a witch, and the slab was put there to keep
her soul in the grave. The truth is almost as
good: It seems her heartbroken husband, a
wealthy man, placed the stone there to keep the
village pigs from grazing on her grave.

At the other end of the graveyard you come
to the **Emerson-Wilcox House**, where you can
buy a combination ticket for all the sites in the

**Fort McClary
  Memorial Park
Route 103
Kittery**

**Fort Foster
Garrish Island
Kittery**

YORK

**Emerson-Wilcox
  House
Lindsay Street
York
207-363-4974**

Old Gaol Museum
Lindsay Road
York

First Parish
  Congregational
  Church
York Street
York
207-363-3758

Jefferds' Tavern
Lindsay Road
York

village. The house was built in 1740 on church land, then leased for 999 years. It was once a tailor shop, tavern, and general store, and then a post office. Today its rooms are furnished in a series of different period styles. One of them boasts a local treasure: the Mary Bulman bed hangings, the only complete set of eighteenth-century American crewelwork hangings in the country.

Across the street you'll find the **Old Gaol Museum**. It was a king's prison from 1719 through the Revolution, and continued to be used as a jail until 1860. You can walk through the jailer's quarters, the cells, and the dungeon—a special treat for children.

From the Old Gaol cross York Street (Route 1) to the **First Parish Congregational Church**, on the green. The Reverend Samuel Moody laid the cornerstone in 1747. The Reverend Joseph Moody, his son, was the subject of one of Hawthorne's short stories, "The Minister's Black Veil." Moody accidentally killed a friend while they were out hunting. He felt so guilty he wore a handkerchief over his face for the rest of his life.

Head back across York Street to the other end of Lindsay Road, near the parking lot. Here you'll find the **Old Schoolhouse**, which was built in 1745, and **Jefferds' Tavern**. The tavern was built in 1750 in Wells, where it was a neighborhood pub and a stagecoach stop. It was moved here in the 1940s and restored. Come inside and look for the mural of the village.

From here you can drive or walk (it's about a mile) down Lindsay Road to the river. The **John Hancock Warehouse** (Hancock was one of the owners) houses an exhibit about life and industry on the York River. The eighteenth-century commercial building—the only surviving one in the area—is set up as a period warehouse. Outside you can enjoy a picnic lunch by the water.

The **Elizabeth Perkins House** sits beside the river at Sewall's Bridge. Perkins, who died in the 1950s, and her mother were largely responsible for the preservation work in the village. The eighteenth-century colonial house, once the Perkins's summer home, is filled with their marvelous collection of furnishings from all over the world.

Elizabeth Perkins House
South Side Road
York

York Harbor's waterfront is bustling. Don't miss **Cliff Walk**, which begins along the boardwalk at the ocean end of Harbor Beach Road, and ends on a rocky beach near Cow Beach Point. Along the way: wonderful views of the coastline (look for Nubble Light to the north) and lovely homes, and the sounds of waves crashing over the rocks.

YORK HARBOR

Follow Route 1A to Nubble Road, to the tip of Cape Neddick. Next to **Nubble Light** is the six-bedroom Victorian lightkeeper's house. Captain Bartholomew Gosnold landed here in 1602, and named the point Savage Rock because of an encounter he had with the Indians on shore. The lighthouse was built in 1879 after the rock had claimed several wrecks.

CAPE NEDDICK

From the point you can see **Boon Island Lighthouse**, 6¹/₂ miles southeast of the cape. Celia Thaxter describes the lonely life of the lightkeeper and his family in *The Watch of Boon Island*.

Continue on Route 1A up the coast to Ogunquit. The 2¹/₂-mile-long beach here is one of the finest in New England—but the water is cold! **Marginal Way**, a path along the ocean, begins at Spar Hawk Motel and ends at Shore Road in **Perkins Cove**. The cove is filled with artists and craftsmen, lobstermen and fishing boats, and lots of good restaurants. Look for the double-leaf draw-footbridge, the only one in

OGUNQUIT

Maine, which is raised for every boat that sounds a horn.

If you're a fan of lobster stop for a meal at **Barnacle Billy's** in Perkins Cove (207-646-5575), where the menu hasn't changed for twenty-six years. The $3^1/2$-ounce lobster roll is just as delicious now as it was then. You can sit outdoors on the sundeck or inside if you wish. Don't be put off by the valet parking—it's necessary to squeeze in as many cars as possible.

The **Ogunquit Playhouse** (Route 1, 207-646-5511) has been delighting people since the 1930s. The playhouse offers well-known musicals and plays.

WELLS

Wells Auto Museum
Route 1
Wells
207-646-9064

Rachel Carson National Wildlife Refuge
Route 9
Wells
207-646-9226

Wells National Estuarine Research Reserve
Route 9
Wells
207-646-4521

KENNEBUNK

Brick Store Museum
117 Main Street
Kennebunk
207-985-4802

Wells is about 5 miles north of Ogunquit, on Route 1. The **Wells Auto Museum** is fun for the whole family. You'll find collections of cars, bicycles, motorcycles, even license plates, and nickelodeons. And you can take a ride in an antique car.

The **Rachel Carson National Wildlife Refuge** is a lovely spot to commune with nature. The white-pine forest stands next to a salt marsh where you can spot herons, kingfishers, and egrets. Trails lead through the woods and into the marsh on a circular route. You can walk part of the way on a boardwalk over the marsh.

Adjacent to the refuge is a new nature center called **The Wells National Estuarine Research Reserve** with headquarters at Laudholm Farm, a well-preserved nineteenth-century saltwater farm. An estuarine environment offers special plants, fish, and wildlife for study. It will be a natural field laboratory for research and education as well as a place for people to enjoy.

Continue up the coast along Route 1 to Kennebunk. Main Street boasts an interesting church and the **Brick Store Museum**, where you'll find a collection of early American pewter, maritime exhibits, old wedding gowns, and antique fire engines. Ask for a map of the other historic homes in town (most aren't open to the public). There's a legend about one of them—the **Wedding Cake House**. The sea captain who built the house created the elaborate trimming for his disappointed bride; they had married so quickly, there wasn't time to bake a wedding cake.

Wedding Cake House
Landing Road
Kennebunk

In Kennebunkport you'll find the oldest commercial building in the area. It began as Perkins' West India Goods, then became a boardinghouse, a post office, a harness shop, a fish market, an artist's studio, and finally a book shop called **Book Port** (207-967-3815). It's in **Dock Square**, a good spot for watching the Kennebunkport world go by.

KENNEBUNKPORT

The **Kennebunkport Historical Society** has exotic treasures brought back by sea captains, exhibits about local shipwrecks, and other memorabilia. Many of the towns along the New England coast had their own ropewalks—long platforms with a spindled wheel at either end. The ropemakers would walk between the wheels, spinning flax as they went. Thomas Goodwin built a ropewalk on Ocean Avenue, Kennebunkport, in 1806. (It's now a yacht club.) The platform here was 600 feet long. Because each wheel had six spindles, six men would have worked spinning flax here.

Kennebunkport
Historical Society
North Street
Kennebunkport
207-967-2751

Stop at the **Seashore Trolley Museum** for a ride on an old-fashioned trolley. Also here: a slide show, exhibits from horsecars to streamliners, and craftsmen at work restoring the collection.

Seashore Trolley
Museum
Log Cabin Road
Kennebunkport
207-967-2712

Don't leave town without stopping for lunch or supper at one of the many restaurants. Our favorites: the **Old Grist Mill** (207-967-4781), built in 1749, on Mill Lane; the **Breakwater** (207-967-3118) on Ocean Avenue; the **White Barn Inn**

(207-967-2321) on Beach Street; and **Arundel Wharf** (207-967-3444) on the waterfront.

PORTLAND

Portland Convention and Visitor's Bureau
142 Free Street
Portland
207-772-4994

From Kennebunkport take Route 9A to I-95, to Portland. Stop at the Convention and Visitor's Bureau for information about the **Portland History Trail** and a free bus tour of the historic area.

Then head for the waterfront and the **Old Port Exchange**. The area, devastated by the Great Fire of 1866, was rebuilt in the 1960s. It's filled with shops, restaurants, pubs, and recreational facilities. Along the wharves you'll see fish-processing plants and warehouses. And the harbor is busy with ferries and boats heading out to Nova Scotia and Casco Bay. You can wander around endlessly, watching the waterfront activity and savoring that Maine smell.

Every morning at eleven a red double-decker bus sets off from the Old Port Exchange for a three-hour tour of Portland's historic area. It's fun and it's free! Call or stop at the Convention and Visitor's Bureau for more information.

There are two good restaurants nearby: the **Inn at Park Spring** (207-774-1059) at 135 Spring Street, and **F. Parker Reidy's** (207-773-4731) on Exchange Street. Or bring a picnic and enjoy the fine view over the bay on **Eastern Promenade**, a good spot for watching Fourth of July fireworks. (Across the harbor, **Falmouth Foreside** offers a fine anchorage for visiting yachts.)

Wadsworth-Longfellow House
481 Congress Street
Portland
207-772-1822

Tate House
1270 Westbrook Street
Portland
207-774-9781

On Congress Street you'll find the **Wadsworth-Longfellow House**, built in 1785 by General Peleg Wadsworth. The house is furnished with pieces used by the family during the hundred years they lived here. At one time only fields separated the house from the sea; today buildings and highways block the view.

The **Tate House** was built in 1755 by Captain George Tate. The house has a center chimney with eight fireplaces and unusually fine paneling on the first floor. Note the distinctive gambrel roof.

The **Victoria Mansion** is also called the Morse-Libby House. This brownstone, built in the Italian villa style, is hard to miss with its soaring square tower. Inside you will see stained glass windows, etched glass, frescoes, and carved woodwork. The furniture is the original Morse collection.

Victoria Mansion
109 Danforth Street
Portland
207-772-4841

For a view of the White Mountains, Casco Bay, and the city of Portland, head for the **Portland Observatory** where you can climb 102 steps for the view. It once served as a signal tower; flags were raised when vessels were spotted approaching the town.

Portland has a number of galleries and museums. The **Portland Museum of Art**, designed by I. M. Pei (Seven Congress Square, 207-775-6148), houses many nineteenth- and twentieth-century works including some by Andrew Wyeth, Winslow Homer, and Marsden Hartley. The **Joan Whitney Payson Gallery of Art** (Westbrook College, 207-797-9546) contains works by Renoir, Picasso, Van Gogh, Chagall, Degas, Gauguin, Monet, and others. The **Stein Glass Gallery** (20 Milk Street, 207-772-9072) offers the largest collection of work by New England glass artists in the United States.

Portland
  Observatory
138 Congress Street
Portland
207-774-5561

From Portland follow I-95 north to Freeport, for a shopping spree at **L. L. Bean** (207-865-4761). Here is everything you could possibly want for camping, fishing, skiing, snowshoeing, and hunting. Even if you're not an outdoorsman, you'll love poking around this fabulous place.

FREEPORT

More than 100 new outlet stores, shops, and restaurants have opened in the past few years in Freeport. "Free" indeed!

BRUNSWICK

Museum of Art
Walker Art
  Building
Brunswick
207-725-3275

Peary-MacMillan
  Arctic Museum
Hubbard Hall
Brunswick
207-725-3416

THE
HARPSWELLS

Continue on I-95 to Brunswick, the home of **Bowdoin College**. On campus stop to see paintings by Stuart, Copley, Homer, and Eakins in the **Museum of Art**. Nearby, exhibits in the **Peary-MacMillan Arctic Museum** outline the history of polar expeditions and display belongings of the two arctic explorers.

Travel along the central Maine coast, from Portland to Bar Harbor, has always been easier by sea than by land. For a glimpse of unspoiled Maine, you must be willing to drive up and down the necks. Here you'll find old saltwater farms, their land split between two or three necks (the dory was as important a tool as the plow), and small coves with lobstermen's houses and piers.

To see some of this country, drive down Route 123 from Brunswick along Harpswell Neck, a narrow finger into the sea, 1¹/₂ miles across at its widest point. In the tiny village of Harpswell Center the 1757 **First Meetinghouse** is a fine example of early church architecture.

The area abounds with legends. You may see a headless horseman riding through South Harpswell. Come at midnight when the moon is bright. Or you might catch the Ghost Ship of Harpswell, fully rigged and under sail. That ship is part of a tragic legend about two young friends, George Leverett and Charles Jose, who fell in love with Sara Soule. Jose left town; Leverett stayed and built a ship he named *Sarah*. He sailed into Portland to pick up cargo, and there saw a black ship armed with a cannon. It was the *Don Pedro*, and it was sailed by his rival, Jose. The *Don Pedro* attacked, and all on board the *Sarah* were killed except Leverett; he was tied to the mast of his ship, and she was pushed out to sea. Now legend says the *Sarah*'s dead crew set sail and turned the ship toward home. The ghostly crew took Leverett ashore and left him with his logbook on the beach, where he was rescued. The *Sarah* was sighted from **Harpswell House** in 1880. She gleamed in the sun, headed straight for the harbor, and then disappeared, as though she'd come home for the last time.

Harpswell House
9 Gilman Avenue
South Harpswell
207-725-7694

The Dead Ship of Harpswell
John Greenleaf Whittier

What flecks the outer gray beyond
 The sundown's golden trail?
The white flash of a sea-bird's wing,
 Or gleam of slanting sail?
Let young eyes watch from Neck and Point,
 And sea-worn elders pray,—
The ghost of what was once a ship
 Is sailing up the bay!

From gray sea-fog, from icy drift,
 From peril and from pain,
The home-bound fisher greets thy lights,
 O hundred-harbored Maine!
But many a keel shall seaward turn,
 And many a sail outstand,
When, tall and white, the Dead Ship looms
 Against the dusk of land.

She rounds the headland's bristling pines;
 She threads the isle-set bay;
No spur of breeze can speed her on,
 Nor ebb of tide delay.
Old men still walk the Isle of Orr
 Who tell her date and name,
Old shipwrights sit in Freeport yards
 Who hewed her oaken frame.

What weary doom of baffled quest,
 Thou sad sea-ghost, is thine?
What makes thee in the haunts of home
 A wonder and a sign?
No foot is on thy silent deck,
 Upon thy helm no hand;
No ripple hath the soundless wind
 That smites thee from the land!

For never comes the ship to port,
　　Howe'er the breeze may be;
Just when she nears the waiting shore
　　She drifts again to sea.
No tack of sail, nor turn of helm,
　　Nor sheer of veering side;
Stern-fore she drives to sea and night,
　　Against the wind and tide.

In vain o'er Harpswell Neck the star
　　Of evening guides her in;
In vain for her the lamps are lit
　　Within thy tower, Seguin!
In vain the harbor-boat shall hail,
　　In vain the pilot call;
No hand shall reef her spectral sail,
　　Or let her anchor fall.

Shake, brown old wives, with dreary joy,
　　Your gray-head hints of ill;
And, over sick-beds whispering low,
　　Your prophecies fulfill.
Some home amid yon birchen trees
　　Shall drape its door with woe;
And slowly where the Dead Ship sails,
　　The burial boat shall row!

From Wolf Neck and from Flying Point,
　　From island and from main,
From sheltered cove and tided creek,
　　Shall glide the funeral train.
The dead-boat with the bearers four,
　　The mourners at her stern,—
And one shall go the silent way
　　Who shall no more return!

And men shall sigh, and women weep,
　　Whose dear ones pale and pine,
And sadly over sunset seas
　　Await the ghostly sign.
They know not that its sails are filled
　　By pity's tender breath,
Nor see the Angel at the helm
　　Who steers the Ship of Death!

Off Route 123 there's a road to the right that takes you to Route 24. Head south through the area where a murdered pirate supposedly stands guard over buried treasure (some say they've seen his light and heard him moaning). Between Orrs Island and Bailey Island, separated by Will Straits, is an uncemented granite-block bridge that's laid out like a honeycomb so that the tides and rushing spring thaws can flow through freely. There's a statue of a Maine lobsterman at **Land's End** on the tip of Bailey Island. After a storm, when the surf is high, or any time, take the cliff walk for superb views of Casco Bay and Halfway Rock Light.

ORRS & BAILEY ISLANDS

Head back up Route 24 to Route 1 or I-95 into Bath, Maine's cradle of shipbuilding. Some five thousand vessels have been launched here, including half of all the wooden sailing vessels built in the United States between 1862 and 1902.

Allow yourself time to visit the **Maine Maritime** at its three sites: Sewall House, the Percy and Small Shipyard, and the Apprenticeshop. **Sewall House**, museum headquarters, is a twenty-eight-room Georgian mansion. Here are collections of ship models and paintings, and exhibits on lobstering, fishing, and sailing. The **Percy and Small Shipyard** is the country's only surviving yard where large wooden sailing ships were once built. The *Seguin*, the oldest wooden steam tug still registered, is being restored here. In the **Apprenticeshop** the museum conducts programs for students who want to learn how to build classic Maine coast skiffs, dories, and sloops.

A *New York Times* article tells the story of a descendant of a Bath shipyard owner who is still trying to recover a Civil War debt from the government. In 1862 the yard built a 300-foot gunboat for the navy; it was commissioned and

BATH

**Maine Maritime Museum
Sewall House
963 Washington Street
207-443-1316**

**Percy and Small Shipyard
263 Washington Street
Bath**

**Apprenticeshop
375 Front Street
Bath**

served for some time. Legitimate cost overruns pushed the final bill over what Congress had appropriated. Although both the navy and the U.S. Board of Claims recommended that the total bill be paid, Congress took no action. And the family has been pursuing the claim for over a hundred years. How much was the bill? In 1862 it came to $11,708.79.

POPHAM BEACH

From Bath take Route 209 south to Popham Beach. Visit the site of Popham Colony, where a hundred English colonists arrived in 1607. Discouraged by the harsh winter and sickness, they stayed just a year, most of them returning to England on the *Virginia*, a ship they built themselves (the very first built in America).

Popham Beach State Park
Route 209
Popham Beach
207-389-1335

At the **Fort Popham Memorial** you'll see the partial construction of a fort that was begun in 1861 and never finished. Displays here interpret the history of the area—the story of Popham Colony, Benedict Arnold's march through Maine, and the fort's construction.

The memorial is in **Popham Beach State Park**, a facility extending along 4½ miles of fine sand. There are tidal pools, dunes, rocky outcroppings, and warm water (for Maine). Come early. Parking is limited.

WISCASSET

Castle Tucker
Lee and High Streets
Wiscasset
207-882-7364

Continue up Route 1 to Wiscasset, one of the prettiest villages in Maine. **Castle Tucker**, where you'll find a freestanding elliptical staircase, has a beautiful view overlooking Wiscasset Harbor. It's furnished with original Victorian pieces. The **Musical Wonder House** has an unusual collection of music boxes, player pianos, gramophones, pipe organs, and period antiques. Many of the furnishings in the **Nickels-Sortwell House** are original. Stop at the **Maine Art Gallery** on Warren Street (207-882-7511). The gallery features work by local artists and hosts a special show during the summer.

Musical Wonder House
18 High Street
Wiscasset
207-882-7163

Nickels-Sortwell House
Main and Federal Streets
Wiscasset

Our favorite site: the resting place of the *Luther Little* and the *Hesper* (not the one that was sunk on Norman's Woe), two four-masted schooners that lie in the harbor tidal flats, picturesque reminders of the days of sail.

The Dismantled Ship
Walt Whitman

In some unused lagoon, some nameless bay,
On sluggish, lonesome waters, anchor'd near the shore,
An old, dismasted, gray and batter'd ship, disabled, done,
After free voyages to all the seas of earth,
haul'd up at last and hawser'd tight,
Lies rusting, mouldering.

Boothbay Harbor is on Route 27 south of Wiscasset. It's one of the finest and busiest of Maine's natural harbors, with commercial fishing boats, excursion boats, windjammers, and deep-sea fishing charters going in and out. In mid-July the harbor is the site of the three-day **Windjammer Festival**, but you can see these marvelous sailing ships here all summer long.

At the **Boothbay Railway Village** you'll find antique cars and fire equipment, railroad society memorabilia, and a collection of antique dolls. When you're through exploring, take a ride on a narrow-gauge railroad.

For more information about the town, stop at the chamber of commerce or the **Boothbay Region Historical Society** on Townsend Avenue.

BOOTHBAY HARBOR

Boothbay Harbor
  Chamber of
  Commerce
Route 27
Boothbay Harbor
207-633-2353

Boothbay Railway
  Village
Route 27
Boothbay Harbor
207-633-4727

Continue on Route 1 to Damariscotta. Stop at the visitors' center on Main Street; then cross the street to the **Chapman-Hall House**. The house, built in 1754, is furnished with period pieces. Also here: a collection of eighteenth-century tools (crafts, farming, and shipbuilding) and an herb garden.

DAMARISCOTTA

Chapman-Hall
  House
Main Street
Damariscotta

PEMAQUID POINT

Pemaquid Point Lighthouse
Lighthouse Road
Pemaquid Point

Are you longing for the coast proper? Head south on Route 129 to Route 130, to Pemaquid Point. **Pemaquid Point Lighthouse**, which towers over the pounding surf, is a glorious spot to spend time. Enjoy the magnificent view, then visit the **Fisherman's Museum** in the lightkeeper's house next door.

Colonial Pemaquid Historic Site
Route 130
Pemaquid Point
207-677-2423

In 1965 archaeologists began uncovering foundations of early Indian settlements and seventeenth-century houses at **Colonial Pemaquid Historic Site**, near Pemaquid Beach. There's a museum displaying much of the material from the site, where several thousand artifacts have been found.

FRIENDSHIP

Continue up Route 1 to Route 220 south, to Friendship, home of the famous Friendship sloop. The **Friendship Sloop Society** schedules a number of rendezvous and races during the summer. In 1987 they sailed together in New London, Connecticut; Southwest Harbor, Friendship, and Boothbay Harbor, Maine; and Marblehead, Massachusetts. For current information contact Reade Brower or Judy Foster, 10 Leland Street, Rockland, ME 04841, (207-596-6696).

TENANTS HARBOR

From Friendship meander through the countryside to Cushing, where Andrew Wyeth summers and paints, and Thomaston, a village of beautiful sea captains' homes. Then go south on Route 131 to Tenants Harbor, a lovely fishing village. Stop for a swim in the magnificent clear quarry. Then buy fresh lobsters for dinner. (There's a distributor down the road from the quarry.)

MONHEGAN ISLAND

Just beyond Tenants Harbor, from Port Clyde, you can take the mailboat *Laura B* (207-372-8848) to Monhegan Island, which lies 9 miles out to sea. Leif Erikson may have landed

BOOTHBAY HARBOR

The Boothbay Central Railroad steams along its tracks at the Rail Road Museum.

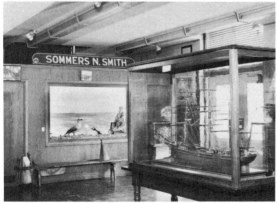

ROCKLAND

The Farnsworth Art Museum of marine art and artifacts.

ACADIA NATIONAL PARK

Consisting of more than 42,000 acres, the park is almost completely surrounded by the sea.

here in the year 1000; we know John Cabot did in 1498. Later Monhegan was a haven for pirates.

You can't bring your car, but the island is only a couple of miles long and a mile wide, and the views along the rugged cliffs on the off-shore side are well worth the walk. While you're exploring, plan a stop at the **Monhegan Museum**, in the former lightkeeper's house. What's here? Indian artifacts, exhibits about the island's wildlife, and an art gallery.

Monhegan Museum
1 Lighthouse Hill
Monhegan

ROCKLAND

Follow Route 131 back to Route 1 and Rockland, where you'll find a large collection of Andrew Wyeth paintings in the **William A. Farnsworth Library and Art Museum**. Also in the museum's collection: the works of other nineteenth- and twentieth-century artists, among them Winslow Homer.

Rockland is the departure point for eight of Maine's windjammers.

William A.
Farnsworth
Library and Art
Museum
19 Elm Street
Rockland
207-596-6457

VINALHAVEN

The **State of Maine Ferry Service** runs a ferry between Rockland and the island of Vinalhaven. On the island, one of the oldest summer colonies in New England, are several interesting houses. Also here: a marvelous area for cruising and an active fishing industry. Stop for a swim in one of the spring-filled granite quarries, explore a small cove, or just sit back and enjoy the view. Across a small strip of water to the north, you can see North Haven Island; to the southwest sits Hurricane Island, where the first Outward Bound School was located.

State of Maine
Ferry Service
517 Main Street
Rockland
207-594-5543

ROCKPORT

Heading up the west shore of Penobscot Bay you come to Rockport, former home of André the Seal. André used to swim 160 miles to Boston to spend the winter at the aquarium there; and then back to Maine again in the spring. His keeper, Harry Goodridge, taught him a number of tricks, which he performed afternoons in his special floating pen near the head of the harbor. André died in 1986 but there's a statue in his memory at the marine park in Rockport.

Continue up Route 1 through Rockport to Camden, one of Maine's most interesting towns. The harbor is a fascinating place, busy with commercial and charter fishing boats, sloops, and a large fleet of windjammers (offering weekly cruises). Contact the **Maine Publicity Bureau** (97 Winthrop Street, Box 2300, Hallowell, ME 04347-2300, 207-289-2423) for a pamphlet listing windjammer cruises.

Stop at the **Camden Information Booth** at the landing for a wealth of information about the area. Then enjoy the shops and restaurants and the view of the waterfalls running through the center of town.

Camden is nestled against the **Camden Hills**, which rise majestically from the shore of the bay. Come for the view or the hiking—both are exceptional. The **Mount Battie South Trail** begins on Megunticook Street (north of the town square). The 1-mile path is steep, but the views from the ledges are worth the climb. Or take the easy way to the top (800 feet): the toll road from **Camden Hills State Park**.

Mount Megunticook Trail (3½ miles) begins at the warden's hut in the park's campgrounds. Enjoy beautiful views of the ocean as you wind your way up to the summit of Mount Megunticook (1,385 feet); then come down on the **Tablelands Trail** to Mount Battie Road.

Bald Rock Mountain Trail starts 4 miles north of the park, on Route 1. (Look for a sign near telephone pole 106.) Follow yellow blazes along a logging trail to Bald Rock Summit (1,100 feet), where there are shelters if you want to spend the night. On a clear day you can see Northport and Lincolnville, Islesboro Island,

CAMDEN

Camden
Information
Booth
Public Landing
Camden
207-236-4404

Camden Hills State
Park
Route 1
Camden
207-236-3109

Deer Isle, and even Pulpit Harbor on North Haven. The trail is 3 miles long.

Maiden Cliff, named for an eleven-year-old girl who fell to her death in May 1864, offers spectacular views of Megunticook Lake and the surrounding countryside. Follow Route 52 west from Camden to the Barrett Place parking lot, where the **Maiden Cliff Trail** begins. At the summit (1,204 feet)—it's marked by a wooden cross—pick up the **Scenic Trail** for your return trip. The total distance is 2½ miles.

Ragged Mountain Trail begins at the Camden Ski Bowl (take John Street from town) and continues up the lift line, right into the woods, and along the ridge to the summit (1,300 feet). You can see the ocean over Oyster River Pond, the Glen Cove area, and Maiden Cliff. Then come down any of the ski runs.

For fine seafood dining, try **Cappy's Chowder House** (207-236-2254) or the **Lobster Pound** (207-789-5550) on Route 1 in Lincolnville.

CASTINE

From Camden continue along Route 1 to Route 175 south, to Route 166A on the Nasket peninsula. Here you'll find Castine, a quiet town with a stormy history. In 1779 Commodore Saltonstall led Paul Revere and other patriots here in the Massachusetts Expedition. The expedition—a mission to dislodge the British from their base at Castine—failed miserably, and all the American boats were lost. Because the abortive mission was such an embarrassment to several prominent patriots, it was never fully documented. And the British? They occupied the town again during the War of 1812.

**Fort George
Wadsworth Cove
Road
Castine**

You can learn more about the area's history at **Fort George**, where fortifications were constructed as early as 1626. The buildings have been razed and rebuilt many times since. Then stroll around the town, reading the historical markers and enjoying the fine examples of colonial architecture.

The **Maine Maritime Academy** offers tours of the *State of Maine*, a training ship. In August the academy also schedules walks (intelligent beachcombing) with staff members. These field trips on the natural history of the seashore last between two and three hours.

**Maine Maritime
  Academy**
Battle Avenue
Castine
207-326-4311

On your way down the Penobscot peninsula to Deer Isle, stop at North Brooksville on Route 175, where a bridge crosses over a rapids in the Bagaduce River. These rapids reverse with the tide. About 2 miles downriver is another reversing rapids, more vigorous than the first, where the current passes through a narrow rocky channel. You can launch a canoe or small boat near the bridge, and run the rapids either up or down the river, depending on the tide.

The stretch of river between the two rapids is a haven for seals. Come on a fine day at low tide, and you'll see them sunning on uncovered rocks.

From Castine take Route 166 to Route 199, to Route 175 south. Continue on Route 175 to Route 15, crossing Eggemoggin Reach on a high suspension bridge. Deer Isle is a great area for exploring, for discovering something new and interesting around the next bend. What's here? Towns climbing into the hills, harbors active with lobstering, and scallop and sardine catches; historic homes; a musicians' retreat; an abandoned silver mine; a granite quarry; lilies floating on Ames Pond; highly skilled craftsmen; and mounds of shells left by the Indians.

DEER ISLE

Friends tell us about a great place to buy fresh fish—right off the boat—for dinner. Driving along Route 15 from the village of Deer Isle toward Stonington, turn left on Oceanville Road (there's a filling station and a used car lot on the corner); then right on the dirt road marked

"Northeast Boat Yard." The wharf is at the end of the road. The fishermen usually return with the day's catch between two and three in the afternoon. Come before the truckers start loading, and you'll find delicious fresh fish. A warning for the fainthearted: The fish are gutted but not cleaned.

ISLE AU HAUT

From Stonington, at the tip of Deer Isle, you can take the mailboat to Isle au Haut, 6 miles out, a part of Acadia National Park. Named by Samuel de Champlain in 1604 for its high land, the island is relatively untouched, with just a few roads and trails around the perimeter. Bring your bike or plan to hike.

MOUNT DESERT ISLAND

Meander up to Ellsworth through the Blue Hill region; then take Route 3 to Mount Desert Island.

This beautiful island was discovered by Champlain, who named it L'Isle des Monts Désert because the mountains looked so barren. In 1613 a group of Jesuits settled on Fernald's Point but were driven out by the British after only a month. That skirmish was the first in a century and a half of fighting between French and British for control of the area.

Acadia National
 Park
Box 177
Bar Harbor 04609
207-288-3338

Today, almost half of the island (along with parts of two nearby islands) makes up **Acadia National Park**. The terrain is varied—wooded valleys, lakes, mountains, and granite shore constantly lashed by the sea—and filled with beautiful trees and wild flowers, and birds and animals. Stop at the visitors' center in Hulls Cove for maps, guidebooks, and information about trails (hiking and biking), self-guided nature walks, and special programs.

A tour of the park? **National Park Tours** (207-288-3327) in Bar Harbor offers a bus trip around the park. Or you can take a cruise from **Frenchman's Bay Boating Company** (207-288-

3322) in Bar Harbor. Or you can rent a tape recorder and taped tour at the visitors' center, and drive yourself.

Bar Harbor is the largest and best known town on Mount Desert Island. At one time a fabulous summer resort, many of the elegant nineteenth-century "cottages" were destroyed in a disastrous fire in 1947. Plan to spend some time shopping; then head for one of the many good restaurants for lunch or dinner. Friends recommend **Testa's Restaurant** (207-288-3327), **Galyn's Galley** (207-288-9706), **George's** (207-288-4505), and the **Island Chowder House** (207-288-4905).

Loop Road Trail begins at Bar Harbor, where several scenic overlooks offer magnificent views of Frenchman's Bay and Bar Harbor itself. **Sieur de Monts Spring,** farther out, has a nature center and a wild flower garden. Nearby, the **Abbe Museum** preserves the Indian history of the area. Not far from the museum, at the picnic area, the road becomes one way.

Hardy souls can stop for a swim at **Sand Beach**, off Ocean Drive, where the average temperature of the water in summer is a brisk 50 to 55 degrees. There is some surf although the beach is in a protected cove. A path from here leads to Otter Cliffs.

Don't miss **Thunder Hole**, where the waves crash in and out with a roar. And the view from **Otter Cliffs**—the highest headlands on the East Coast—is spectacular!

As you drive along the Atlantic shore, you can see **Cadillac Mountain** rising from the interior. You can reach the 1,530-foot mountain, the highest point on the Atlantic coast north of Rio de Janeiro, by heading north on Jordan Pond Road. From the summit you can see sparkling **Eagle Lake** to the northwest and **Somes Sound** to the west. The sound, the only natural fjord on the East Coast, creeps in so far that the island is almost cut in two. Swimmers: try **Sand Beach**

Abbe Museum of Maine Indian Artifacts
Loop Road
Bar Harbor
207-288-3519

(above) or **Seal Harbor Beach**, a community beach off Route 3, where the water temperature hovers around 57 degrees in summer. The surf is gentle; the drop-off, gradual. Less hardy souls can try swimming at the head of the sound in Somesville, where the water is actually warm.

For hikers, Mount Desert is paradise. At the eastern end of the island you can walk the Champlain Mountains from south to north on the **Gorham Mountain Trail**. The 6-mile trail begins a mile north of Otter Cliffs at the Monument Cove parking area. The **South Ridge Trail** (7 miles) takes you to the summit of Cadillac Mountain. It begins at the campground on Otter Cove. Shorter trails to the top: the **West Face Trail** from Jordan Pond Road and the **North Ridge Trail** from the Bar Harbor side of Ocean Drive. Watch out for cars!

Pemetic Mountain Trail, an easy 2 miles, begins at the north end of Bubble Pond, off Jordan Pond Road, and goes along the ridge to the top of Pemetic Mountain (1,218 feet).

The Penobscot and Sargent mountains run along the west side of Jordan Pond. The **Jordan Cliffs Trail** begins at the **Jordan Pond House** (207-276-3316), a restaurant just north of Seal Harbor. The distance, if you circle back on the **Penobscot Mountain Trail**, is about 5 miles. Enjoy long views over Blue Hill Bay, the Atlantic, even Frenchman's Bay; then stop for lunch on your way out.

Norumbega Mountain Trail begins on Route 198 near Upper Hadlock Pond, and extends almost 3 miles. From the top (852 feet) you can see South-West Harbor and Tremont. Be sure to bring along a pail or a basket if you're hiking in blueberry season.

Acadia Mountain Trail offers an easy walk through an area rich in history. An early French colony was formed here, on Saint Sauveur

Mountain, but was later destroyed by the English. English patrols used to come to **Man o' War Brook** to fill their casks with fresh water, and to hunt and fish. The trail is 2¹/₂ miles long, and begins on Robinson Road, off Route 102, across from Echo Lake. Look for the sign to the summit (644 feet).

Or you can choose to head northwest on Route 1 to Bangor, then take I-95 to Route 201 north to Maine's lake country (Itinerary L).

ITINERARY L: THE LAKES AND MOUNTAINS OF MAINE

RANGELEY LAKES

ITINERARY L

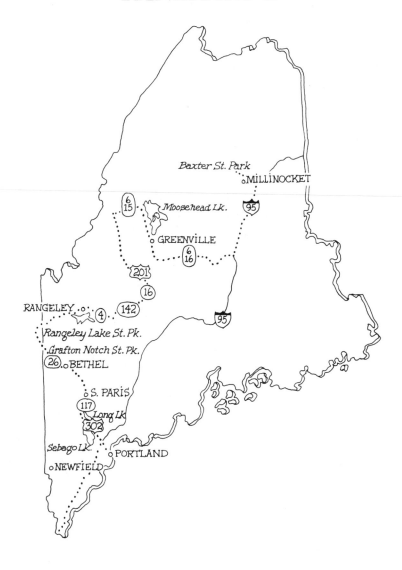

Baxter St. Park

MILLINOCKET

6
15

Moosehead Lk.

95

GREENVILLE

6
16

201

16

RANGELEY

4

142

95

Rangeley Lake St. Pk.

Grafton Notch St. Pk.

26

BETHEL

S. PARIS

117

Long Lk.

302

Sebago Lk.

PORTLAND

NEWFIELD

The Lakes and Mountains of Maine

Many people think of Maine in terms of the coastline alone, but the vast interior of the state contains a multitude of crystal clear lakes, several mountain ranges, and more untroubled wilderness than the rest of New England put together. Vacationers can enjoy this part of Maine year-round, with water sports, fishing, and hiking in the summer and skiing in the winter. Families find that camping by lakes and mountains makes vacations affordable and memorable. Major lake regions include those around Sebago Lake, the Rangeley Lakes, Moosehead Lake, and the Allagash Wilderness Waterway. The Longfellow Mountains run from Rangeley all the way to Baxter State Park. Our route begins in the Sebago Lake region to the south and wanders northward and eastward through the mountains all the way to Baxter State Park. You can combine any part of this itinerary with seacoast pleasures by connecting to the previous itinerary.

SEBAGO LAKE

Maine's second-largest lake is a resort community especially famous for its landlocked salmon, as well as squaretail trout, togue, and black bass. There are villages around the shores offering accommodations, and camping is available in **Sebago Lake State Park**. Antique and craft shops dot the area.

Jones Gallery of Glass and Ceramics
Route 107
Sebago
207-787-3370

Nearby, on Douglas Hill, **The Jones Gallery of Glass and Ceramics** houses an extensive collection built up over the years by Dorothy Jones. The museum offers changing exhibits, a gallery shop that includes some antique pieces, tours, a lecture program, and a library.

Daniel Marrett House
Route 25
Standish
207-642-4094

Two miles south of the lake in Standish, the **Daniel Marrett House** played an important part in the War of 1812. Fearing that the British would capture Portland, the town fathers took money from Portland banks and stored it in the house. This part Georgian, part Greek Revival-style home is furnished with eighteenth- and nineteenth-century family furniture.

Hikers recommend the view from the top of Douglas Mountain. At 1,415 feet you can see Sebago Lake, the surrounding lakes, and the White Mountains of New Hampshire.

Route 25 west and Route 11 southwest to Newfield leads you to **Willowbrook at Newfield**, a restored nineteenth-century village. Twenty-seven buildings house a collection of the "trades of yesteryear" exhibit, restored sleighs and carriages, tools, and farm implements.

Willowbrook at Newfield
Route 11
Newfield
207-793-2784

Just north of Sebago Lake sits **Songo Lock**, built in 1830 as part of the Cumberland-Oxford Canal from Portland to Harrison. It's fun to help open or close the hand-operated lock, or just watch the procedure. The Songo River flows between Sebago Lake and Long Lake, extending the range for sailors and boaters. If you didn't bring a boat, you can take a cruise on the Mississippi River paddlewheeler, *Songo River Queen II*, located on Route 302 at the causeway in Naples (207-693-6861), or help deliver the mail on the U.S. Mail boat from the causeway.

PARIS

Drive into the town of Paris, off Route 25 above South Paris, along a street lined with old white houses with lovely gardens. These houses are open on a house tour sponsored by Stephens Memorial Hospital once a year. The birthplace of Hannibal Hamlin, who was vice-president under Abraham Lincoln, is located just beyond the Hamlin Memorial Library. The library was once the Old Stone Jail, dating from 1828. From Paris Hill look to the west for spectacular views of the White Mountains.

This area is a destination for rockhunters because there are several mines to visit. Or you can see gems at the Maine Mineral Store in West Paris.

BETHEL

From the Sebago/Long Lake area head north on Routes 117 and 26 to Bethel. Built on the banks of the Androscoggin River, the town is set in the foothills of the White Mountains. Settled in 1774, it is one of the oldest towns in the region. Besides serving as the center of a lumber-

Sunday River Ski Resort
Route 2
Bethel
207-824-2410

ing and farming region, Bethel attracts visitors for fishing, boating, rockhounding in local mines, and skiing. **Sunday River Ski Resort** is only 6 miles away. Just beyond the Sunday River Bridge is the famed "Artists Bridge," a covered bridge dating from 1870 that is popular with both painters and photographers.

Grafton Notch State Park is located 25 miles northwest on Route 26. Visitors enjoy views of Old Speck Mountain to the west, Baldpate Mountain to the east, Moose Cave, Screw Auger Falls with its 25-foot-deep holes worn into the rock of the riverbed, and Mother Walker Falls. The Appalachian Trail passes through the park and continues for 277 miles to the top of Mount Katahdin.

RANGELEY LAKES

Continue north on Route 26 to Errol and take Route 16 to the Rangeley Lakes region. Or for an especially scenic drive, take Route 26 from Bethel, Route 2 east to Rumford, and Route 17 north to the Rangeley Lakes. If you go through Rumford, a papermill town, look for Penacook Falls in the middle of town. Route 17 is the spectacular section of this route, following along the Swift River, which is popular with gold panners. Views of lakes and mountains unfold as you drive north along this road.

Rangeley Lake State Park
Rangeley
207-864-3858

The Rangeley chain of lakes includes Rangeley, Quimby Pond, Dodge Pond, Kennebago, Loon, Saddleback, Mooselookmeguntic, Cupsuptic, Upper and Lower Richardson, Aziscohos, and Umbagog. Streams connect the lakes to provide a network for boaters and fishermen.

Rangeley Lake State Park offers swimming, fishing, boating, picnicking, and camping.

Saddleback Mountain Ski Area
Route 4
Rangeley
207-864-3380 or
207-864-5364

East of the town of Rangeley, **Saddleback Mountain Ski Area** has a vertical drop of 1,800 feet. **Sugarloaf Mountain Ski Area** is the largest ski area in the state. Because it is in the snowbelt the slopes hold their cover through late spring. A friend calls it Maine's undiscovered secret.

Sugarloaf Mountain Ski Area
Routes 16 and 27
Kingfield
207-237-2000

RANGELEY LAKES

Maine's Rangeley Lake region offers the desirable combination of tranquil lakes surrounded by unspoiled mountains.

KINGFIELD

Sugarloaf Mountain in Kingfield has a summer side with its well-groomed golf courses.

SUGARLOAF MOUNTAIN

Kingfield's Sugarloaf ski area gives skiers a wide variety of trails to choose from, many with spectacular views.

MOOSEHEAD LAKE

From Rangeley take Routes 4, 142, and 16 east to North Anson, then Route 16 and Scenic Route 201 to Jackman. Did you know that Benedict Arnold took this route along the Kennebec River on his tragic expedition to Quebec? Look for interpretive markers along the way. At Jackman turn onto Routes 6 and 15 to Moosehead Lake. As the largest lake in Maine, Moosehead offers a wealth of wilderness to explore. Visitors gather for whitewater canoeing, hiking, moose-watching, hunting, fishing, camping, ice fishing, cross-country skiing, and snowshoeing. Take the 46-mile "Bow Trip" on the Moose River for a wilderness trip you won't forget.

Greenville, at the southern end of Moosehead Lake, is the home of the *Katahdin*, a 1914 lake steamship. Besides offering cruises on the lake, "Kate" also serves as the **Moosehead Marine Museum**. There you can peruse exhibits on steamboats and logging.

Mount Kineo, which ascends from the lakeshore, was favored by Indians as a source of stone for tools and weapons. Try some of the trails for spectacular views of the lake and area.

BAXTER STATE PARK

From Greenville head south on Routes 6 and 15 to Abbot Village, where you join Route 16 heading east to Lagrange and Routes 155 and 6 to I-95. Head north to Millinocket and the entrance to Baxter State Park.

There, **Mount Katahdin**, at 5,267 feet, is one of the highest peaks in the eastern United States. The Appalachian Trail, which begins in Georgia, ends here.

In 1930 Perceval P. Baxter bought the land and gave it "for the benefit of the people of Maine," to enjoy in its natural state. And enjoy it you will. You can swim, hike (be sure to check trail conditions with a park ranger), picnic, fish, canoe, and camp here. Write to Box 540, Millinocket (203-723-5140), or stop at the park office at 64 Balsam Drive for maps, information, and a list of rules.

Canoeing enthusiasts dream about a lengthy trip along the **Allagash Wilderness Waterway**, a 95-mile stretch through lakes, rivers, and forests. Chamberlain Thoroughfare, which lies between Lakes Chamberlain and Telos, is the best place to launch your canoe. The long paddle ends in Allagash Village, north of Allagash Falls. At this point the Allagash flows into the St. John River. You must register before beginning on this trip because rangers want to know where you are. Contact the Bureau of Parks & Recreation (Call 207-289-3821 or write Maine Department of Conservation, Statehouse Station 22, Augusta, ME 04333).

Your exploration of the lakes and mountains of Maine is complete. Head back to the coast along I-95.

ITINERARY M: THE GREEN MOUNTAINS OF VERMONT

STOWE

ITINERARY M

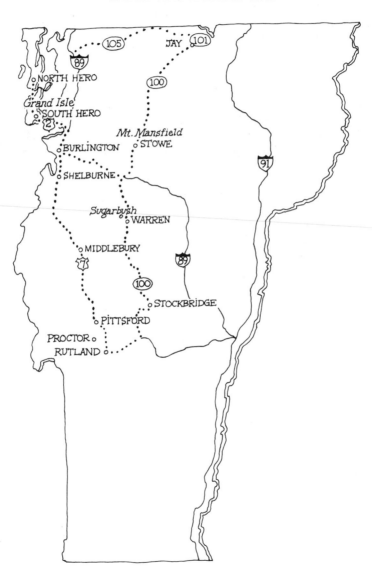

The Green Mountains of Vermont and the Champlain Valley

The early history of man in Vermont begins with the Algonquians about 2000 B.C. Later the Algonquians, Iroquois, Mohicans, and Abnakis used Vermont as a trail from Massachusetts to New York. This Indian heritage is still very much present in the names around the state: Quechee, Bomoseen, Passumpsic, Winooski, Jamaica.

On July 4, 1609, Samuel de Champlain led the Algonquian Indians against the Iroquois. He killed two Iroquois chiefs and a number of warriors, incurring the wrath of the Iroquois for years to come. While here he named a mountain Le Lion Couchant (the crouching lion); it's known today as Camel's Hump. And he called the largest island in Lake Champlain Grand Isle. This French influence is also evident in other regional names: Montpelier, Vergennes, St. Johnsbury, Danville.

The first English settlement in the area was Fort Dummer, near Brattleboro, in 1724. The land was bought at auction by Sir William Dummer and Colonel William Brattle (Dummerston and Brattleboro were named for them). At that time Vermont was part of New York, which didn't keep New Hampshire from annexing land there. The matter was settled by King George II, who maintained that the land belonged to New York. In 1770 Ethan Allen and his Green Mountain Boys rallied to drive off the "Yorkers" who were following up on that claim. The same group responded to the call against the British during the Revolution. In 1777 Vermont declared itself an independent republic, which it remained for fourteen years before becoming a state.

The Green Mountains are probably the remains of the oldest mountain range in New England, dating back 440 million years. Erosion worked folds into the bedrock on a north-south axis, producing an even, rolling range with no jagged peaks or deep valleys. This *peneplain*, or flat plain, is interspersed with *monadnocks*, isolated mountains made up of very hard bedrock that did not erode as much as the land around it.

There are not many lakes in the Green Mountains, possibly because the movement of the glaciers was along the folds southward instead of across them. There was, however, one large glacial lake, Lake Vermont, which covered the Champlain lowland up to 700 feet above the present level of Lake Champlain.

Although the Green Mountains are fairly flat in the south, in the northern section they divide into three parallel ranges more rugged in appearance and filled with more separate peaks. Mount Killington, Mount Ellen, Camel's Hump, and Mount Mansfield are all over 4,000 feet. Some geologists believe that the mountains in the south were once much higher. They claim that the Taconic Mountains, which stretch between northern Connecticut and central Vermont on a north-south axis, were once the tops of the southern Green Mountains, which detached and moved a number of miles to the west. (This is called a *thrust fault*—an older rock formation settled over a younger one.)

One of the picturesque attractions of Vermont is the covered bridge. And there are more than fifty to find. See the Vermont state map for their locations.

Burlington is a good place to begin this route through the Green Mountains and the Champlain Valley. Then head west to Grand Isle for some Revolutionary War history. Striking out northeast from Burlington will take you to Jay Peak, for a ride to the top and a view you won't believe. A drive east from Burlington will bring you to Stowe and towering Mount Mansfield. You can head south from Burlington to Sugarbush Valley and down the backbone of the Green Mountains. And yet another alternative is to visit the Shelburne Museum, then continue south to Middlebury, Ripton, Pittsford, and Proctor.

BURLINGTON

Lake Champlain
Regional
Chamber of
Commerce
209 Battery Street
Burlington
802-863-3489

Lake Champlain
Transportation
King Street Dock
Burlington
802-864-9804

Burlington, the largest city in Vermont, is a college town with a busy industrial area. Contact the chamber of commerce or stop at one of the information booths—there are three: at Main Street and South Willard, at Burlington Square, and at University Mall—for area news.

Burlington sits on the eastern shore of Lake Champlain. From the waterfront you can take a cruise on a gaff-rigged windjammer, the *Homer W. Dixon* (802-862-6918). Or you can take an hour-long ferry ride from the King Street Dock to Port Kent, New York.

On the water, keep your eyes open. There are sea monsters in the lake! Way back in 1609, Champlain wrote about a creature he spotted that was 20 feet long and as thick as a barrel, with a head like a horse and a body like a serpent. In the 1870s "Champ" was sighted by hundreds of steamer passengers. And in 1977 a woman took a photograph of something that looks very much like "Champ." So watch closely!

**North Beach
Institute Road
Burlington**

**Ethan Allen Park
North Avenue
Burlington**

Battery Park, on the waterfront at Pearl Street, was the scene of defensive shooting at British warships during the War of 1812. Sit back and enjoy the fine view of the Adirondacks across the lake. For swimming, picnicking, and camping, drive out North Avenue, to Institute Road, to **North Beach**. Continue on North Avenue to **Ethan Allen Park**, part of the farm once owned by the fascinating leader of the Green Mountain Boys.

Legends about Ethan Allen mix fact and fabrication. Once when he was walking through the woods a huge bobcat sprang and landed on his back; Allen reached behind and wrenched the cat onto the ground, then strangled it. When he arrived where he was going he explained his delay by blaming the "Yorkers" for training and setting varmints against him. Another time he was said to have killed a bear by jamming his powderhorn down the animal's throat! Even a rattlesnake didn't get the better of Ethan Allen. One night after too much elbow-bending, Allen and a friend stopped for a nap. A rattler coiled on Allen's chest, struck him several times, then rolled off, staggered, burped, and fell asleep. The next morning Allen complained about the pesky "mosquito" that kept biting him during the night.

Allen's drinking caused him some trouble at home too. His wife, Fanny, finally worked out her own method for checking his sobriety. She pounded a nail high on the wall of their bedroom. In the morning, if she found his watch hanging on the nail, she knew he'd come home sober; if not, he was in for it. It didn't take Allen long to put one and one together. And after a while, no matter how much he was weaving about, he'd get that watch hooked on before he went to sleep.

When news leaked out of an impending real estate auction, Allen, his brother Ira, and the sheriff announced the sale would be delayed until one the next day. And it was—until one in the morning! Just after midnight the three men met. And at the stroke of one Ethan bid a dollar for the house, barn, and hundred acres; Ira bid two dollars; and the gavel fell.

Back in town, stop at the **Robert Hull Fleming Museum**. There's an Egyptian mummy, a Kang Hsi vase, and seventeenth-century Persian miniatures, and galleries with lots of exhibits.

Robert Hull Fleming Museum
Colchester Avenue
Burlington
802-656-2090

If you're in Burlington between June and October, enjoy the **Mozart Festival**. Write ahead or call for a schedule of concerts. And every summer the **Champlain Shakespeare Festival** takes place at the **Royall Tyler Theater** on the University of Vermont campus.

Mozart Festival
Box 512
Burlington
802-862-7352

Champlain Shakespeare Festival
University of Vermont
Burlington
802-656-2095

Burlington offers gastronomic delights for everyone—in all tastes and price ranges.

The **Ice House** (802-864-1800) on Battery Street, right on the lake, is a pleasant place to spend some time. It features an oyster bar, creative salads, daily seafood specials, and a superb Sunday brunch. Like sandwiches? Try one at **Carbur's Restaurant** (802-862-4106) on Saint Paul Street. Vermont's largest sandwich menu offers over a hundred unbelievable concoctions, among them the Flashback, the Swinger Club, the Tricky Dick, the Oregon Plan, and the Pyramid Maul. If you can finish the Queen City Special, you've got quite an appetite! At **Ben & Jerry's Ice Cream** (802-862-9620) on Cherry Street, you get, not only terrific ice cream, but also your choice of homemade soups, crepes, salads, sandwiches, cappuccino, and espresso. Like to shop? Try the **Church Street Marketplace**, which features craft fairs and a sidewalk cafe.

From the city take I-89 north to Route 2; then follow the signs across the bridge to Grand Isle. This quiet island is a wonderful place to

GRAND ISLE

**Department of
  Forests and Parks**
Montpelier
802-828-3375

relax. Three parks—**Grand Isle State Park, Knight Point State Park,** and **North Hero State Park**—offer swimming, boating, and camping. Contact the **Department of Forests and Parks** for information about them.

Rent a boat and set off for **Valcour Island,** on the west side of the lake between Port Kent and Plattsburgh. The first major naval battle of the Revolutionary War was fought here on October 11, 1776.

In September of that year General Benedict Arnold assembled his naval forces between Valcour Island and the New York mainland. His fleet included the sloop *Enterprise*, the schooners *Royal Savage* and *Revenge*, and a number of smaller vessels. Captain Thomas Pringle led the British fleet—the schooners *Maria* and *Carleton*, and several dozen smaller ships. On the first day the British held the advantage, then tried to maintain a line south of the island to hold the Americans in place. But, in dense fog that night the Americans sailed north around the island, then south all the way to Crown Point (16 miles north of Ticonderoga). Eventually the British destroyed the American fleet, but General Arnold and his men escaped to Fort Ticonderoga. This battle upset British plans to capture the fort in 1776; instead they withdrew to Canada. In the meantime the Americans were able to strengthen their forces, and were victorious at Saratoga in 1777, the turning point in the war.

Today the island's 950 acres are uninhabited, preserved in their natural state. For birdwatchers there's a large rookery for great blue herons in the southeast corner; for hikers and campers there are 7 miles of trails and camping sites scattered around the island. For information, contact the New York State Environmental Conservation Department (518-474-2121).

Stop at **Allenholm Farm** (802-372-5566) in South Hero for apples (the island abounds with orchards), cheeses, jellies, and gifts. Driving along Route 2 you'll pass the **Hyde Log Cabin**, which is maintained by the historical society. It was built in 1783, the oldest log cabin in the country.

When you're through exploring, you can follow Route 2 through North Hero and Alburg Center to Route 78 to Swanton, to Route 36 along the east shore of the lake, back to Burlington. Or, if time's a problem, retrace your steps on Route 2 and I-89 into the city.

Burlington is a good jumping-off place for ski country. If you'd like to try the northernmost ski area in Vermont head for **Jay Peak**. One way to get there is to drive I-89 north to St. Albans, then turn east on Routes 104, 105, 118 and 242. The vertical drop is 2,150 feet and lifts include a sixty-passenger aerial tramway, a triple chairlift, two double chairlifts, and two T-bars. You can ski at Jay from early November to early May.

Expert skiers will head for the "Jet" triple chair and zoom down Derrick Hot Shot, Haynes, U.N., The Jet, and Kitzbuehel. They mean it when they label those runs black! Beginners will find trails concentrated around the Queen's Highway T-bar, as well as Northway, which leads them from the summit all the way down. Watch carefully if you ride the Green Mountain Chair, because while the trails may sport green circles partway down, the top is definitely blue squared. Intermediates will enjoy Northway for an easy first run, and then should try Ullr's Dream that is nice and very wide at the top, and slightly narrower but smooth and winding all the way down. If you want to try the "Jet" triple chair, take Montrealer, Hell's Crossing, and Northway to the bottom. If you need to get back to the main base lodge at the end of the day, there is only one way short of a long walk: take the Queen's Highway T-Bar and ski the Queen's Highway across.

JAY

Jay Peak Ski Resort
Route 242
Jay 05859
800-451-4449 or
802-988-2611

M•283

Cross-country skiing is available at **Jay Peak Touring Center** (from outside Vermont, 800-451-4449 or 802-988-2611 from inside Vermont), **Hazen's Notch Touring Center** (800-326-4708), and **Heermansmith Farm Touring Center** (802-754-8866).

If you're there during other seasons you can ride the **Jay Peak Aerial Tramway** for a view of four states and Canada from 4,000 feet up. The Long Trail crosses the summit of Jay Peak; hikers find the view worth the climb. Fishing is available nearby in the Willoughby and Black rivers where you can expect to catch salmon, lake trout, rainbow trout, brook trout, bass, northern pike, and walleyes.

STOWE

The closest major ski area to Burlington is, of course, that old favorite, Stowe. Take I-89 from Burlington until you reach Route 100 heading north to Stowe. Dating from a rope tow in 1936, Stowe continues to expand and attract skiers from everywhere. The twin peaks, Mount Mansfield and Spruce Peak, offer enough variety to suit any family.

Mount Mansfield, at 4,393 feet the highest mountain in the state, looms over the surrounding countryside. There are several stories that explain the mountain's strikingly human look. One tells of a man named Mansfield who fell off the Camel's Hump when the camel knelt to drink, and now lies face up, a mountain profile. Another legend says the profile is the face of Mishawaka, the son of an Indian chief, who crawled up to the peak to prove his courage, and died there.

Mount Mansfield's vertical drop is 2,350 and the longest run is 4½ miles. The mountain boasts the first quad chairlift in the area, plus a gondola, triple chairlift, and two double chairlifts. Spruce Peak has 1,550 feet of vertical drop and is serviced by four double chairlifts.

Mount Mansfield has attracted expert skiers for years, who like to try their luck on the "Front Four" or Starr, Goat, Liftline, and National; another option is taking the gondola up to try Chin Clip. Beginners prefer Meadows and Easy Street on Spruce Peak, building up to some of the runs from the top of the Mount Mansfield Quad such as Toll Road, Lullaby Lane, and Easy Mile. Intermediate skiers will find wonderful runs on both sides, including Perry Merrill from the top of the gondola or those old favorites, Tyro, T-Line, Gulch, North Slope, and, most of all, Standard from the triple chair. From the Octagon at the top of the Mt. Mansfield Quad you can wind your way down Lord and cross over on Toll Road to Skimeister or Sunrise leading to North Slope or any number of other trails to the bottom. Spruce Peak also offers fun to the intermediate with its Main Street—nice and wide—and the narrower but more interesting Smugglers and Sterling trails, all the way down.

Cross-country skiers have many areas to choose from at Stowe, including **Mount Mansfield Touring Center** (802-253-7311), **Trapp Family Lodge Ski Touring Center** (802-253-8511), **Topnotch Ski Touring Center** (802-253-8585), and Edson Hill Ski Touring Center (802-253-8954). You'll find that they interconnect so you can really go out for a full day of exercise.

You may not know that Stowe has been a summer vacation area since before the Civil War. Now you can ride up on a lift or drive your car on the Mountain Auto Road to the summit. Hiking in the mountains is popular as well as a myriad of summer sports.

Did you love *The Sound of Music*? If you did, you have to stop at the **Traff Family Lodge** (802-253-8511). The building is new—the original was destroyed by fire in 1981—but the family's spirit is still here. The inn, nestled in mountains not unlike those in the Trapps' native Austria, is off Route 108.

Hungry? There are more restaurants in Stowe than you can sample in one trip; some of our favorites are: **Ten Acres Lodge** (802-253-7638), **The Partridge Inn** (802-253-8000), **Restaurant Swisspot** (802-253-4622), **Topnotch at Stowe** (802-253-7638), and **Trapp Family Lodge** (802-253-8511).

Shopping is available all up and down Mountain Road. If you like Moriarty hats stop in their shop on Mountain Road (802-253-4052) to update yours or add a sweater or two. The range of colors and combinations is mind-boggling, but go ahead and choose!

SUGARBUSH VALLEY

Another ski area is Sugarbush Valley. From Burlington take I-89 South to Route 100, then head south to signs for Sugarbush Valley. Sugarbush and Sugarbush North are two separate areas that will eventually be connected. You can ski either area on one ticket. The vertical drop is 2,600 feet. Sugarbush lifts include three triple chairlifts, four double chairs, and a couple of poma lifts. Sugarbush North (originally called Glen Ellen) offers five double chairs, a poma, and a T-bar.

Intermediate skiers need to plan carefully when riding the lifts from the Valley Base Lodge at Sugarbush. There is a comfortable trail down from the top of each lift, but if it should be closed you won't be happy on an expert trail. Try the Spring Fling Triple Chair leading to Snowball for starters; Sugar Bravo Triple Chair leads to Domino or Downspout and then into Jester. The Gate House Double Chair offers Sleeper, Pushover, or Slowpoke. Or you can take Village Run all the way down to Sugarbush Village. Sugarbush North offers Elbow or Lookin' Good to Glen House, then Which Way or Cruiser to the bottom of North Ridge Double Chair. The Inverness Double Chair leads to Inverness, Brambles, or Semi-Tough.

The Old Champlain Steamer Ticonderoga at the Shelburne Museum.

SHELBURNE

A secret fishing hole along a trout stream in Vermont.

NORTHWESTERN VERMONT

Mountains provide a scenic backdrop for Lake Champlain sailing.

BURLINGTON

Cross-country skiers will find trails at **Sugarbush Inn** (802-583-2301), **Tucker Hill** (802-496-3203), or **Mad River Barn** (802-496-3310).

When you're ready for a good meal head for **Sam Rupert's** (802-583-2421) for the best lobster bisque in town, followed by delicious entrees and homemade desserts. Other possibilities include **The Phoenix** (802-583-2777), and **Waitsfield Inn** (802-496-3979). All these restaurants are located on Mountain Road.

SHELBURNE

Shelburne Museum
Route 7
Shelburne
802-985-3344

If you're not looking for ski country, take Route 7 south from Burlington to Shelburne. Here you'll find the **Shelburne Museum**, with a remarkably extensive and varied collection of Americana. The thirty-five buildings, spread out on 45 acres of land, house collections of quilts, textiles, tools, glass, ceramics, scrimshaw, furniture, dolls, carriages, and wagons. There are seven period homes, a general store, a blacksmith shop, a schoolhouse, a church, a livery stable, a smokehouse, the 220-foot sidewheeler *SS Ticonderoga*, a steam train, a railroad car, and galleries. Wear comfortable shoes (there is a shuttle bus for the foot-weary) and plan to spend the day.

MIDDLEBURY

Vermont State
 Craft Center
Frog Hollow Lane
Middlebury
802-388-3177

Morgan Horse
 Farm
Weybridge Road
Middlebury
802-388-2011

Continue south on Route 7 to Middlebury, the home of **Middlebury College**. The lovely old Georgian and nineteenth-century buildings make this "college on the hill" just what a New England college should be.

One of our favorite stops is the **Vermont State Craft Center**, just off Main Street. Here you'll find crafts exhibitions, classes, and wonderful collections of wooden toys, stained glass, jewelry, pottery, pewter, and more—all for the buying.

To reach the **Morgan Horse Farm**, which is managed by the University of Vermont, head out Route 125 west to Route 23, and follow the signs.

There is an audio-visual presentation about the Morgan Horse Farm and a tour of the stables.

Continue south on Route 7. About 4 miles beyond Middlebury turn left on Route 125, to Ripton. Robert Frost lived here from 1939 until his death in 1963. His home, the **Homer Noble Farm**, is 2 miles east of the town. You can visit the house and the cabin behind it, where Frost worked. Through the years, the poet became involved in the Breadloaf Writer's Conference at Middlebury College's summer campus, a few miles farther along Route 125. The **Robert Frost Interpretive Trail** begins at the farm and ends at the Breadloaf campus. You can read seven of his poems on plaques along the way.

RIPTON

Homer Noble Farm
Route 125
Ripton

Head back to Route 7, and follow it south into Pittsford. Here maple syrup aficionados will enjoy the **New England Maple Museum**. The museum houses a collection of antique sugaring equipment and a wall of panel displays that depict the development of the industry. There's also a ten-minute slide show about modern production methods. When you're through looking, step into the tasting area for a spoonful of fresh syrup.

PITTSFORD

New England
  Maple Museum
Route 7
Pittsford
802-483-9414

At Pittsford Mills turn off Route 7 to Proctor, the center of another local industry—marble. Head for the **Vermont Marble Exhibit** on the grounds of the Vermont Marble Company, a couple of miles north of town. What's here? Samples of marble from all over the world, a view of the massive factory, a look at a sculptor at work, and movies that explain the quarrying process.

Between the Taconic Mountains and the Green Mountains, widening into Lake Champlain, lies the Champlain Valley. You can see marble in the rock all along the valley, where heat

PROCTOR

Vermont Marble
  Exhibit
Route 3
Proctor
802-459-3311

and pressure have combined with limestone. Vermont is one of the largest producers of marble in the nation. The best commercial marble in the state lies on a north/south axis between Brandon and Dorset, and many of the quarries in the area—including the one in Proctor—are open for visits.

The town of Proctor was named for Colonel Redford Proctor, a descendant of Captain Leonard Proctor, who settled in Cavendish, Vermont, in 1780. Captain Proctor had a feud going with Salmon Dutton over Dutton's "turnpike," a toll road Proctor didn't see the need for. (In fact he built himself a "shunpike" through the same area—just to avoid paying Dutton's toll!) The family feud lasted seventy-five years, until Redford laid it to rest by marrying Emily Dutton in 1858.

From the town take West Proctor Road a mile south to **Wilson Castle**. The thirty-two-room nineteenth-century mansion sits on 115 acres. In the house are stained-glass windows, furnishings from Europe and the Orient, and an art gallery.

Wilson Castle
West Proctor Road
Proctor
802-773-3284

Now that you have completed a swing through the Champlain Valley and the Green Mountains, head south a few miles on Route 3 or Route 7 to Rutland to join Itinerary N.

WINDHAM COUNTY COURTHOUSE

ITINERARY N

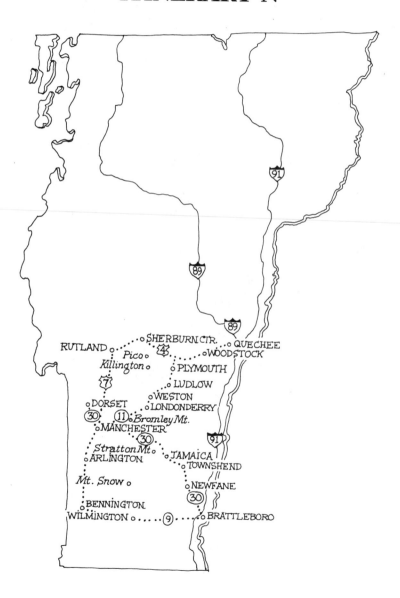

Southern Vermont

The Song of the Vermonters, 1779
John Greenleaf Whittier

Ho—all to the borders! Vermonters, come down,
    With your breeches of deerskin and jackets of brown;
With your red woollen caps, and your moccasins, come,
    To the gathering summons of trumpet and drum.

Does the "old Bay State" threaten?
    Does Congress complain?
Swarms Hampshire in arms on our borders again?
    Bark the war-dogs of Britain aloud on the lake—
Let 'em come; what they can they are welcome to take.

Yet we owe no allegiance, we bow to no throne,
    Our ruler is law, and the law is our own;
Our leaders themselves are our own fellow-men,
    Who can handle the sword, or the scythe, or the pen.

Hurrah for Vermont! For the land which we till
    Must have sons to defend her from valley and hill;
Leave the harvest to rot on the fields where it grows,
    And the reaping of wheat for the reaping of foes.

Come York or come Hampshire, come traitors or knaves,
    If ye rule o'er our land, ye shall rule o'er our graves;
Our vow is recorded—our banner unfurled,
    In the name of Vermont we defy all the world!

You can tour southern Vermont in a number of sensible ways. In case you have just come from New Hampshire, you might want to begin at Quechee; the next stop is Woodstock, then Plymouth and points south. You will probably want to spend some time in the Killington area, and if you do, be sure to ride the gondola to the top. Heading south again, go through Ludlow and Weston to Manchester, again a wonderful place to spend some time. Then head north to Dorset and Merck Forest or south to Arlington and Bennington. From Bennington you can cross the southern tier of the state to Brattleboro on the Molly Stark Trail, with a side trip through Newfane and Townshend. There are a number of ski areas in this region, with appropriate peaks and hiking trails, including Okemo, Bromley, Stratton, and Mount Snow. Wherever you want to begin this itinerary will do. Just pick up the town of your choice and carry on. Having crisscrossed the state many times, we have found that there is no single "best" way to enjoy the subtle combination of mountains and valleys of southern Vermont.

If you begin to explore southern Vermont from White River Junction, take Route 4 west to Quechee. **Quechee Gorge**, Vermont's Little Grand Canyon, rises 165 feet over the Ottauquechee River. Stop for a good view of the gorge from the bridge on Route 4. Or hike along the **Quechee Gorge Trail**, which begins a third of a mile beyond the gorge near the state park entrance. Watch for the sign marked with blue blazes. The views along the trail are spectacular.

Continue along Route 4 to Woodstock, one of the loveliest towns in New England. Take time to walk around the green to enjoy the beauty of many authentic facades on the houses. Nearby, the **Woodstock Historical Society** has nine restored rooms with collections of silver, glass, paintings, and period furniture, and a landscaped garden. The house was built by Charles Dana in 1807. Don't miss the dolls and dollhouses, some belonging to local Woodstock families.

**Woodstock
Historical Society
26 Elm Street
Woodstock
802-457-1822**

On Central Street, antique shops, galleries, bookstores, and boutiques now occupy restored eighteenth- and nineteenth-century buildings. Don't miss the last covered bridge constructed in Vermont, located across the green from the Woodstock Inn.

Billings Farm and Museum has been restored recently. George Perkins Marsh, a linguist and diplomat, lived on the farm in the 1830s; his book *Man and Nature* reinforces the importance of what we now call ecology. Today the farm operates both as a dairy farm and as a museum. Life in 1890 on a Vermont farm is illustrated by exhibits about tasks such as clearing land, planting, threshing, cutting ice in winter, and making cheese and butter. Necessary tools and equip-

**Billings Farm and
Museum
River Road
Woodstock
802-457-2355**

ment are also on display. Jersey cattle, like the ones Frederick Billings bought in 1871, still win blue ribbons.

Restaurants abound in Woodstock. Our favorites include the **Woodstock Inn** (on the green, 802-457-1100), **The Village Inn of Woodstock** (41 Pleasant Street, Route 4, 802-457-1255), **Spooner's at Sunset Farm** (Route 4, 802-457-4022), and **The Prince & The Pauper** (24 Elm Street, 802-457-1818).

Woodstock Chamber of Commerce 4 Central Street Woodstock 802-457-3555

There is much to discover in this town, a town that has valued and preserved its heritage while adapting it to modern living. Contact the chamber of commerce for more information about historic sites. It's the place, too, for information about nearby nature trails, **Faulkner** and **Mount Peg**.

John Freiden has written a wonderful book, *20 Bicycle Tours in Vermont*, about bicycle trips in Vermont. And one of those trips begins and ends in Woodstock, with stops at South Pomfret, Hewetts Corners, and West Hartford. Bring the book and your bike for full enjoyment.

Or, if you'd like to join a group bicycle tour, contact **Vermont Bicycle Touring** (Box 711, Bristol, VT 05443; 802-453-4811). In the winter, cross-country skiers enjoy the trails at **Woodstock Ski Touring Center** (Route 106, 802-457-2114).

BRIDGEWATER CORNERS
Calvin Coolidge State Forest Route 100A Bridgewater Corners 802-672-3612

Follow Route 4 into Bridgewater Corners; then turn left on Route 100A. The **Calvin Coolidge State Forest** outside town offers picnicking, hiking, and camping.

PLYMOUTH

Continue on Route 100A to Plymouth, where Calvin Coolidge was born in 1872. You can visit the **Coolidge Birthplace** and then head to the **Coolidge Homestead**, where the president was sworn in. When President Harding died early in the morning of August 3, 1923, the news was carried from Bridgewater to the homestead by the telephone operator's husband—the Coolidges didn't have a phone! Well, they may not have had a phone, but they did have a notary public handy for the swearing in—Colonel John Coolidge, the vice-president's father. Someone later asked the colonel how he knew he could administer the oath of office to his own son. His reply: "I didn't know that I couldn't."

The former president's son, John Coolidge, still lives in town during the summer. He runs **Plymouth Cheese** (802-672-3650), a cheese factory where everything is made by hand. Stop in to watch or buy.

Coolidge Birthplace and Homestead
Route 100A
Plymouth
802-828-3226

About a mile west of Plymouth, pick up Route 100 north, which rejoins Route 4 at West Bridgewater. This stretch of road takes you into the **Killington Ski Area.** You can ride a gondola to the top of **Killington Peak**—a 4,241-foot ride, straight up. Killington Peak was the site of the christening of the state of Vermont. In 1763 the Reverend Samuel Peters and friends climbed to the top of Mt. Pisgah (later named Killington), carrying a bottle of champagne. When they reached the top, instead of enjoying a bubbly drink, Peters broke the bottle on a rock and christened it "Verd Mont" (French for "Green Mountain").

We hope the wind doesn't gust up to 70 miles per hour, as it sometimes does, when you reach the summit. On a clear day you can see the White Mountains of New Hampshire, including Mount Washington. To the northwest the high peaks of the Adirondacks in New York stand out. Look north along the backbone of the state, the Green Mountains, to Mount Mansfield. Hikers can take the Killington Nature Trail, which circles around the peak.

SHERBURNE CENTER

Killington Ski Area
Killington Road
Sherburne Center
802-422-3333

Drive a little farther up Route 4 to the 5-mile access road to the largest ski area in the Northeast and one of the largest in the United States. When you ski Killington you're not skiing just one mountain—but six. Furthermore they all interconnect by means of trails for all skiing levels. The vertical drop is 3,160 feet, and eighteen lifts (including a gondola, quads, trips, double chairs, and a poma lift) service the area. Depending on snowfall, Killington is open from late October into June.

Lest you think that Killington is too big and complex to enjoy, remember that you will be skiing one area at a time, getting to know your favorites before moving on. You can stay up on the mountain most of the day, choosing trails that are less crowded, rather than waiting in line at the bottom. The trail map has been improved, and the use of color has simplified the pattern.

Beginners will love the Snowshed area, which is perfectly groomed with not a steep slope or mogul anywhere. The intermediate skier will enjoy Snowdon Mountain with its Mouse Run, Bunny Buster, and Chute. Ram's Head has been a favorite for years, with lovely, winding Timberline when there is enough snow cover, or the Swirl and Header (the latter has snowmaking). From Killington Peak try West Glade and East Glade, which lead to Snowdon and the Mouse Run again. South Ridge Triple Chairlift offers Pipe Dream and Wanderer, which are great confidence builders for anyone. Sunrise Mountain has several easy winding trails, including Sun Dog, Sunrise Trail, and Juggernaut Too. If the snow is good, don't forget to take your long run down the Great Eastern or the 4-mile trail to the gondola base—pure pleasure for continuous, easy skiing.

There's plenty to do even when the slopes are bare. Come in summer for golf, riding, or tennis. The **Killington Playhouse** (802-422-3333), based at Snowshed Lodge, schedules performances during July and August. Snowshed also hosts the Vermont State Craft Fair, Vermont Antique Show, Vermont Gallery Showcase, and the Sportsman's Exposition.

Cross-country skiing is available at **Mountain Meadows Ski Touring Center** (Route 4, 802-775-7077). Trails wander around Kent Lake and through the forest. It is located at the foot of Killington Road.

Restaurants pop up along the Killington Road frequently. Our favorites include **Charity's 1887 Saloon** (802-422-3800), **Claude's and Choices** (two restaurants under one roof, 802-422-3970), the **Grist Mill** (802-422-3970), **Mother Shapiro's** (802-422-9933), **Pogonips** (in Snowshed Lodge), 802-422-7880), and **The Wobbly Barn Steakhouse** (802-422-3392).

Living in the shadow of Killington, **Pico** is the place to go if you're not fond of crowds. Sometimes the snow is better at Pico and yet skiers drive on by, not knowing what they're missing. Families and those interested in relaxing skiing days enjoy Pico. There are ten expert trails, fourteen intermediate, and seven beginner. The vertical drop is 1,967 feet; seven chairlifts service the area as well as two T-bars.

Pico Ski Resort
Sherburne Pass
Rutland
802-775-4345

Experts will head for the Summit chair. Beginners may want to start off on the Pico T-Bar II, on the left face, or Bonanza Chairlift, on the right face. Intermediates might take the Triple Chair on the right face to ski the first run down Triple Slope, then try Ace of Clubs and Sundowner. The Outpost Chair leading to the Wrangler is nice if there is enough snow cover. Take the Summit Chair to the top and ski Easy Street to Lower Pike. There is a new intermediate area located between the Summit and Outpost Chairs serviced by the Golden Express.

And of course there's hiking. Try the trail over Deer Leap Mountain, which begins at Long Trail Lodge on Route 4 at the top of Sherburne Pass. You start out on a section of the mountain with fine views, and rejoin the Long Trail; then climb steeply to the south peak.

A word of caution: Don't head out on a trail with a guidebook as your only source of information. All hikers, regardless of their experience, need good topographic maps of the area they're exploring. **U.S. Geological Survey** maps are available at most bookstores and stationery shops. Or you can write directly for them. The **National Survey** in Chester, Vermont, is another source of good maps.

The **Bucklin Trail** to Killington peak begins at Brewers Corners on the west face of the mountain, and ascends through some old flat logging roads, then some steeper rocks. It crosses Brewers Brook several times, winds in and out of Calvin Coolidge State Forest, then joins the Long Trail until it bears right, up to the peak. On a clear day you can see the Green Mountains stretching north from Pico Peak to distant Mount Mansfield; Glastenbury Mountain to the south; the Presidential Range to the east; and, the Taconic Mountains and the Adirondacks to the west. To reach the trail, follow Route 4 to Mendon, and turn left on Wheelerville Road. About 4 miles up you'll see a parking lot and the blue-blazed signs marking the path.

The **Long Trail** is a 263-mile footpath that stretches from Williamstown, Massachusetts, to the Canadian border near North Troy, Vermont. James Taylor, headmaster of Vermont Academy, came up with the idea for the trail in 1909. He organized a group of volunteers to clear a path linking the northern and southern peaks of the Green Mountains. His volunteers carried their equipment in pack baskets, clearing and building shelters as they went northward—a project that took twenty-two years.

Today the trail is maintained by the **Green Mountain Club**, which awards end-to-end emblems to those who walk the trail completely. (Over twelve hundred have been presented.) There are sixty-five shelters along the way, each no more than a day's hike apart. The north end is marked by a marble monument, one side reading "United States"; the other, "Canada."

RUTLAND

Take Route 4 right into Rutland. The second largest city in Vermont was chartered in 1761 by Governor Benning Wentworth of New Hampshire. In the 1770s Rutland prospered as a frontier town, with both a gristmill and a sawmill. Later it, and the area, became famous for its superb marble. The New York Public Library, the John F. Kennedy Memorial, and the Supreme Court Building were all built from marble quarried here.

Stop for a meal at **Back Home Cafe** (Center Street, 802-775-2104), **Casa Bianca** (Grove Street, 802-773-7401), **Sirloin Saloon** (Main Street, 802-773-7900), and **Governor Williams' House** (corner of Routes 4 and 7, 802-773-9336).

LUDLOW

Okemo Mountain Resort
315 Mountain Road
Ludlow
802-228-4041

From Rutland follow Route 7 to Route 103, into Ludlow. **Okemo Mountain,** on your way into town, offers fine skiing in the winter.

For those who remember skiing Okemo years ago, as we do, the changes in the area will seem startling, but the expansion of the mountain has been carefully planned and executed. The vertical drop is 2,150 feet. There are now nine chairlifts, many of them triples and quads, and a poma serving sixty-eight slopes and trails.

The expansion to Solitude Peak, with its new quad chair, opens up a new area for intermediates and experts.

The mountain is full of pleasant runs for the intermediate skier. You might begin by taking the Sachem Chair and skiing down Upper and Lower Sachem. Then take Sachem up again and ski Link and Lower World Cup. Move over one chair to Northeast Summit Triple to Nor'Easter. Again from Northeast try Upper Chief and Upper World Cup, which are rated expert but are within the range of advanced intermediate skiers. Move over again to Green Ridge Chair to try Tomahawk leading into Lower Arrow. The new quad chair, Solitude, will take you to Coleman Brook and Heaven's Gate. Exhibition, under the lift, is rated expert although it has intermediate pitch.

When you're ready for a good meal on the Okemo slopes, head for **Clock Works** (802-228-2800), which is well known for Sunday brunch as well as lunch or dinner. More casual spots on the mountain include **The Sitting Bull** in the base lodge, which serves Mexican fare plus soup and sandwiches, or **The Sugar House**, located on the lower slopes of the mountain, which offers salads and daily specials.

Cross-country skiers can go across the road to **Fox Run** (Routes 103 and 100, 802-228-8871), which has trails along the river. Nearby **Hawk of Vermont** (Route 100, Pittsfield, 802-672-3811) offers a large network of trails along the Black River as well as up on the mountain.

If you want to go out for dinner try **Michael's** (Route 103, 802-228-5622) for seafood and steak, **Nikki's** (Route 103, 802-228-7797) for American regional cuisine, **Castle Inn** (Route 103 and 31, Proctorsville, 802-226-7222) for gourmet fare in a castle atmosphere, or **Echo Lake Inn** (Route 100, Tyson, 802-228-8602) for a "presidential dinner at an historic inn in Coolidge country."

From Ludlow follow Route 100 west to Weston, a charming village slightly off the main line. The **Farrar-Mansur House**, built in 1797, is just off the common. Once a tavern, it's now a museum. Nearby the **Weston Playhouse** (802-824-5288) offers summer theater.

There are several shops in town. Our favorites: the **Vermont Country Store** (802-824-3184), the **Weston Village Store** (802-824-5477), and the **Weston Bowl Mill** (802-824-6219), where you'll find a large selection of wooden items and bins full of seconds.

WESTON

From Weston head south on Route 100 to Londonderry, where you turn right on Route 11, to Manchester. Pick up Route 7A and follow it into Manchester Center. At the junction of Routes 11 and 7A, stop in one of the most complete bookstores anywhere—**Northshire Bookstore**—which has a stock appropriate to a major city bookstore.

MANCHESTER

The old town on the hill is an impressive collection of stately colonial homes. Mary Todd Lincoln and her son Robert were visitors here, and Robert came back to stay until he died in 1926. You can visit his home, **Hildene**, which was occupied by direct descendants of the family until 1975. The furnishings are original, and everywhere one finds memorabilia of the Lincoln family.

**Hildene
Route 7
Manchester
802-362-1788**

"Welcome back" was the message from the town as the historic **Equinox Hotel** reopened after a ten-year period of silence. We remember driving by the massive block-long structure during the late 1970s, wondering if it would ever be restored and reopened. The first hotel on the site was built in 1769; since that time historic events have swirled around it. On the green stands a statue of one of Ethan Allen's Green Mountain Boys; a group of them met there just before the Battle of Bennington in 1777. In 1863 Mrs. Lincoln and two of her sons stayed in the Equinox. The hotel redecorated a suite of rooms in anticipation of a second visit for both President and Mrs. Lincoln in 1865, but he was assassinated a few months before the proposed visit.

Visitors walk back in time as they enter the Victorian parlor and walk across its colorful floral carpeting to listen to piano music and have a drink or light meal in Marsh Tavern or dinner in one of the dining rooms. The chef, who was already well known when he came to the Equinox from another prestigious inn, produces mouthwatering fare. Call 800-362-4747 (outside Vermont) or 802-362-4700 (in Vermont) for reservations.

The Manchester area is filled with opportunities for outdoor activities: hiking, swimming, boating, and fishing. Fishermen everywhere know the town because the **Orvis Company** (802-362-3881) is located here. You can visit the famous producer of fishing equipment at the plant on Route 7A between Manchester and Manchester Center.

Spring is really on the way when the canoes start appearing on the Batten Kill. The river flows south through the Vermont Valley, between the Green Mountains and Mount Equinox. From the town square in Manchester, follow Union Street east about three quarters of a mile to the Union Street Bridge—your launching area. Oh, you may receive some glares from fishermen and leave a little paint on the rocks, but this river, with its very mild white water, is a joy to run. Where to stop? There's a campground north of Arlington, and another near Shushan, New York—both good spots to end your trip.

Don't leave town without stopping at the **Jelly Mill** (802-362-3494) on Route 7. There are three floors filled with gifts of every description. When you've shopped to your heart's content, treat your stomach to lunch upstairs in the **Buttery**. Friends recommend the **Reluctant Panther Inn** (802-362-2568) for fresh seafood, quail, and lamb; **Grabber's Restaurant** (802-362-3394) for beef and seafood; and **The Black Swan** (802-362-3807) for continental cuisine with a California flair.

There are many ways to continue your exploration of southern Vermont from Manchester, each one appealing. Heading north on Route 7 and northwest on Route 30 leads to East Dorset and Dorset. Heading southeast on Route 30 leads to Brattleboro, passing through archetypal Vermont towns and close by two major ski areas, Bromley and Stratton. Route 7A heads south through Sunderland and Arlington to Bennington. From there you can drive the historic Molly Stark Trail (Route 9) from Bennington to Brattleboro.

EAST DORSET

To explore the area north of Manchester, take Route 7 north to East Dorset. There's a fine area for hiking near **Emerald Lake State Park**. Instead of going into the park, bear right at the sign for **Natural Bridge**. Leave your car in the parking lot. The climb is steep, leading up to a deep gorge spanned at the top by a 2-foot-wide natural bridge that's almost as thick.

Emerald Lake State Park
Route 7
East Dorset

DORSET AND EAST RUPERT

Alternatively, from Manchester take Route 30 northwest to Dorset. This charming village, with well-kept colonial houses, was the site of the first marble quarry in the country. The **Dorset Playhouse** (802-867-2223) is an established theater of professional caliber. Call for a schedule of performances. The **Dorset Inn** (802-867-5500) is just what you think of when you think of an inn in Vermont. Stay for the night, or just a meal.

Merck Forest
Route 315
East Rupert
802-394-7836

Continue north on Route 30 into East Rupert; then take Route 315 for 2½ miles to the sign for **Merck Forest**. This 2,600-acre forest, a treasure for hikers, was given to the town by George W. Merck in 1950. There is a year-round program of reforestation and logging, and signs at seven stations along the main trail describe the wildlife in the area. Before you start, register at the information booth and pick up a pamphlet. After Station 3, you come to a barn, the center of the educational program. There are a number of trails to follow, including the steep trail to Mount Antone, and there are nine overnight shelters that can be used with a permit. The forest is open all year and offers one of the finest cross-country ski terrains in Vermont.

Bromley
Mountain
Manchester
802-824-5522

If you're ready for skiing or hiking head southeast on Route 30 to Bromley and Stratton mountains, then south on Route 100 to Mt. Snow.

The vertical drop at Bromley is 1,334 feet. Bromley has six double chairlifts and one T-bar. It is open from mid-November into April. We love the sunshine on those pleasant south slopes. Intermediates will come into their own at Bromley with the whole mountain to explore. Snow Ranger to Upper Thruway or Shincracker lead into the easier slopes at the bottom, or you can choose to shoot down all the way under the lift on Upper Twister and Lower Twister.

If you're around during the summer try the first alpine slide in North America. Ride up on the chairlift and then choose one of three tracks for your slide down to the bottom. You control the speed of your sled! Or you can choose to take the chairlift to the summit.

Nearby sits ever-popular Stratton Mountain. The vertical drop is 2,003. Lifts include three quad chairlifts, one triple chairlift, and six double chairlifts. One of the distinctive features of Stratton is the village, reminiscent of European alpine ski centers. The Clock Tower in the square is a good place to meet at the end of the day. Dating from the early 1960s, Stratton has attracted people who wanted to build second homes right next to the ski area. As you ski down the slopes you can glimpse one chalet after another waiting for their owners to come in after a day of skiing and put their feet up beside a roaring fire.

Stratton Mountain
Stratton
802-297-2200

Expert skiers will be challenged by World Cup on the Upper Mountain and Upper Down Easter in the Sun Bowl. Beginners have their own special place located between the base lodge and Sun Bowl. For intermediates, this ski area is wonderful; you can choose between low intermediate and intermediate by checking the symbols. Favorites include the following trails: from the top of the Snow Bowl Quad Chair take Upper Wanderer to West and East Meadow, leading to Drifter Link and Old Log Road. Or try Upper Drifter, Interstate, and Lower Standard. Also from the top, Black Bear is nice and wide. In the Sun Bowl try Sunriser Supertrail or Gentle Ben.

All summer long, you can play tennis, golf, or join a special program in conjunction with the Orvis Company if you like to fish. The Volvo International Tennis Tournament is held at Stratton in the summer. The Stratton Sports Center offers both summer and winter activity with fifteen outdoor tennis courts, four indoor tennis courts, three racquetball courts, a fitness center, steam room, suntan parlor, and a sports shop.

Follow Route 100 to Mount Snow (802-464-3333). For many years Mount Snow has offered

Mount Snow
802-464-3333

wide smooth trails with the sun on them in the morning—the best way to encourage new and not-so-new skiers. We well remember the unique two-person gondola that looks like a red, blue, or yellow egg with your skis hanging out the bottom. Over the years Mount Snow has become more sophisticated, even to the point of using computer-monitored snowmaking facilities. The adjoining area of Carinthia adds more dimension to Mount Snow skiing.

The vertical drop is 1,700 feet. Lifts include the gondola, five triple chairlifts, eight double chairlifts, a T-bar, and a rope tow. The main mountain is almost completely covered with snowmaking equipment, which makes beginning and intermediate skiers very happy.

Many expert skiers head to the North Face for black diamond runs such as Free Fall, Challenger, Fallen Timbers, P.D.F. (Pretty Damned Fast), and Jaws of Death—they do sound ominous! Beginners can start at the Learning Center, then graduate to the Mixing Bowl area, Beaver Hill, and Sundance. Mount Snow is heavily stacked toward the intermediate skier with the entire main mountain so rated. The trails are wide, beautifully groomed, with a few dips here and there for a challenge. Snowdance is a wide field that can make anyone feel euphoric.

Mount Snow in the summer offers the 3-mile round-trip gondola ride to the top of the mountain, a golf school, tennis, swimming, horseback riding, sailing, windsurfing, and fishing. There are lots of activities such as antique and flea markets, an air show, a music festival and crafts fairs in the area.

Perhaps you prefer to take a different route from Manchester. Follow Route 7A south about 5 miles to Sunderland. Watch for the entrance to **Skyline Drive**, a steep narrow toll road to the top of **Mount Equinox**. The view from the 3,835-

First Congregational Church and cemetery, where poet Robert Frost is buried.

BENNINGTON

The Killington Gondola, the longest ski lift in North America, transports passengers up 4241 ft. Killington Peak. The 7-mile round trip offers 360 degree views of 5 states and Canada.

KILLINGTON

57 trails spread over 3 mountain faces give a variety of terrain for all levels of ability at Mount Snow. The ski season runs from mid-November through early May.

MOUNT SNOW

N•309

foot peak includes the spine of the Green Mountains, the backbone of Vermont and New York.

Continue south to Arlington for a gourmet meal at **The Inn at Arlington** (802-375-6532), a Greek Revival mansion with appropriate interior decoration. Diners drive from many miles away to enjoy the Sunday brunch as well as memorable dinners.

BENNINGTON

Continue south on Route 7 to Bennington, the home of Ethan Allen's Green Mountain Boys—the Bennington Mob. On August 16, 1777, the Battle of Bennington was fought nearby (the actual battle site is near Walloomaac, New York). That battle marked a turning point in the war, weakening the British and forcing them to retreat.

Bennington Battle Monument
Monument Road
Bennington
802-447-0550

The **Bennington Battle Monument**, a 300-foot-high obelisk built in 1891, commemorates General Stark's victory over the British led by General John Burgoyne. If you're here in late August you can witness the celebrations of Bennington Battle Day Weekend. Take an elevator to the top of the monument for a view of the countryside. Farther up Monument Avenue, you can walk around Old Bennington and enjoy the lovely colonial homes, the green, and **Old First Church**. This white clapboard structure has an unusual steeple with three tiers. Inside, each of the six columns was developed from one tree. Vaulted ceilings and box pews complete this interesting period building.

Stroll through the **Old Burying Ground**, next to the church, to see the graves of five Vermont governors, the founders of Bennington, and the grave of Robert Frost. His epitaph represents his life: "I had a lover's quarrel with the world."

Bennington Museum
Route 9
Bennington
802-447-1571

About a mile beyond the center is the **Bennington Museum** and its collections of Bennington pottery, blown and pressed glass, paintings by Grandma Moses, costumes, and furnishings.

The **Grandma Moses Schoolhouse** is located next door to the museum. Some of her paintings and mementos are on display in the Schoolhouse. Grandma Moses began painting at the age of 70 and continued until she died at 101.

Don't leave without stopping at **Bennington Pottery** (802-447-7531) on County Street. You'll find a lovely gift shop, good buys on seconds, and, next door, a wonderful cafe for lunch. You might also eat at the **Publyk House** (Harwood Hill, Route 7A, 802-422-8301) or **The Squires** (421 Main Street, 802-442-2767).

Follow Route 67A out of Bennington to North Bennington, where you'll find the **Parke-McCullough House**. The Victorian mansion is furnished with period pieces. During the year, craft fairs, art exhibits, square dances, and other events are held here.

NORTH BENNINGTON

Parke-McCullough House
West and Park Streets
North Bennington
802-447-2747

For an interesting side trip, drive east on Route 9 out of Bennington on Molly Stark Trail to signs for **Molly Stark State Park**. Molly Stark was the wife of General John Stark, who was called out of retirement during the Revolution to lead a thousand men across Vermont, to protect munitions stored in Bennington. Stark wrote his wife:

WILMINGTON

Molly Stark State Park
Route 9
Wilmington
802-464-5460

> Dear Molly: In less than a week, the British forces will be ours. Send every man from the farm that will come and let the haying go.

She did as he asked and more; she sent two hundred townspeople along too. As he went into battle, General Stark said, "There are the Redcoats, and they are ours, or this night Molly Stark sleeps a widow." But she didn't. He won the battle and brought home a brass cannon, one of six taken from the British. (It's still on display in New Boston, New Hampshire, and is fired every Fourth of July.)

From Wilmington continue on Route 9 to pick up the itinerary in Brattleboro.

JAMAICA

As another alternative from Manchester, head southeast on Route 30 to Jamaica, where the whitewater canoe and kayak championships are held each spring. Stop for a meal at **Three Mountain Inn** (Route 30, 802-874-4140). In 1983 the U.S. Whitewater Kayak team stayed there and were fed high-energy meals to spur them on to victory.

TOWNSHEND

Continue on to Townshend. Here you'll find the longest covered bridge in Vermont—**Scott Bridge**—spanning West River. It was built in 1870 and extends 276 feet. In town the **Congregational Church** is the archetypical New England church. It was built in 1790, and it is very beautiful. It's also a favorite of jigsaw puzzle manufacturers—so you may already be familiar with it.

NEWFANE

Newfane, 4 miles south of Townshend on Route 30, is one of the loveliest towns in the state. The **Windham County Court House**, a Greek Revival structure, was built in 1825.

Stop for a meal at the **Newfane Inn** (802-365-4427), right on Route 30. The inn is lovely (it was built in 1787), and so is the food. Then walk across the street to the **Newfane Country Store** (802-365-7916). Its four rooms are filled with kitchen accessories, foods (the bread is delicious), quilts, and all kinds of country gifts. If you're looking for older treasures, come on a Sunday between May and October for the **Newfane Flea Market**.

Follow Route 30 into Brattleboro. Brattleboro is the site of the first settlement in Vermont, in 1724 at Fort Dummer. The town was once home to Rudyard Kipling. In 1892 the author married Caroline Starr Balestier of Brattleboro. On her family's estate they built **Naulahka**, a home that Kipling described as a ship with the propeller (furnace) and kitchen at the stern, his study and a piazza at the bow. It was here that he wrote *The Jungle Book, The Seven Seas,* and *Captains Courageous*. During a family quarrel over land rights, Beatty Balestier, Kipling's brother-in-law, made threats on his life. Balestier was arrested, and Kipling and his family moved to England. Today you can see Naulahka from a distance, but it is not open to the public.

This itinerary through southern Vermont is complete. Brattleboro is on the New Hampshire border and is an easy trip to the towns that end Itinerary I. It also is not far from Greenfield, Massachusetts, in Itinerary G.

BRATTLEBORO

Naulahka
19 Terrace Street
Brattleboro

APPENDIX I: INNS AND BED & BREAKFAST

HOPKINS INN

INNS AND BED & BREAKFAST
IN NEW ENGLAND

The following list of inns and bed and breakfast accommodations includes a selection ranging from those that are inexpensive to establishments worthy of a "big splurge" occasion. We have tried to include those with an interesting historical past or a beautiful setting.

On the whole, inns and B&Bs in the United States are more expensive than their counterparts in Europe, but they are more appealing than comparable motel accommodations. Some of them offer special rates during their off-peak times, such as weekends in cities and weekdays in the country, or at quiet times in their seasonal cycle through the year. Prices will vary, but all of them offer personal attention to make your stay pleasant; for once you will be something more than twenty to forty bytes on a computerized reservation list. Your host or hostess may offer you a glass of sherry, fresh fruit in your room, flowers, bath oil in the bathroom, or a foil-wrapped chocolate on your pillow. On the other hand, don't be disappointed by the lack of one of these gestures. You may find that your hosts will offer you an hour of conversation during an evening, and you may become friends and return year after year. Inns and B&B hosts and guests share one quality that appeals more and more to most Americans: They like to talk and to meet new friends in each region they visit, so it is no wonder that those who have traveled widely prefer staying in someone's home rather than in an anonymous hotel owned by a corporate chain. Almost all of the inns and B&Bs serve a complimentary breakfast, but only the inns serve lunch and dinner. Occasionally we have listed accommodations that do not fit the criteria for inns or B&Bs but are nevertheless the most appealing in the area.

Everywhere on the scene are the condominiums springing up in vacation areas. Many beach and ski areas offer "condo" living throughout the year, and during off-seasons the rates drop considerably. Retirees with homes in the South often rent an inexpensive ski-area condo in the cool mountains for the summer. But even in high seasons, for leaf watching in the fall or skiing during the winter, condos may provide substantial savings for families who can cook their own meals rather than paying much higher restaurant prices. The initial price of the condo, which seems much higher than a lodge or motel, may be a bargain in the long run.

In no case do we pretend or intend to be comprehensive. We recommend good places that we know something of without prejudice to equally good places that we are ignorant of, many of which we hope to discover in future travels. Our listings of accommodations are neither inclusive nor exclusive—but only an adjunct to the book's itineraries for the convenience of those who do not wish to spend much of their time finding a good place to sleep.

Reservation Services and Directories

A list of B&B reservation services follows; the rationale for these services is comparable to that of a travel agent, since each one offers to secure and guarantee reservations in advance. Some are national, some state, and others regional; each of them has a range of accommodations to offer. Some will help you plan your trip by reserving rooms along your route. Others will offer suggestions for specific areas you wish to visit or a directory to help you choose your own accommodations. Membership fees apply in some cases, but not all.

NATIONAL	Bed & Breakfast, The National Network, P.O. Box 4616, Springfield, MA 01101.
	The National Bed and Breakfast Association, P.O. Box 332, Norwalk, CT 06852. Phone: 203-847-6196.
	Pineapple Hospitality, 47 North Second Street, Suite 3A, New Bedford, MA 02740. Phone: 617-990-1696.
	Bed and Breakfast, Ltd., Box 216, New Haven, CT 06513. Phone: 203-469-3260.
CONNECTICUT	Covered Bridge Bed and Breakfast, West Cornwall, CT 06796. Phone: 203-672-6052.

Bed & Breakfast Down East, Ltd., Box 547B, Macomber Mill Road, Eastbrook, ME 04534. Phone: 207-565-3517.

MAINE

Bed and Breakfast Cape Cod, Box 341, West Hyannisport, MA 02672. Phone: 617-775-2772.

MASSACHUSETTS

Bed and Breakfast Associates, P.O. Box 166, Babson Park Branch, Boston, MA 02157. Phone: 617-449-5302.

Bed & Breakfast, Cambridge & Greater Boston, Box 665, Cambridge, MA 02140. Phone: 617-576-1492.

New Hampshire Bed & Breakfast, RFD 3, Box 53, Laconia, NH 03246. Phone: 603-279-8348.

NEW HAMPSHIRE

Bed & Breakfast of Rhode Island, P.O. Box 312, Barrington, R.I. 02806. Phone: 401-246-0142.

RHODE ISLAND

Vermont Bed & Breakfast, Box 139, Browns Trace, East Fairfield, VT 05465. Phone: 802-827-3827.

VERMONT

Accommodations by State

Bishopsgate Inn, Goodspeed Landing, East Haddam, CT 06423. Phone: 203-873-1677. This is an 1818 shipbuilder's home with lots of fireplaces. In fact, you can have dinner in front of your own fireplace in your room! The inn is furnished with period pieces and family antiques. Breakfast features home-baked specialties and pantry preserves.

CONNECTICUT

East Haddam

The Griswold Inn, Main Street, Essex, CT 06426. Phone: 203-767-0991. Dating from 1776, the popular Griswold Inn has the charm of the past along with modern conveniences. Governor

Essex

Trumbull and Oliver Cromwell loved it, and suites were named after them. Besides offering accommodations, the "Gris" is well known for wonderful food; the famous Hunt Breakfast was begun when the British occupied the inn during the War of 1812.

Glastonbury

Butternut Farm, 1654 Main Street, Glastonbury, CT 06033. Phone: 203-633-7197. Here is an eighteenth-century jewel of a colonial home, furnished with antiques collected by the owner. Breakfast is served beside a long, paneled fireplace, where there is a collection of English Delft to look at.

Groton Long Point

Shore Inne, 54 East Shore Road, Groton Long Point, CT 06340. Phone: 203-536-1180. Beautiful views of the water are offered from this lovely residential setting. The rooms have handmade bedspreads; one room has hand-stencilled walls.

Litchfield

Toll Gate Inn, P.O. Box 1339, Litchfield, CT 06759. Phone: 203-482-6116. Built in 1745, it became an inn on the road from Hartford to Litchfield and was also known as the Captain William Bull Tavern. In 1923 the building was moved to Toll Gate Hill. Some of the bedrooms have fireplaces, canopied bed, and loveseats. Dinner is served in one of the original rooms of the house or in the large ballroom that contains a fiddler's loft.

Kent

1741 Saltbox Inn, P.O. Box 677, Route 7 and Studio Hill Road, Kent, CT 06757. Phone: 203-927-4376. Also called the John Beebe House, the inn is listed as a National Register Historic Property. The center chimney vents five fireplaces; the one in the kitchen is one of the largest in Connecticut. Bedrooms are furnished with colonial pieces, and each room has a fireplace.

The Inn at Mystic, Routes 1 and 27, Mystic, **Mystic**
CT 06335. Phone: 203-536-9604. A variety of
accommodations are available in the Inn (a 1904
Colonial Revival mansion where Humphrey Bo-
gart and Lauren Bacall stayed on their honey-
moon), in the Gate House overlooking the
orchards, and in a motor inn. The Flood Tide
Restaurant serves meals with style.

The Old Mystic Inn, 58 Main Street, Old
Mystic, CT 06372. Phone: 203-572-9422. Dating
from the early 1800s, the building once con-
tained the Old Mystic Book Shop. Recently renovated and decorated, three of the four guest
rooms have working fireplaces.

Red Brook Inn, P.O. Box 237, Old Mystic,
CT 06372. Phone: 203-572-0349. There are two
buildings at Red Brook. In 1768 stagecoach travelers looked forward to stopping at the Haley
Tavern. Rooms are furnished with canopied or
poster beds and period pieces. The Crary Homestead, just down the hill, was built by a Mystic
merchant sea captain during the late 1700s.

Boulders Inn, New Preston, CT 06777. **New Preston**
Phone: 203-868-7918. Built in 1895 for a family,
the house has a view of Lake Waramaug at the
bottom of the hill. Rooms on the second floor
are furnished with antiques. The property has
been expanded to include cottages with working
fireplaces.

The Hopkins Inn, New Preston, CT 06777.
Phone: 203-868-7295. This Federal-style inn
overlooks Lake Waramaug, adjoining vineyards,
and farmland. It was built in 1847 as a summer
guest house. The rooms are furnished with country antiques.

Greenwoods Gate, Norfolk, CT 06058. **Norfolk**
Phone: 203-542-5439. This 1797 colonial has
been renovated and decorated in a different style
in each room—from a floral room with lacy pil-

lows and brass bed to a Victorian room with a loft bed. You can even have your breakfast in bed.

Norwalk

Silvermine Tavern, Norwalk, CT 06850. Phone: 203-847-4558. The Coach House, the Old Mill, the Gatehouse, and the Tavern are all within earshot of a wonderful waterfall. You can feed the swans and wild ducks who stay all winter to nibble. Rooms are furnished with antiques. Don't miss Miss Abigail, the only woman permitted by Connecticut law to stand within three feet of a bar.

Old Lyme

Bee and Thistle Inn, 100 Lyme Street, Old Lyme, CT 06371. Phone: 203-434-1667. Dating from 1756, the house contains many fireplaces. Rooms include canopied or four-poster beds, quilts, and Early American furnishings. Guests may have breakfast in their rooms, on a porch, or in front of the fire in the dining room.

Old Lyme Inn, Lyme Street, Old Lyme, CT 06371. Phone: 203-434-2600. The building dates from the 1850s when it was a working farm of 300 acres. Recently renovated, the inn contains Empire and Victorian period antiques. Paintings reflect the Old Lyme school of artists who once lived in Florence Griswold's home just across the street.

Salisbury

Under Mountain Inn, Route 41, Salisbury, CT 06068. Phone: 203-435-0242. Built in the 1700s, this inn is shaded by a thorned locust tree, thought to be the oldest in the state. Rooms are all decorated differently—some with brass beds, print wallpaper, and wing chairs. Don't miss the English pub with its paneling that was found under the attic floorboards (the lumber was supposed to have been turned over to the king of England).

Cabin in the Woods, P.O. Box 3291, Stony Creek, CT 06405. Phone: 203-488-5284. This new, modern, knotty-pine cabin contains oriental rugs, a club kitchen, a living room with a woodburning stove, and a birdfeeder outside the window.

Stony Creek

MAINE

Hearthside Inn, 7 High Street, Bar Harbor, ME 04609. Phone: 207-288-4533. This three-story weathered-shingled house was built around 1900 for a local doctor. Recently redecorated, the house has a lovely fireplace and collection of Victorian furniture.

Bar Harbor

Four Seasons Inn, Box 390, Bethel, ME 04217. Phone: 207-824-2755. This 1895 Victorian B&B is in the center of town. Rooms are filled with antiques and decorated with fresh flowers and fruit baskets.

Bethel

L'Auberge Country Inn, Box 21, Bethel, ME 04217. Phone: 207-824-2774. L'Auberge is located in a garden at the edge of town. This old-fashioned inn offers comfortable rooms as well as a dormitory.

The Cornish Inn, Route 25, Box 266, Cornish, ME 04020. Phone: 207-625-8501. This restored, old-fashioned, village inn is located in the Lakes Region of Maine. Guest rooms are decorated with antiques and stencilled walls.

Cornish

High Meadows Bed & Breakfast, Route 101, Eliot, ME 03903. Phone: 207-439-0590. This lovely colonial house was built on a hill in 1736 by a merchant shipbuilder and captain. Some of the bedrooms contain four-poster beds, fireplace, and period furniture. Guests are invited to relax on the porch or in the living room in front of the fireplace.

Eliot

Isle Au Haut   The Keeper's House, P.O. Box 26, Isle Au Haut, ME 04645. Phone: 207-677-3678. This is a new inn in a lighthouse. Arrangements need to be made in advance for a 40-minute trip on the mailboat from Stonington. For an authentic light show you shouldn't miss the action on the top of the 48-foot lighthouse.

Kennebunk   The Kennebunk Inn, 45 Main Street, Kennebunk, ME 04043. Phone: 207-985-3351. Dating from 1799, the inn has been completely restored by the owners. Some of the rooms feature a Victorian sofa, oriental rug, and brass bed. The patio, with its colorful geraniums, is a pleasant place to relax.

Kennebunkport   The Chetwynd House Inn, Chestnut Street, Box 130, Kennebunkport, ME 04046. Phone: 207-967-2235. This home was built in 1840 by Captain Seavey. It is in the village and the ocean is nearby. The house features ceiling-to-floor windows and wide-board pine floors.

North Windham   Sebago Lake Lodge, White's Bridge Road, North Windham, ME 04062. Phone: 207-892-2698. The lodge is located right on the lake. Two white buildings are brightened with blue shutters. Boats are available for guests.

Pemaquid Falls   Little River Inn, Route 130, Pemaquid Falls, ME 04558. Phone: 207-677-2845. Located on top of Pemaquid Falls, this house has both river and saltwater views. It was built in 1840 as a farmhouse. "Banquet" breakfasts are a special treat.

Rangeley   Rangeley Inn, Box 398, Main Street, Rangeley, ME 04970. Phone: 207-864-3341. This turn-of-the-century inn is located on the eastern shore of the lake. The wood-beam pub is part of the original 1877 building. Rooms range from doubles to quadruples, with antiques and brass beds.

York Beach

Jo-Mar Bed and Breakfast, 41 Freeman Street, P.O. Box 838, York Beach, ME 03910. Phone: 207-363-2958. Located on the ocean, this house offers appealing views up to Nubble Light. It is located on a bluff overlooking Short Sands Beach. Breakfast includes blueberry muffins or coffee cake.

MASSACHUSETTS

Boston

The Eliot Hotel, 370 Commonwealth Avenue, Boston, MA 02215. Phone: 617-267-1607. This hotel, next to the Harvard Club, has been renovated to include suites with kitchenettes.

Brookline

Beacon Street Guest House, 1047 Beacon Street, Brookline, MA 02146. Phone: 617-232-0292. This Victorian townhouse offers some rooms with fireplaces. It is located just outside Kenmore Square, close to Fenway Park.

Brookline Manor Guest House, 32 Centre Street, Brookline, MA 02146. Phone: 617-232-0003. Three separate houses, built in the early 1900s, have been converted into this guest house.

Cambridge

A Cambridge House Bed & Breakfast, Box 211, Cambridge, MA 02140. Phone: 617-491-6300. This 1892 Federal-style home is listed on the National Register of Historic Places. Guests may sink into comfortable chairs in front of the fireplace and listen to classical music from the stereo, or sip sherry and have a bite of fruitcake in the adjacent Victorian parlor. Bedrooms are decorated with coordinated prints and include easy chairs with a coffee table. Breakfasts offer special recipes to keep guests going all morning.

Cape Cod

Chatham

Chatham Wayside Inn, 512 Main Street, P.O. Box 749, Chatham, MA 02633. Phone: 617–945–1800. Originally a coach inn, the Wayside still has a pub that is popular with local residents. Pub fare is available in the tavern, while a full menu is offered in the dining room. Bedrooms are in the process of being renovated.

The Queen Anne Inn, 70 Queen Anne Road, Chatham, MA 02633. Phone: 617-945-0394. This 145-year-old inn offers a view of Oyster Pond Bay, a complimentary cruise around the harbor, use of bicycles, tennis courts, and a spa/hot tub. Each bedroom is furnished with antiques and comfortable chairs, and some have a fireplace, whirlpool bath, and balcony. Dining in the "Earl of Chatham" is a real treat.

Dennis

Isaiah B. Hall House, 152 Whig Street, Dennis, MA 02638. Phone: 617-385-9928. This Greek Revival farmhouse was built in 1857 by a cooper (barrel-maker). His barrels were used to ship cranberries from the adjacent bog. Rooms are decorated with antiques, orientals, stained glass, and quilts. Some rooms have balconies.

East Brewster

Old Sea Pines Inn, 2553 Main Street, P.O. Box 1026, East Brewster, MA 02631. Phone: 617-896-6114. This inn was once the Sea Pines School of Charm and Personality for Young Women, founded in 1907. Its furnishings reflect the twenties and thirties, with priscilla curtains, brass beds, and print wallpaper.

East Orleans

Ship's Knees Inn, Beach Road, East Orleans, MA 02643. Phone: 617-255-1312. Did you know that a "ship's knee" is a piece of wood cut into a bracket shape, holding deck beams to the frame of the ship? This sea captain's home is furnished with antiques. One bedroom has a fireplace, and many rooms have ocean views.

Capt. Tom Lawrence House, 75 Locust Street, Falmouth, MA 02540. Phone: 617-540-1445. Built as a whaling captain's home, the house is now shaded by two tall maple trees. Guests may play the Steinway piano or sit by the fire. Guest rooms feature down comforters.

Coonamessett Inn, Jones Road and Gifford Street, Falmouth, MA 02541. Phone: 617-548-2300. Although guests don't really expect to see a mermaid on the patio, there is a bit of water—a quiet pond, colorful with fall colors when we were there. Dating from 1796, the house contains original paneling and fireplaces built from "ballast brick" carried on schooners from Europe. Rooms are furnished with pine and cherry colonial furnishings. Meals are offered in several rooms in the main building.

Mostly Hall Bed & Breakfast Inn, 27 Main Street, Falmouth, MA 02540. Phone: 617-548-3786. Built as a summer home in 1849, the house is elegant, the grounds lush. Guest rooms are furnished with canopied beds, and each room has a reading area. Don't miss the "Widow's Walk Room" at the very top. Guests may borrow a bicycle and head off on the Shining Sea Bikeway.

The Palmer House Inn, 81 Palmer Avenue, Falmouth, MA 02540. Phone: 617-548-1230. This Victorian-style inn contains stained glass windows and period furnishings. The guest rooms contain four-poster, brass, or sleigh beds and are colorful with quilts, silk flowers, and old photos.

The Village Green Inn, 40 West Main Street, Falmouth, MA 02540. Phone: 617-548-5621. Right on the green, the house offers two large porches where guests can rock and relax. Some of the guest rooms have fireplaces.

Sea Witch Inn, 363 Sea Street, Hyannis, MA 02601. Phone: 617-771-4261 or 617-775-3608.

Built in 1900, this home features a wraparound porch. The rooms are furnished with antiques, including brass beds. Guests may use the refrigerator and outdoor grill.

Provincetown

The Joshua Paine House, 15 Tremont Street, Provincetown, MA 02657. Phone: 617-487-1551. The descendants of Joshua Paine sold this house to its present owners. It is furnished with antiques and is just one block from the water.

Twelve Center Guest House, 12 Center Street, Provincetown, MA 02657. Phone: 617-487-0381. Captain Josiah Snow built this Victorian house in 1872. The rooms are large and each is decorated in a different color scheme. Breakfast includes home-baked muffins.

Woods Hole

The Grey Whale Inn, 565 Woods Hole Road, Woods Hole, MA 02543. Phone: 617-548-7692. Dating from 1804, this inn is located on Little Harbor overlooking Vineyard Sound. You can have breakfast while watching yachts and ferries head out to sea.

Concord

Hawthorne Inn, 462 Lexington Road, Concord, MA 02554. Phone: 617-369-5610. Originally this land belonged to Ralph Waldo Emerson, who deeded it to Bronson Alcott and later to Nathaniel Hawthorne. The larch trees planted by Hawthorne are still standing. The house is furnished with antiques, orientals, paintings, and some Japanese block prints from the 1800s.

The Anderson-Wheeler Homestead, 154 Fitchburg Turnpike, Concord, MA 01742. Phone: 617-369-3756. In 1858 Edwin Wheeler bought the property, which had been known as Whipple Tavern since 1831. After a fire a house and barn were built on the site; over the years the property has been passed down through the same family to the present owners. There are five fireplaces; it is pleasant to have breakfast beside one. A new bath has two skylights, a tub with claw feet, and a large tiled walk-in shower.

Candlelight Inn, 53 Walker Street, Lenox, MA 01240. Phone: 413-637-1555. The inn is a popular place to dine, in one of the four dining rooms or outside in the courtyard during the summer. Guest rooms are individually decorated with print wallpaper, antiques, floral arrangements on skirted tables, quilts, and paintings.

Lenox

Deerfield Inn, The Street, Deerfield, MA 01342. Phone: 413-774-5587. This white clapboard inn is right in the center of things in historic Deerfield. You can tour the houses in small doses and return to your room to rest. The inn has its own collection of antique furnishings. Guest rooms offer canopied beds, print fabrics, and nice paintings. Don't miss the Beehive Parlor's reproduction wallpaper dating from the early nineteenth century. Visitors can have a light lunch downstairs, or in the dining room by reservation.

Deerfield

Blue Shutters Inn, 1 Nautilus Road, Gloucester, MA 01930. Phone: 617-281-2706. This inn has attractive landscaping around rocks leading up to the front door as well as a view of the lovely sandy beach and water across the road. Plush blue carpeting in the living room leads to comfortable sofas in front of the fireplace. All guest rooms have a view of the water.

Gloucester

Williams Guest House, 136 Bass Avenue, Gloucester, MA 01930. Phone: 617-283-4931. This Colonial Revival home is located right on Good Harbor beach. Some of the rooms have balconies. There are a cottage and two apartments for longer stays.

Marblehead

The Harbor Light Inn, 58 Washington Street, Marblehead, MA 01945. Phone: 617-631-2186. The living room is elegant with a large oriental rug, antiques, and a glowing fireplace. Each of the guest rooms has its own character with china vases on the mantel, a selection of books, oriental rug, canopied bed, fireplace, and reading area. Some even feature a jacuzzi, plants, and a skylight.

Martha's Vineyard

Edgartown

The Daggett House, 59 North Water Street, Edgartown, MA 02539. Phone: 617-627-4600. This shingled colonial house has a secret stairway . . . somewhere. There are two more buildings on the property: the Captain Warren House across the street and the Garden Cottage on the water. There is a paneled fireplace in the breakfast room where a full country breakfast is served.

The Kelley House, Kelley Street, Edgartown, MA 02539. Phone: 617-627-4394. The original building dates back to 1742; a three-story section has been added. Guests enjoy the public rooms, which are decorated in colonial fashion. Roses grow in gardens on the grounds, and there is a pool.

The Victorian Inn, South Water Street, P.O. Box 947, Edgartown, MA 02539. Phone: 617-627-4784. Located in the midst of sea captains' homes, this inn is across from the famous Pagoda Tree. The guest rooms have four-poster beds and antiques. Some of them have balconies.

Nantucket

The Carlisle House Inn, 26 North Water Street, Nantucket, MA 02554. Phone: 617-228-0720. Dating from 1765, this inn has been in business for over 100 years. Some bedrooms are very simple; some have canopied beds, oriental rugs, stencilled wallpaper, and working fireplaces.

Nantucket Roosts, Nine Cliff Road, Nantucket, MA 02554. Phone: 617-228-9480. Here are not one but two guest houses to choose from. Cliff Lodge Guest House is a former sea captain's home built over 200 years ago. The living room is filled with antiques, and the bedrooms have been newly redecorated with Laura Ashley wallpaper. Still Dock contains apartments with kitchens, nice for longer stays.

The Roberts House Inn, 11 India Street, Nantucket, MA 02554. Phone: 617-228-9009, 617-228-0600, or 800-992-2899. This Greek Revival inn, dating from 1846, offers rocking chairs on the front porch for complete relaxation. Bedrooms range from small rooms to family suites. Canopied beds and antiques are in many rooms. The Manor House next door was acquired in mid-1987.

Newburyport

The Morrill Place Inn, 209 High Street, Newburyport, MA 01950. Phone: 617-462-2808. This home features a staircase with six-inch rises built when women wore hoop skirts. There are a music room, library, and porches for guests. Afternoon tea and a continental breakfast are offered.

Rockport

Linden Tree Inn, 26 King Street, Rockport, MA 01966. Phone: 617-546-2494. This white Victorian house is 150 years old. It is on a side street and has a pleasant porch from which guests can enjoy the view. The living room has been renovated, and there is a glass-front wood stove for spring and fall warmth. The beach is 2½ blocks away.

The Seafarer, 86 Marmion Way, Rockport, MA 01966. Phone: 617-546-6248. Located on the easternmost point of Cape Ann, this house has a 180-degree view of the water. Cool breezes waft even when the temperature soars in town. Each room has at least three paintings by local artists. Several apartments are also available.

The Yankee Clipper Inn, P.O. Box 2399, Rockport, MA 01966. Phone: 617-546-3407. This inn consists of three buildings that were once private residences. The inn is an oceanfront mansion with bedrooms, the dining room, and glass-enclosed porches. The Quarterdeck is also on the water. The Bullfinch House is up the hill away from the water, but guests use the same facilities, such as the dining room and swimming pool. Antiques and period furnishings decorate all three houses.

Stockbridge

The Red Lion Inn, Stockbridge, MA 01262. Phone: 413-298-5545. Originally built in 1773 as a tavern and a stagecoach stop, the Red Lion was purchased by the Treadway family in 1862. During the ninety years it remained in the family, collections of antiques, china, and pewter were built up; much is still on display today. Five presidents have stayed there: Cleveland, McKinley, Theodore Roosevelt, Coolidge, and Franklin D. Roosevelt. Bedrooms are pleasant with print wallpaper and antiques. Guests may dine in the Widow Bingham Tavern or in the dining room.

Swampscott

Cap'n Jack's Waterfront Inn, 253 Humphrey Street, Swampscott, MA 01907. Phone: 617-595-7910, 617-595-9734. The house overlooks the harbor, which is filled with many sailboats in the summer. There are a pool and a sauna. Boats are available for your use.

Williamstown

The House on Main Street, 1120 Main Street, Williamstown, MA 01267. Phone: 413-458-3031. This 1804 home is located in the center of town, off Field Park. It is furnished with antiques and oriental rugs.

The Steele Homestead Inn, RR 1, Box 78, Antrim, NH 03440. Phone: 603-588-6772. Built in 1810 as a home by James Steele, the inn sits on a slope on four acres of land, which are colorful with gardens and a fruit orchard. Guests may relax in front of the fireplace surrounded by family antiques. Guest rooms are all decorated differently, and two of them have fireplaces.

Pinestead Farm Lodge, Route 116, Franconia, NH 03580. Phone: 603-823-8121. The views from this working farm include a meadow with cows, Cannon Mountain, and Kinsman Ridge. Rooms are in groups of three in separate sections of the house; each group has its own bath and kitchen. They may be rented individually or as a group for a family.

The New Grayhurst, 11 F Street, Hampton Beach, NH 03842. Phone: 603-926-2584. This 1890 gambrel-roofed beach house has flower boxes totaling thirty feet in length. Accommodations include a cottage, apartment, studios, rooms, and suites.

The Inn on Golden Pond, Route 3, Box 126, Holderness, NH 03245. Phone: 603-968-7269. Dating from 1879, the inn property includes 55 acres, which are perfect for cross-country skiers. After a day of skiing, guests enjoy relaxing by a fire in the sitting room. If you loved *Golden Pond*, you'll love this inn's location—the lake where the movie was filmed, Squam Lake, is across the road. Guest rooms have views of the grounds.

The Manor on Golden Pond, Box T, Route 3, Holderness, NH 03245. Phone: 603-968-3348. Built in 1903 by an Englishman, this inn maintains the charm of an English country estate. Carved and paneled walls and fireplaces set the tone for this mansion. Guests can read by the fire or have a drink in the Tapestry Lounge. Meals are served in the Candlelight Room.

Jackson

The Blake House, Route 16, Jackson, NH 03846. Phone: 603-383-9057. Here is an intimate guest house in European tradition, with cozy bedrooms, paneled living room, fieldstone fireplace, and cathedral ceilings. A full breakfast is served buffet-style.

Jaffrey Center

The Monadnock Inn, Main Street, Jaffrey Center, NH 03454. Phone: 603-532-7001. This inn has rocking chairs all along the front porch for guests to use. Guests can also curl up with a book in front of the fireplace in the living room.

Lincoln

The Mill House Inn, Lincoln, NH 03251. Phone: 603-745-6261. The inn is part of the historic Mill at Loon Mountain, a newly renovated complex including the Tavern in the former mill drying shed. The three-level restaurant has a three-sided view of the mountains as well. Millfront Marketplace offers lots of boutiques, a bookstore, and a gallery. The guest rooms are comfortable and there are an indoor pool, jacuzzi, and sauna.

Meredith

The Inn at Mill Falls, Mill Falls Marketplace, Route 3, Meredith, NH 03253. Phone: 603-279-7006. In the early 1800s a gristmill and a sawmill were in full operation here, but they closed down before 1816. From the windows in the inn you can watch water cascade down through a series of channels. Guests enjoy the comfortable bedrooms, pool, sauna, and whirlpool spa.

North Conway

Nereledge Inn, River Road, North Conway, NH 03860. Phone: 603-356-2831. This 1787 home includes a dining room and English-style pub where you can play darts, backgammon, and cribbage, or just relax. The guest rooms have English eiderdowns and rocking chairs. Guests can enjoy views of Cathedral Ledge while having breakfast.

Wildflowers Guest House, North Main Street, North Conway, NH 03860. Phone: 603-356-2224. This century-old country home has a lovely view of Mount Washington. The wildflower theme is carried out into the bedrooms; each has a different wildflower wallpaper. Guests are invited to enjoy the living room during the evenings. The complimentary breakfast includes home-baked coffee cakes and special breads.

North Woodstock

Woodstock Inn Bed & Breakfast, Box 118, Route 3, Main Street, North Woodstock, NH 03262. Phone: 603-745-3931. Accommodations are in two houses. The Main House, a 100-year-old Victorian, is decorated with antiques. We liked the antique skis on the wall and also the stencilling around the windows. The Woodstock Inn Riverside overlooks the Pemigewasset River and has a porch for river-watching. The Clement Room offers breakfast and dinner, including a number of specialties. Adjacent Woodstock Station, where you can have a casual lunch or dinner, was Lincoln's original railroad station.

Waterville Valley

Black Bear Lodge, Waterville Valley, NH 03223. Phone: 800-258-8988 (in NH, 800-552-4767) or 603-236-8371. The lodge offers one-bedroom suites with a kitchen. Other amenities include an indoor-outdoor pool, whirlpool, sauna, steamroom, and gameroom.

Snowy Owl Inn, Waterville Valley, NH 03223. Phone: 800-258-8988 (in NH, 800-552-5767) or 603-236-8383. The inn offers rooms, studios, and suites; a complimentary breakfast and wine and cheese or hot chocolate and cookies after 4:00 p.m. are included. Guests can curl up with a book in the library, sing-along in front of the 1890s grand piano, have a drink before the fire in the Brookside Room, or enjoy the pool, whirlpool, and recreation room.

RHODE ISLAND

Block Island

Gables Inn & Gables II, Box 516, Dodge Street, Block Island, RI 02807. Phone 401-466-2213, 401-466-7721. Both houses have been restored and furnished with antiques and floral wallpaper. Beaches are just across the street. New apartments and a cottage are also available.

Narragansett

The Seagull, 50 Narragansett Avenue, Narragansett, RI 02882. Phone: 401-783-4636. This Victorian house was built in 1904. It is located one block from the beach.

The Summer House Inn, 87 Narragansett Avenue, Narragansett, RI 02882. Phone: 401-783-0123. This inn is located 1000 feet from the ocean. Guest rooms are furnished with white iron beds, country-print wallpaper, and antique bureaus. Guests can relax on the porch, which wraps around the front of the house.

Newport

Admiral Farragut Inn, 31 Clarke Street, Newport, RI 02840. Phone: 401-849-0006. You can't miss the great snowy egret painted on the wall just inside the door of this colonial inn. Guest rooms offer Shaker-style four-poster beds, painted armoires with stencilling, imported English antiques, and nautical prints on the walls. Breakfast is served on the banquet board in the Great Room.

Benjamin Mason House, 25 Brewer Street, Newport, RI 02840. Phone: 401-847-8427. Built by Benjamin Mason in 1740, the house is located in a row of historic houses on a side street up the hill from Thames Street. Two single bedrooms are available, both furnished with colonial pieces. Breakfast is served on the patio, weather permitting, or in the colonial dining room.

Cliffside Inn, Two Seaview Avenue, Newport, RI 02840. Phone: 401-847-1811. Built in 1880 by Governor Swann of Maryland as a summer residence, the inn overlooks the Atlantic; Cliff Walk is nearby. Guest rooms are furnished with antiques, oriental rugs, china pieces on the mantel, and paintings.

The Yankee Peddler Harborside Inn, Christie's Landing, Newport, RI 02840. Phone: 401-846-6600. This inn is located right on the wharf—a wonderful place to watch yachts come and go if you are in one of the waterside units. Or you can watch the action from the landing. Suites offer a sleeping loft, deck, refrigerator, and wet bar.

The Jailhouse Inn, 13 Marlborough Street, Newport, RI 02840. Phone: 401-847-4638. If you've wondered what it might be like in a jailhouse, you can stay in the authentic 1772 Newport Jail. However, this one has been completely renovated, and the rooms are light and airy instead of dingy and dark. A few black jail-like gates and lawmaking signs are around for atmosphere. The inn opened in August 1987.

Ma Gallagher's Guest House, 348 Thames Street, Newport, RI 02840. Phone: 401-849-3975. This guest house is located above the Ark Restaurant. The Victorian-style structure was built in the late 1890s and is listed in the National Register of Historic Places. During its early days Mary Gallagher cooked for the men who lived upstairs. The guest rooms are furnished with Victorian antiques and period pieces.

The Pilgrim House, 123 Spring Street, Newport, RI 02840. Phone: 401-846-0040. Built in 1809, this Victorian house is located in the Historic Hill district. There is a third floor deck overlooking the harbor. In warm months breakfast is served there; at other times it is served beside the fire.

Providence

337

The Old Court, 144 Benefit Street, Providence, RI 02903. Phone: 401-751-2002. Designed in 1863 as a rectory for St. John's Episcopal Church, the house has been renovated and decorated. The front hall is elegant with a crystal chandelier, and two living rooms are furnished with antique pieces. Guest rooms are attractive with brass bed, white lace bedspread, several mirrors, and antique pieces; all rooms are different. Breakfast is served in the downstairs cafe amidst ferns and hanging plants. We loved the cappuccino.

VERMONT

Arlington

The Arlington Inn, Route 7A, Arlington, VT 05250. Phone: 802-375-6532. This Greek Revival mansion was built in 1848 by Martin Chester Deming, a railroad magnate and Vermont politician. The inn looks elegant as you approach over the lawn, and it is. The living room, hall, and dining rooms are filled with antiques and oriental rugs. Guest rooms and suites are attractive with antique pieces. Guests have breakfast in the solarian, also a popular room for weddings. The inn has a reputation for wonderful meals, and it's well earned.

Barrows House, Dorset, VT 05251. Phone: 802-867-4455. This inn is almost 200 years old. It is a pleasant place to stay in the winter when you can go cross-country skiing right on the property. During the summer guests may use the pool and tennis court and borrow bicycles. The inn is furnished with antiques, including rockers in front of the fireplace.

East Middlebury

Waybury Inn, East Middlebury, VT 05740. Phone: 802-388-4015. Originally built as a stagecoach stop, the inn has been open for over 150 years. Guest rooms are individually decorated with four-poster canopied or brass beds. Meals include Sunday brunch.

Three Mountain Inn, Jamaica, VT 05343. **Jamaica**
Phone: 802-874-4140. Dating from the 1780s,
the inn has walls and floors of wide, planked
pine, a fireplace, and a library for reading. The
guest rooms are individually decorated, some
with four-posters and some with a balcony. The
owner took a course at the Culinary Institute and
meals are memorable.

Cortina Inn, Route 4, Killington, VT 05751. **Killington**
Phone: 802-773-3331. After a day of skiing,
skiers enjoy soaking in the inn's pool. The lobby
contains a large open-hearth fireplace, and there
is an art gallery upstairs.

Inn at Long Trail, Route 4, Killington, VT
05751. Phone: 802-775-7181. This inn was the
first ski lodge in Vermont, built in 1938. Located
between Killington and Pico, it offers accommo-
dation all year. McGrath's Irish Pub offers Guin-
ness on tap.

Killington Village Condominiums, The Village Lodging Center, Killington, VT 05751.
Phone: 802-422-3101. Six groupings of condominiums cluster in the woods at the base of Killington. Each unit has a fireplace and kitchen;
nice to come home to after a day of exercise.

Killington Village Inn, 5 Killington Road,
Box 153, Killington, VT 05751. Phone: 802-422-
3301. This inn's lounge, with its plaid carpeting
and fieldstone fireplace, is a cozy place after hiking or skiing all day.

The Summit, Mountain Road, Killington,
VT 05751. Phone: 800-635-6343 or 802-422-
3535. Two Saint Bernards recline in the living
room of this inn. Hand-hewn beams and four
fireplaces add to the charm.

The Highland House, Route 100, London- **Londonderry**
derry, VT 05148. Phone: 802-824-3019. This
house is located on a hill with a view of Magic
Mountain. There are 26 acres to roam in, includ-

ing five kilometers of wooded cross-country trails. Rooms are individually decorated. Guests may use the swimming pool and tennis courts on the grounds.

Ludlow

Echo Lake Inn, Box 154, Ludlow, VT 05149. Phone: 802-228-8602. This inn includes rooms, suites, and new condominiums built in an old cheese factory. We visited on Thanksgiving morning when the aroma of roast turkey wafted through the house; breakfast, lunch, and dinner are available here. Guest rooms are individually decorated.

Okemo Trailside Condominiums, Box 165, Ludlow, VT 05149. Phone: 802-228-8255. If you like to ski right to your door this is the place. After a day of skiing or hiking, you can return to your condominium and build a fire in the fireplace. Each unit includes a complete kitchen.

Manchester

Brook-n-Hearth Bed & Breakfast Inn, Box 508, Manchester Center, VT 05255. Phone: 802-362-3604. This homey, family-style house is perfect for winter or summer visitors. You can cross-country ski or hike all over the property. There is also a trout stream. Enjoy the views of the countryside, including Mount Equinox.

The Equinox, Manchester Village, VT 05254. Phone: 800-362-4747 (outside VT) or 802-362-4700. The Equinox is back—more resplendent than ever. (There is a description of this historic inn and its renovation in Itinerary N.) The Victorian furnishings and green velvet draperies in the lobby are set off by a brightly colored floral carpeting. The guest rooms are comfortable, and the suites are individually decorated and named. The health spa on the grounds offers individual programs as well as classes in aerobics, tennis, and calisthenics. You can even have a "spa" diet meal in the dining room.

1811 House, Manchester Village, VT 05254. Phone: 802-362-1811. This house once belonged to Abraham Lincoln's granddaughter. English and American antiques, fireplaces, oriental rugs, and canopied beds make the house inviting. There is a pub where guests can play darts; they also can play chess in the library.

The Inn at Manchester, Box 41, Manchester, VT 05254. Phone: 802-352-1793. Dating from 1890, this Victorian home features old prints and posters on the walls, antiques, and a fireplace to relax by.

Plymouth

Farmbrook Motel, Route 100A, Plymouth, VT 05056. Phone: 802-672-3621. If you like the sound of rushing water, here's the place. A stream gurgles and cascades right in front of you. Nestled on the side of a hill with woods all around, this motel feels like Vermont should.

Hawk Inn and Mountain Resort, Route 100, Plymouth, VT 05056. Phone: 800-451-4109, 802-672-3811. The Hawk offers a chance to get away for a special vacation. Rustically elegant stone and timber units are scattered throughout the woods; there are also rooms in the inn. The inn offers a restaurant, a health spa, swimming pool, and sauna.

Rutland

The Hillcrest Tourist House, McKinley Avenue, Rutland, VT 05740. Phone: 802-388-4015. This 100-year-old farmhouse is furnished with country antiques. Continental breakfast is included.

South Wallingford

Green Mountain Tea Room and Guest House, Route 7, South Wallingford, VT 05771. Phone: 802-446-2611. This house was built in 1792 as a stagecoach stop. Home-cooked meals are available. You can swim and fish in Otter Creek on the edge of the property.

Stowe

Fiddler's Green Inn, Route 108, Stowe, VT 05672. Phone: 802-253-8124. This homey Vermont farmhouse offers guests the chance to play chess or Scrabble in front of the fieldstone fireplace after a day of skiing. Paneling, comfortable sofas, a rocker, German mugs, and a fiddle on the mantel set the scene. Breakfast is served on long trestle tables in the dining room, which has a view of birdfeeders and the river.

Stoweflake, Mountain Road, Route 108, Stowe, VT 05672. Phone: 802-253-7355. This all-season resort provides a swimming pool, health spa, tennis, golf, fishing, and skiing. A variety of guest rooms are available. Charlie B's offers light food and drinks in front of the fireplace. Winfield's features Continental–American cuisine.

Ten Acres Lodge, Luce Hill Road, Stowe, VT 05672. Phone: 802-253-7638. The lodge's living rooms have fireplaces and views out the bay windows over cross-country trails to the mountains. Accommodations include rooms in the main lodge and two cottages. Candlelight dinners are a specialty.

Timberholm, Cottage Club Road, Stowe, VT 05672. Phone: 802-253-7603. The views from this home include the valley and the Worcester Mountain range. The living room has a large fieldstone fireplace and plenty of comfortable chairs. Homemade soup is served for skiers who return with hearty appetites in the afternoon.

Topnotch at Stowe, Mt. Mansfield Road, Stowe, VT 05672. Phone: 800-451-8686 (from Northeastern U.S.) or 802-253-8585. This conference and resort center offers every activity a guest could want: tennis, swimming, horseback riding, games, racquetball, golf, billiards, lawn croquet, and a health spa. Cross-country skiing is available in winter on the grounds. Guest rooms have Americana antique furnishings. The Sunday brunch contains an amazing array of good things on two lengthy tables.

Trapp Family Lodge, Stowe, VT 05672. Phone: 802-253-8511. Completely rebuilt after a fire, this lodge offers a library, fireplace in the lounge, and Austrian and American cuisine. A variety of guest rooms are available in the main lodge or the lower lodge. Cross-country skiing is available on the grounds. Read more description in Itinerary M.

Stratton Mountain

Stratton Mountain Lodging, Stratton Mountain, VT 05155. Phone: 800-843-6867. Guests may stay at Stratton Mountain Inn, Stratton Village Lodge, Liftline Lodge, or Birkenhaus. If you like to ski from your door, you can do it here. There are several restaurants to try right on site. The Stratton Sports Center is the place to go for swimming, Nautilus, racquetball, tennis, and jacuzzi.

Sunderland

The Inn at Sunderland, Sunderland, VT 05250. Phone: 802-362-4213. Built in 1840, this Victorian farmhouse has marble fireplaces, chestnut and cherry woodwork, and fireplaces. The guest rooms contain country-style antiques, including ornate carving on some of the beds. Wreaths decorate the doors and flowers decorate the rooms. The owners have an amusing collection of toy pigs scattered around the house.

Weston

The Darling Family Inn, Route 100, Weston, VT 05161. Phone: 802-824-3223. This restored 1830 farmhouse exhibits both European and American antiques. Some of the guest rooms have quilts and a wreath on the door. Housekeeping cottages are also available.

Wilmington

Nutmeg Inn, Route 9, Wilmington, VT 05363. Phone: 802-464-3351. This 1700s farmhouse has been restored and furnished with antiques. Guests may relax in front of the fireplace in the living room, complete with rocking chairs.

Woodstock

The Woodstock Inn, Woodstock, VT 05091. Phone: 802-457-1100. Built on the site of the original 1793 inn, the Woodstock Inn is massive but blends in with the New England decor of this charming town. There is a new sports center as well as golf course and tennis courts. The 10-foot fireplace welcomes guests after a day outdoors in pure Vermont air.

APPENDIX II: CAMPING

FRANCONIA NOTCH STATE PARK

CAMPING IN NEW ENGLAND

Over the past 28 years of traveling together, with children of varying ages, we have found that camping multiplies vacations, extending the time we can afford and increasing our range. Although campsite fees have risen since earlier days when we traveled across country with babies, they are still a bargain. A family can travel comfortably for a fraction of the cost of a motel trip with meals out, thereby freeing unspent money for sports and entertainment. The hidden benefits of this mode of travel are many. You can dress casually, eat at your own convenience, avoid the hassle of checking in and out (plus springing your car from exorbitant garage rates in large cities), change your mind, leave earlier or stay longer without worrying about accommodations, explore beaches and mountains in areas that are remote, choose the campsite with a view that suits you, and enjoy cooking and relaxing with your family. Travel more while paying less and enjoy the ultimate vacation luxury of complete freedom.

Of course, there are times when it is not fun to camp. We had one horrendous night pitching tents in a howling gale after midnight, but the sun did come out the next morning and we quickly dried out our belongings and went off for a day that was truly appreciated after the night before. The "good camper award" went to the best sport that night! On another occasion, while camping at North Truro on the Cape, our long weekend coincided with a particularly nasty three-day northeaster. We simply shifted from spending days on the beach to discovering museums and shops. One time, early in our camping days, we made the mistake of pitching the tent on a slight incline with the entrance on the high side. After spending the day in museums while the storm raged, we returned to find several inches of water lapping along the low side of the tent— inside. Another learning experience!

Campgrounds

Campground facilities vary from minimal pit toilets to imitations of city life, including tables, hot showers, playgrounds, fireplaces, rec rooms, stores, laundries, and swimming pools. Many privately owned campgrounds offer hookups for electricity, water, and sewer.

Campers may want to consider making advance reservations for a base camp if traveling in peak season. We suggest using a base camp for each regional area to avoid making and breaking camp often. Some campgrounds will accept reservations and some will not. If you do not have a reservation, try to stop early enough to be sure of finding a campsite. Many campgrounds have a "holding" area where you can stay overnight until a vacancy opens.

Following is a state by state listing of campgrounds that we have found to be desirable. We have listed available facilities and special features for each campground. These lists are selective rather than complete. You may want to check the current *Rand McNally Campground Guide* for a full listing of sites and facilities. State tourist offices often have listings of private campgrounds. You can also make reservations by calling "Camper 800," a computerized system. For a fee of $1 charged to a credit card number, you can obtain a confirmation immediately. Even if you do not know names of specific campgrounds in the area you wish to visit, the service will make arrangements for you. Call 800-828-9280 (in New York 800-462-9220).

CONNECTICUT

Cornwall Bridge

Housatonic Meadows State Park, Box 105, Cornwall Bridge, CT 06754. Phone: 203-672-6772. 1 mile north on Route 7. Offers 104 sites on 451 acres, flush toilets, showers (charge), hiking, and fishing. A good base for canoe trips on the Housatonic. Reservations accepted.

East Haddam

Devil's Hopyard State Park, East Haddam, CT 06423. Phone: 203-873-8566. 3 miles north of the junction of Routes 82 and 156. Offers 20 sites on 860 acres, pit toilets, and stream fishing. A wooded setting near scenic Chapman Falls. Reservations accepted.

Litchfield   White Memorial Foundation Family Campground, Box 368, Litchfield, CT 06759. Phone: 203-567-0089. Between Litchfield and Bantam off Route 202. Offers sites in Windmill Hill area (wooded) and Point Folly area (waterfront), pit toilets, store, and boating. Reservations with a deposit accepted.

Madison   Hammonasset Beach State Park, Box 271, Madison, CT 06443. Phone: 203-245-2785. Exit 62 from I-95, 1 mile south on Route 1. Offers 558 sites on 923 acres, flush toilets, showers (charge), snack bar, store, swimming, and fishing. The park sits on Long Island Sound. Reservations accepted.

Mystic   Seaport Campground, Mystic, CT 06372. Phone: 203-536-4044. From I-95, 1½ miles north on Route 27; then a half mile east on Route 184. Offers 72 tent and 130 trailer sites on 30 acres, flush toilets, electricity hookups (charge), water hookups, laundry, store, recreation hall, swimming pool, and fishing. Reservations accepted.

New Preston   Lake Waramaug State Park, New Preston, CT 06777. Phone: 203-868-2592. From Route 45, 2 miles west on town roads. Offers 88 wooded sites on 95 acres, flush toilets, showers (charge), snack bar, swimming, scuba diving, and fishing. Reservations accepted.

Niantic   Rocky Neck State Park, Box 676, Niantic, CT 06357. Phone: 203-739-5471. Exit 72 from I-95, 1 mile south on Route 156. Offers 169 sites on 710 acres, flush toilets, showers (charge), snack bar, swimming, and fishing. Sandy beach a short walk away. Reservations accepted.

Pleasant Valley   American Legion State Forest, Box 161, Pleasant Valley, CT 06063. Phone: 203-379-

0922. From Route 318, 2 miles north on West River Road. Offers 30 sites on 738 acres, flush toilets, showers, and hiking trails. Fishing and canoeing on the Farmington River. Reservations accepted with application.

Taylor Brook-Burr Pond State Park, Torrington, CT 06790. Phone: 203-379-0172. Exit 46 from Route 8, 1 mile west on town road. Offers 40 sites on 438 acres, flush toilets, showers, hiking, swimming, and fishing. Reservations accepted.

MAINE

Pownal

Bradbury Mountain State Park, Pownal, ME 04069. Phone: 207-688-4712. Freeport exit from I-95, 2 miles west. Offers 54 sites on 272 acres, pit toilets, nature trails, and a playground. Features a view of Casco Bay and the White Mountains from the mountaintop (an easy hike). No reservations.

Damariscotta

Lake Pemaquid Camping, Box 599, Damariscotta, ME 04543. Phone: 207-563-5202. From Damariscotta, 1 mile north to Biscay Road (Route 32), 2 miles south to Egypt Road. Offers 200 sites on 150 acres, flush toilets, showers (charge), electricity and water hookups, laundry, swimming, fishing, boating, tennis, and a playground. The spring-fed lake is 7 miles long with a sandy beach. Reservations accepted.

Camden

Camden Hills State Park, Camden, ME 04843. Phone: 207-236-3109. From Camden, 2 miles north on Route 1. Offers 112 sites on 5,474 acres, flush toilets, showers, and nature trails. The area features scenic views of Maiden Cliff, the Megunticook range, and 1,700 feet of typical rocky Maine coastline. No reservations.

Bar Harbor

Black Woods National Park, RFD 1, Box 1, Bar Harbor, ME 04609. Phone: 207-288-3274.

From Bar Harbor, 5 miles south on Route 3.
Offers 297 sites, flush toilets, swimming, fishing,
boating, riding, and recreational programs. Reservations required.

Millinocket

Baxter State Park. There are several campgrounds in the park. For information write: Reservation Clerk, Baxter Park Authority, 64
Balsam Drive, Millinocket, ME 04462. Mount
Katahdin, the Appalachian Trail, and the many
lakes make this a beautiful place to camp and
hike.

MASSACHUSETTS

Boston

Boston Harbor Island State Park, c/o Wompatuck State Park, Union Street, Hingham, MA
02043. Phone: 617-749-7160. Accessible by boat.
Sites on Lovells, Bumpkin, and Grape islands.
Permits required.

Brewster

Sweetwater Forest, Drawer FF, Brewster,
MA 02631. Phone: 617-896-3773. Exit 10 from
Route 6, 3 miles north on Route 124. Offers 250
sites (a few on the lake), on 60 acres. Flush toilets, showers, electricity and water hookups
(charge), swimming pool and children's beach,
fishing, boating, and a playground. Reservations
with a deposit accepted.

Charlemont

Mohawk Trail State Forest, Box 7, Charlemont, MA 01339. Phone: 413-339-5504. From
Charlemont, 5 miles west on Route 2. Offers 56
sites on 6,457 acres, flush toilets, store, hiking
trails, swimming, and fishing. Spectacular
mountain scenery. No reservations.

East Brewster

Nickerson State Park, Box 787, East Brewster, MA 02631. Phone: 617-896-7695. From
Brewster, 2 miles east on Route 6A. Offers 400
wooded sites on 1,788 acres, flush toilets,
showers, store, nature trails, swimming, fishing,
boat-launching facility, and bike rentals. Features

separate camping areas surrounding ponds with swimming, boating, and fishing. No reservations.

Sippewissett Cabins/Family Campground, **Falmouth** 836 Palmer Avenue, Falmouth, MA 02540. Phone: 617-548-2542. From Bourne Bridge, 12 miles south on Route 28; exit at Sippewissett cutoff, left at blinker, driveway on right. Offers 95 wooded sites and several cabins on 13 acres, flush toilets, showers, electricity and water hookups, laundry, and a playground. The area is wooded with access to the ocean. Reservations with a deposit accepted.

Savoy Mountain State Forest, Florida, MA **Florida** 01247. Phone: 413-663-8469. From North Adams, 5 miles on Route 2, 3 miles south on Route 116. Offers 45 sites on 11,721 acres, flush toilets, showers, hiking trails, swimming, fishing, and bridle paths. No reservations.

Wompatuck State Park, Union Street, **Hingham** Hingham, MA 02043. Phone: 617-749-7160. Exit 30 from Route 3, 7 miles north on Route 228. Offers 400 sites on 2,900 acres, flush toilets, showers, electricity hookup (charge), visitor center, nature trails, riding, and bike paths. No reservations.

Greylock Mountain State Reservation, Box **Lanesboro** 138, Lanesboro, MA 10237. Phone: 413-499-4262. From North Adams, 1½ miles west on Route 2, 5 miles south on Route 8. Offers 35 sites on 11,119 acres, pit toilets, hiking trails, fishing, riding, and bike paths. No reservations.

October Mountain State Forest, Woodland **Lee** Road, Lee, MA 01238. Phone: 413-243-1778. 3 miles north on Route 20. Offers 50 sites on 15,711 acres, flush toilets, showers, hiking, fishing, boating, and riding. Views of streams and mountains. No reservations.

Littleton

Minuteman KOA Kampground, Box 122, Littleton, MA 01460. Phone: 617-772-0042. From I-495, 3 miles west on Route 110. Offers 5 sites on 20 acres, flush toilets, showers, electricity hookup (charge), water hookup, laundry, store, recreation hall, swimming pool, and a playground. Reservations with deposit accepted.

North Reading

Harold Parker State Forest, North Reading, MA 01810. Phone: 617-686-3391. 3 miles north of Middleton on Route 114. Offers 134 sites on 2,800 acres, flush toilets, snack bar, store, swimming, fishing in five stocked ponds, boating, and riding.

North Truro

Horton's Park, Box 308, North Truro, MA 02652. Phone: 617-487-1220. From Route 6, 1 mile east on South Highland Road. Offers 200 wooded sites (some with a view of the bay) on 40 acres, flush toilets, showers (charge), electricity and water hookups (charge), laundry, snack bar, store, and a playground. Within the National Seashore, next to a nine-hole golf course and a mile from an ocean beach. Reservations with a deposit accepted.

North Truro Camping Area, Highland Road, North Truro, MA 02652. Phone: 617-487-1847. From Truro, Route 6 to Highland Road. Offers 250 wooded sites on 20 acres, flush toilets, showers (charge), electricity and water hookups (charge), laundry, and a store. Access to the ocean. Reservations accepted.

Plymouth

Indianhead Campground, RFD 8, Plymouth, MA 02360. Phone: 617-888-3688. Exit 2 from Route 3, 2 miles north on Route 3A. Offers 200 sites on 100 acres, flush toilets, showers (charge), electricity and water hookups, laundry, snack bar, store, fishing, boating, and a playground. Ocean swimming nearby. Reservations with a deposit accepted.

Provincetown

Dune's Edge, Box 875, Provincetown, MA 02657. Phone: 617-487-9815. From Provincetown, a half mile west on Route 6. Offers 100 sites on 13 acres, flush toilets, showers (charge), electricity hookup (charge), store, and a playground. Access to the ocean. Reservations with a deposit accepted.

Rochester

Cape Cod KOA Kampground, High Street, Box 265, Rochester, MA 02770. Phone: 617-763-5911. Exit 20 from I-95, north on Route 105, 4 miles east on county road. Offers 200 sites on 80 acres, flush toilets, showers (charge), electricity hookup (charge), water hookup, laundry, store, swimming pool, fishing, boating, tennis, and a playground. Reservations with deposit accepted.

Sagamore

Scusset Beach State Reservation, Box 65, Sagamore, MA 02561. Phone: 617-888-0859. From Route 3, 2 miles east on Scusset Beach Road. Offers 196 sites on 380 acres, flush toilets, showers, electricity and water hookups, snack bar, swimming, fishing, and a playground. Friends recommend the jetty for pollock fishing; also great boat watching on the canal! No reservations. Two-week stay limit.

Salisbury

Salisbury Beach State Reservation, Salisbury, MA 01950. Phone: 617-462-4481. 2 miles east of Salisbury on Route 1A. Offers 500 sites on 520 acres, flush toilets, showers, snack bar, visitors' center, swimming, fishing, boat-launching facilities, and a playground. No reservations.

Sandwich

Peters Pond Park, Box 999, Sandwich, MA 02563. Phone: 617-477-1775. Exit 2 off Route 6, right for 2 miles on Route 130, left on Cotuit Road. Offers 498 sites (some shaded and some along the lake) on 87 acres, flush toilets, showers, electricity and water hookups (charge), store, swimming, fishing, boating, and a playground. Site located on a lovely spring-fed lake. Reservations with deposit accepted.

South Carver

Myles Standish State Forest, Box 66, South Carver, MA 02366. Phone: 617-866-2526. 3 miles southeast of South Carver (follow signs). Offers 475 sites on 16,000 acres, flush toilets, showers, snack bar, hiking and nature trails, swimming, fishing, boat-launching facilities, and bike paths. No reservations.

Vineyard Haven

Martha's Vineyard Family Campground, Box 1557, Vineyard Haven, MA 02568. Phone: 617-693-3772. From Vineyard Haven ferry dock, 1¹/₂ miles on the road to the airport. Offers 175 sites on 20 acres, flush toilets, showers, electricity and water hookups, laundry, store, and a playground. The area is wooded with access to the ocean. Reservations accepted.

Webb's Camping Area, RFD, Vineyard Haven, MA 02568. Phone: 617-693-0233. From Vineyard Haven, 3 miles east on Edgartown Road, a quarter mile north on Barnes Road. Offers 177 sites (a few overlooking the pond) on 90 acres, flush toilets, showers, electricity and water hookups, laundry, store, and a playground. Reservations with a deposit accepted.

Westport Point

Horseneck Beach State Reservation, Westport Point, MA 02791. Phone: 617-636-8816. From I-95 south on Route 88. Offers 200 sites on 560 acres, flush toilets, showers, swimming, and fishing. No reservations.

Moose Brook State Park, RFD 1, Berlin, NH 03570. Phone: 603-466-3860. From Gorham, 2 miles west on Route 2. Offers 42 sites on 755 acres, flush toilets, showers (charge), hiking trails and swimming. Nearby Pine Mountain offers a particularly lovely climb with spectacular views. No reservations.

Eastern Slope Camping Area, Conway, NH 03818. Phone: 603-447-5092. From Conway, 1 mile north on Route 16. Offers 488 sites on 32 acres, flush toilets, showers (charge), store, tennis, and a playground. Good for small children. Spectacular scenery. Reservations accepted.

Lafayette Campground, Franconia Notch State Park, Franconia, NH 03580. Phone: 603-823-5563. From North Woodstock, 8 miles north on Route 3. Offers 98 campsites on 6,440 acres, flush toilets, showers, hiking trails, fishing, playground, and a naturalist program. No reservations.

Saco River Camping Ground, Box 546, North Conway, NH 03860. Phone: 603-356-3360. From North Conway, 1 mile south on Route 16. Offers 148 sites on 50 acres, flush toilets, showers (charge), electricity and water hookups (charge), laundry, store, recreational hall, swimming, fishing, square dancing, and community sings. Reservations accepted.

Burlingame State Park, Cookestown Road, Charlestown, RI 02813. Phone: 401-322-7337. Off Route 1. Offers 755 sites on 2,100 acres, flush toilets, showers, laundry, swimming, fishing, and boating. The area is wooded, only a few minutes drive from ocean beaches and the Ninigret Wildlife Refuge. For privacy, you may prefer the north camp, which is on the far side of Watchaug Pond. No reservations.

Narragansett

Fisherman's Memorial State Park, Point Judith Road, Narragansett, RI 02882. Phone: 401-789-8374. From Route 1 south on Route 108 to Galilee Road; then west to the campground. Offers 182 sites on 91 acres, flush toilets, showers, electricity and water hookups, swimming, tennis, basketball, volleyball, and a playground. Reservations accepted for a minimum of two days.

Long Cove Marina, RR 9, Box 76, Narragansett, RI 02882. Phone: 401-783-4902. From Route 1, south on Route 108 beyond Fisherman's Memorial State Park. Offers 150 sites on 100 acres, flush toilets, showers, electricity and water hookups (charge), fishing, and boat-launching facilities. Ocean swimming nearby. On the grounds is a native stone house and an old factory that once made bayberry wax. Reservations with deposit accepted.

VERMONT

Arlington

Camping on the Batten Kill, Arlington, VT 05250. Phone: 802-375-6663. From Arlington, 1 mile north on Route 7. Offers 151 sites on 35 acres, flush toilets, showers, electricity hookups (charge), water hookups, swimming, fishing, and a playground. Both shaded and open sites available. Reservations accepted.

Bennington

Woodford State Park, Bennington, VT 05201. Phone: 802-447-7169. From Bennington, 11 miles east on Route 9. Offers 190 sites on 400 acres, flush toilets, showers (charge), hiking and nature trails, swimming, fishing, and boating. Reservations accepted.

Brattleboro

Fort Dummer State Park, RD 3, Brattleboro, VT 05301. Phone: 802-254-2610. From

Brattleboro, drive north on Route 5 to the first traffic light, a half mile east on Fairground Road, 1 mile south on South Main Street and Old Guilford Road. Offers 113 sites and 9 lean-tos on 217 acres, flush toilets, showers (charge), and hiking trails. These sites are large, well screened, and wooded, and more private than many campgrounds. Reservations accepted.

Burlington

Burlington Beach, Superintendent of Parks, City Hall, Burlington, VT 05401. Phone: 802-862-0942. From Burlington follow "City Beach Campsite" signs north on Route 2, left on North Street, right on North Avenue, left on Institute Road. Offers 112 sites on 65 acres, flush toilets, showers, electricity and water hookups (charge), snack bar, boathouse, and a playground. Right on Lake Champlain.

East Dorset

Emerald Lake State Park, East Dorset, VT 05253. Phone: 802-362-1655. From Danby, 6 miles south on Route 7. Offers 105 sites and 36 lean-tos on 430 acres, flush toilets, showers (charge), museum, snack bar, hiking and nature trails, and boating. There is a sandy beach with roped-in shallow area perfect for toddlers. Reservations for a minimum of six nights.

Grand Isle

Grand Isle State Park, Grand Isle, VT 05458. Phone: 802-362-1655. From South Hero, 3 miles north on Route 2, 1 mile east on unpaved access road. Offers 174 sites and 30 lean-tos on 226 acres, flush toilets, showers (charge), snack bar, store, recreation hall, swimming, and boating. Right on the water, with scenic views, a center green for playing, and secluded sites. Reservations are accepted.

Silent Cedars Campground, Route 314, Grand Isle, VT 05458. Phone 802-372-5938. From Route 2, 3 miles west on Route 314. Offers

89 sites and 4 cottages on 20 acres, flush toilets, showers (charge), electricity and water hookups (charge), laundry, swimming, fishing, boat-launching facilities, and a playground. Some sites on the lake, others in the orchard.

Killington

Gifford Woods, Killington, VT 05751. Phone: 802-775-5354. From Rutland, 10 miles east on Route 4, half a mile north on Route 100. Offers 47 sites on 114 acres, flush toilets, showers (charge), and boat-launching facilities. Reservations accepted.

North Ferrisburg

Mount Philo State Park, North Ferrisburg, VT 05473. Phone: 802-425-2390. From Vergennes, 1 mile north on Route 22A, 6 miles north on Route 7, 1 mile east on town road. The entrance road is steep and not recommended for large trailers and RVs. Offers 16 sites on 163 acres, flush toilets, picnic area, and a recreation building. Scenic views.

North Hero

North Hero State Park, North Hero, VT 05474. Phone: 802-372-8727. From North Hero, 8 miles north on Route 2 and a town road. Offers 117 sites and 9 lean-tos on 399 acres, flush toilets, showers (charge), nature trail, swimming, fishing, and boat-launching facilities.

St. Albans Bay

Burton Island State Park, Box 123, St. Albans Bay, VT 05481. Phone: 802-524-6353. On an island in the upper part of Lake Champlain, accessible by boat or ferry from the Kill Kare Area. Offers 42 sites and 19 lean-tos on 253 acres, flush toilets, showers (charge), museum, hiking trails, swimming, fishing, and a marina. Reservations accepted.

South Hero

Apple Tree Bay Campground and Marina, South Hero, VT 05486. Phone: 802-372-5398. Exit 17 from I-89, 6 miles west on Route 2. Offers 250 sites on 200 acres, flush toilets, showers, electricity and water hookups (charge), laundry, store, recreation hall, swimming pool, fishing, marine, and a playground. The lake is across the road. Reservations accepted.

Waterbury Little River Camping Area, Box 86, RD 1, Waterbury, VT 05676. Phone: 802-244-7103. Exit 10 from I-89, 1½ miles west on Route 2, 3½ miles southwest on town road. Offers 195 sites and 6 lean-tos in Mount Mansfield State Forest, flush toilets, showers (charge), museum, hiking and nature trails, swimming, fishing, boating, and a playground. Reservations accepted.

White River Junction Quechee Gorge RA, RFD, White River Junction, VT 05001. Phone: 802-295-2990. From White River Junction, 7 miles west on Route 4. Offers 60 sites on 76 acres, flush toilets, and showers (charge). Reservations accepted.

Wilmington Molly Stark State Park, Wilmington, VT 05363. Phone: 802-464-5460. From Brattleboro, west on Route 9. Offers 60 sites on 158 acres, flush toilets, showers (charge), hiking trails, swimming, and boating. Reservations accepted.

National Parks

For information on national parks you may want to write to:

National Park Service, North Atlantic Region, 15 State Street, Boston, MA 02109.

National Park Service, U.S. Department of the Interior, Washington, D.C. 20240.

National Forest Service, U.S. Department of Agriculture, Washington, D.C. 20250.

The National Park Service charges entrance fees at designated national parks, monuments, recreation areas, seashores, historic sites, and memorial parks. You can purchase a "Golden Eagle Passport" for $10, which is valid for one year and covers entrance fees in any of the designated areas. The fees range from $.50 to $3 at each site. Persons who are over 62 years of age may receive a free lifetime entrance permit to the designated areas. The permit holder, his spouse, and children are all included when traveling together. If you are over 62 years of age bring proof of age. "Passports" and permits are available at most federally operated recreation areas. They cover entrance to parks but not campground fees.

State Parks

Some of the best campsites in New England are located in state parks. Reservation procedures vary by state. For full information on locations, facilities, and reservation policies, write to:

Connecticut: Department of Environmental Protection, Office of Parks & Recreation, 165 Capitol Avenue, Hartford, CT 06115.

Maine: Bureau of Parks & Recreation, State Office Building, Augusta, ME 04333.

Massachusetts: Department of Environmental Management, Division of Forests and Parks, 100 Cambridge Street, Boston, MA 02202.

New Hampshire: Division of Parks & Recreation, Box 856, Concord, NH 03301.

Rhode Island: Division of Parks & Recreation, 83 Park Street, Providence, RI 02903.

Vermont: Department of Forests, Parks & Recreation, Montpelier, VT 05602.

Appalachian Mountain Club

The Appalachian Mountain Club offers bunks in huts located in the White Mountains National Forest of New Hampshire, one of the most magnificent mountain hiking regions in the East. You can make reservations by writing: Reservations Secretary, AMC Pinkham Notch Camp, Gorham, NH 03581. The Pinkham Notch Camp serves as AMC headquarters for that area. Check for special discounts that are often available.

Index to Attractions and Restaurants